Object Oriented Simulation

José M. Garrido

Object Oriented Simulation

A Modeling and Programming Perspective

 Springer

José M. Garrido
Department of Computer & Information Systems
Kennesaw State University
1000 Chastain Road
Kennesaw, GA 30144-5591
USA
jgarrido@kennesaw.edu

ISBN 978-1-4419-5500-5   e-ISBN 978-1-4419-0516-1
DOI 10.1007/978-1-4419-0516-1
Springer Dordrecht Heidelberg London New York

Printed on acid-free paper

Springer is part of Springer Science+Business Media (www.springer.com)

Preface

The primary goal of this book is to introduce students to the basic principles of object-oriented modeling, design and implementation of simulation models. Emphasis is on model implementation by reinforcing OO modeling and programming. The treatment of statistics is left to a minimum.

For undergraduate students (of science and engineering), another goal is to provide relevant material for easy understanding of object orientation and simulation as early as possible in their curricula.

To accomplish the goals mentioned previously, the book consists of three parts. Part 1 presents a basic introduction to general modeling and simulation development, then introduces modern commercial graphical simulation and animation software: Arena and Flexsim. Other commercial simulation software, such as Extend and ProModel are mentioned but are not explained in the book.

The second part presents an overview of Object Oriented modeling and programming and introduces OOP with a high-level programming and simulation language, OOSimL. In this part, the book basically explains object-oriented modeling and techniques for designing and implementing problem solutions.

This part of the book presents a review of the basic principles and techniques of OO programming, and helps to clarify most of the important object oriented concepts taught in programming courses. The problem solving principles and techniques are illustrated by introducing problem modeling and their solutions, which are implemented in OOSimL. The OOSimL language is based on Java and the design of its simulation facilities were influenced by the Simula language and DEMOS classes.

The third part of the book, presents the principles of discrete-event simulation with an object-oriented modeling and programming focus using the OOSimL language. The process style of simulation is emphasized. All the basic OO programming principles explained in Part 2 are applied to the simulation concepts and techniques.

This book takes the "objects early" approach; it presents the object-oriented principles from the beginning, and provides the reader with a stronger foundation with objects and classes. A few models are described with the Unified Modeling Language (UML), other models are described with DEMOS diagrams and extensions developed by Pooley and Hughes.

The basic language constructs of OOSimL are presented gradually with the various programming principles and in an incremental manner. Most conventional textbooks on programming stress too much syntax of the programming language, e.g., Java, from the beginning. This results in unnecessary difficulty for the student in understanding the underlying concepts in problem solution and programming.

Standard pseudo-code constructs are explained and applied to various case studies. These are coded with the pseudo-code-like and high-level notation of OOSimL. For some examples with OOSimL, the Java implementation follows the explanation. General descriptions of the data structures needed in problem solutions are also discussed. All the object-oriented modeling and programming concepts are also applicable to the Java programming language.

The most recent version of the OOSimL simulation software, and the set of simulation models discussed in this book are available from the Web site:

```
http://science.kennesaw.edu/~jgarrido/oosiml.html.
```

There are very few books on object oriented simulation. This book and its associated software and models, were originally designed as a teaching tool. Professional practitioners can use the book to clarify and review the important practical concepts of performance modeling with simulation and some advanced application of programming in OOSimL and Java.

The book does not present the detailed theory of statistical treatment that appears in standard textbooks on system simulation. It is not a complete reference on performance measures of systems. The book only includes the necessary basic theory of probability to support the understanding of applying the appropriate probability distribution in the construction of the simulation models. The book also includes basic material that briefly presents the concepts and techniques of verification and validation of simulation models. Most other books on conventional discrete-event simulation include a more complete treatment on simulation theory, statistical analysis, validation, and on performance issues.

This book is aimed at college students in: computer science, mathematics, science, engineering, and management science.

The material presented in the book can also be used as a textbook for an applied course in object-oriented programming. More appropriately, this book can be used as a supplemental book for courses in advanced performance modeling and analysis. The main features of the book are the following:

- The basic principles of performance measures are applied to several types of systems using object-oriented modeling and the process interaction approach to simulation. Performance and Functional models are introduced.
- The process interaction approach to modeling and simulation are emphasized.
- The understanding of large and complex systems is facilitated.
- The understanding of modeling complex concepts and problems is simplified. This is applicable in modeling systems dealing with concurrency and timing constraints.

- The practical use of object-oriented concepts to solve real problems.
- The use of the simulation software as part of a larger integrated software development effort.
- An introduction to understand the complexities of modeling and simulation with OOSimL and Java. This may be convenient before deciding to acquire a more comprehensive and expensive simulation software system.

While teaching in the Department of Computer Science and Information Systems of Kennesaw State University, my colleagues and I have acquired experience in teaching object oriented programming at various levels. Discrete-event simulation has been taught, up until now, in an elective course at the senior level. Some of the difficulties encountered are the following:

- The teaching approach, which includes inappropriate material content for teaching students with no previous programming knowledge, the sequence of topics is not necessarily adequate, lack of basic software engineering principles in the course contents, and other factors.
- The textbooks on programming, which are mainly language-syntax oriented.
- The programming languages, most of which is mainly C++ or Java, are difficult to learn.
- The textbooks on simulation, most of which are too mathematical-oriented based mainly on statistical analysis.
- The development environment and other tools, which are difficult to learn and/or were designed for an industrial setting.

This book addresses part of these difficulties by providing material for improving the overall approach in teaching programming principles and adopting an "early introduction" approach to discrete-event simulation.

Problem solving and programming principles are emphasized from the beginning with pseudo-code. Pseudo-code is used for most program design. The OOSimL compiler is used to convert a program written in OOSimL into a Java program.

The construction of complete programs is carried out in the high-level language, OOSimL. This language has several advantages, it:

- Is higher-level and much more easy to read and maintain than Java or C++
- Enforces good structuring and documenting of programs
- Includes standard object-oriented constructs that are easy to apply
- Includes standard design structures for algorithm design
- Allows abstraction
- Is compatible with Java and provide a smooth transition to Java.
- It is used to implemented object-oriented discrete-event simulation models

Another goal of the book is to provide programmers a smooth transition to object-oriented modeling and a gradual introduction to object-oriented simulation.

For every topic discussed, one or more complete case studies are presented and explained with the corresponding case study implemented in the OOSimL (and Java) programming languages.

The book includes summaries, examples, and problems in every chapter. The case studies presented as simulation models, the simulation software, and the corresponding PowerPoint slides, will be available on the book Web page.

Acknowledgements

In developing the software, simulation models, case studies, and writing this book, I have had support from my NSF CPATH grant, which I share with Dr. Pamila Dembla.

I have received direct support from the Chair of the Department of Computer Science and Information Systems (CSIS), Dr. Donald Amoroso. I acknowledge direct and indirect help from faculty of CSIS through discussions on programming and various applications of simulation with several of my colleagues: Ben Setzer, Richard Gayler, Ken Hoganson, Chong-Wei Xu, Richard Schlesinger, among others.

Two of my students, Ernesto DiMarco and Ernesto Tham, initially investigated and developed the procedure and tests to configure the Eclipse environment for use with the OOSimL simulation language.

Marietta, Georgia   *José M. Garrido*
February 2009

Contents

Part III Discrete-Event Simulation

Part I
Basic Concepts of Modeling and Simulation

This part presents a basic introduction to modeling and simulation – concepts and principles. It also introduces the block-structuring facilities of modern commercial integrated simulation software: Arena and Flexsim.

Chapter 1
Models and Simulation

1.1 Introduction

This chapter introduces the general concepts of modeling systems and simulation. The basic structure and behavior of systems and models are discussed. Other important topics discussed are: the various stages of a complete simulation study, the performance of a system estimated by running the simulation model, the general approaches for simulation modeling, and the simulation support software available.

1.2 Systems and Models

A system is composed of a collection of components or *entities* that interact and exhibit some type of behavior and together achieve a specific goal. The system usually interacts with its environment, which is the part of the real world that surrounds but is not part of the system. The system can be described as separated from the rest of its environment.

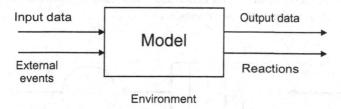

Fig. 1.1 A high-level black-box model of a system

A *model* is an abstract representation of a real system. The model is simpler than the real system, but it should be equivalent to the real system in all relevant as-

J.M. Garrido, *Object Oriented Simulation: A Modeling and Programming Perspective*,
DOI: 10.1007/978-1-4419-0516-1_1,
© Springer Science + Business Media, LLC 2009

pects. The task of developing a model of a system is known as *modeling*. Figure 1.1 illustrates a general black-box model of a system surrounded by its environment.

A model is built to gain more and better understanding about the system it represents. Every model has a specific purpose and goal. A model includes only those aspects of the real system that were decided as being important, according to the initial requirements of the model. Therefore, the limitations of the model have to be clearly understood and documented.

The relevant structure and behavior of a real system are very conveniently represented in its model using object-oriented modeling techniques.

Abstraction is used in modeling and involves including in the model only the important aspects of the system. This results in less detail in the model than in the real system. Abstraction is very useful in modeling large and complex systems.

There are many types of models of interest; the most general categories of models are:

- Physical models
- Graphical models
- Mathematical models

Mathematical models are those in which the components and their relationships and behavior of the real system are represented by mathematical expressions. These models are very flexible, convenient, and powerful to use in problem solving. The types of models studied in this book – simulation models – belong to the category of mathematical models.

1.3 Simulation

Simulation is a set of techniques, methods, and tools for developing a simulation model of a system and using the simulation model to study the system.

The purpose of simulation is develop a simulation model, run experiments with the simulation model, and to gain better and understanding about the behavior of the real system that the model represents.

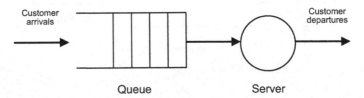

Fig. 1.2 A simple model of a single-server system

Figure 1.2 illustrates the high-level representation of a simple system that has arriving customers, a queue, and a server. An example of such a system is a barbershop with only one barber.

A dynamic system exhibits behavior that evolves over time; this includes various state changes at different points in time. The state of a system is the set of variables that are necessary to describe the system at a particular time. A (dynamic) system has:

- Structure
- Behavior

As previously mentioned, the system behavior depends on the inputs from the environment. For a simulation model to be useful, the model should allow the user to:

- Manipulate the model by supplying it with a corresponding set of inputs
- Observe its behavior or output
- Predict the behavior of the real system from the behavior of the model, under the same circumstances.

Most practical systems are very large and complex. The study of the dynamic behavior and the performance of such systems are very difficult. The development of a simulation model for studying a real-world system has two main purposes:

1. To study some relevant aspects by observing the operation of the model from the simulation runs
2. To estimate various performance measures

The output of the simulation model depends on its reaction to the following types of input:

- The passage of time
- Data from the environment
- Events (signals) from the environment.

The various components in a simulation model are usually classified in the following manner:

- *Flow entities*, these represent entities that flow through the system. These entities enter the system, are processed by various service components in the system, and exit at some other part of the system. The flow entities in the model represent the *customers* in the system as shown in Figure 1.2.
- *Servers*, these entities represent service components that provide some type of processing (or service) to the flow entities.
- *Queues*, these objects are used to place flow entities waiting for service or for one or more resources. Usually, there are one or more queues for each server.
- *Resources*, these are objects that can be acquired (or seized) and released by the flow entities.

Some of the terms discussed are not used universally; different terms are used in the various simulation support software and are not entirely standard. In FlexSim, the flow entities are known as *flowitems*. In Arena, a flow entity is known simply as an *entity*. A server is simply known as a resource in both Arena and Flexsim.

1.3.1 Computer Simulation Models

A simulation model is one implemented as a set of procedures that when executed in a computer, *mimic* the behavior (in some relevant aspects) and the static structure of the real system. This type of models uses empirical methods as possibly the only way to achieve a solution. Simulation models include as much detail as necessary; the representation of arbitrary complexity. These models can be much more accurate than analytical models because potentially, any desired level of detail can be achieved in the solution. Figure 1.3 shows a model of a multi-server system.

The general purpose of a simulation model is to study the dynamic behavior of a system, i.e., the state changes of the model as time advances. The state of the model is defined by the values of its attributes, which are represented by state variables. For example, the number of waiting customers to be processed by a simple barbershop is represented as a state variable (an attribute), which changes its value with time. Whenever this attribute changes value, the system changes its state.

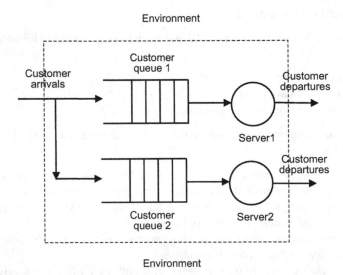

Fig. 1.3 A model of a multi-server system

There are several reasons for developing a simulation model and carrying out simulation runs:

- It may be too difficult, dangerous, and/or expensive to experiment with the real system.
- The real system is non-existing; simulations are used to study the behavior of a future system (to be built).

Simulation is applied in a wide variety of areas, some of these are:

- Computer systems
- Networks
- Systems security
- Medical systems
- Complex defense systems and war-gaming
- Stock market
- Weather prediction
- Computational fluid dynamics
- Traffic management
- Manufacturing
- Astrophysics
- Molecular dynamics
- Business enterprise
- Equipment training

1.3.2 Simulation Results

A simulation run is an experiment carried on the simulation model for some period of observation; the time dimension is one of the most important in simulation. Several simulation runs are usually necessary; in order to achieve some desired solution.

The results of experimenting with simulation models, i.e., simulation runs, can be broken down into two sets of outputs:

1. Trace of all the events that occur during the simulation period and all the information about the state of the model at the instants of the events; this directly reflects the dynamic behavior of the model
2. Performance measures (or metrics), which are the summary results of the simulation run.

The trace allows the users to verify that the model is actually interacting in the manner according to the model's requirements. The performance measures are the outputs that are analyzed for estimates used for capacity planning or for improving the current real system.

1.3.3 Models with Random Behavior

Models that are solved by empirical (or numeric) methods can be further divided into two categories:

1. Deterministic models
2. Stochastic models

A deterministic model displays a completely predictable behavior. A stochastic model includes some uncertainty implemented with random variables, whose values follow a probabilistic distribution. Most simulation models are stochastic because the real systems being modeled usually exhibits inherent uncertainty properties.

A model of a simple barbershop in which all the customers arrive at exact instants, and all have exact specified execution periods of service, is a *deterministic* simulation model because the behavior of the model can be completely and exactly determined.

A model with randomly varying arriving instances, varying service demand from each customer, is a *stochastic* model if only the averages of these parameters are specified together with a probability distribution for the variability of these parameters (workload) in the model. Uncertainty is included in this model because these parameter values cannot be exactly determined.

1.3.4 Discrete-Event Simulation Models

Simulation models can be divided into two general categories:

1. Continuous models
2. Discrete-event models

A continuous model is one in which the changes of state in the model occur continuously with time. Often the state variables in the model are represented as continuous functions of time.

For example, a model that represents the temperature in a boiler as part of a power plant can be considered a continuous model because the state variable that represents the temperature of the boiler is implemented as a continuous function of time. These types of models are usually deterministic and are modeled as a set of partial differential equations.

A discrete-event model is one representing a system that changes its states at discrete points in time, i.e., at specific instants. The simple model of a barbershop is a discrete-event model because when an arrival event occurs, there is a change in the state variable that represents the number of customers waiting to receive service from the barber (the server). This state variable and any other only change state when an event occurs, at discrete instants.

1.4 Input Parameters and Performance

The performance study of a system gives an indication of how well (or badly) is the system carrying out its functions, considering some particular aspect. A performance metric is a measure related to the efficiency and effectiveness of the system. Usually, a set of several different performance measures is necessary, one for every aspect considered.

There are three approaches that can be followed in studying the performance of systems:

1. Measurements
2. Simulation models
3. Analytical (mathematical) models

The last two approaches require the development of performance models. Performance modeling involves the construction of a simulation model or a mathematical analytical model for the purpose of determining some specified performance measures.

A complete performance study includes the definition of the following components:

- A set of relevant objectives and goals
- The performance metrics
- The system parameters
- The system factors
- The system workloads

The capacity planning of any system is determined by its maximum performance. Functionality is the ability of the system to perform correctly. In today's complex environment, the use and demand of computers and computer networks is increasing at an extremely rapid rate, so the capacity planning and performance modeling are very important for the design and operation of these systems.

1.4.1 Workload and System Parameters

The workload consists of a list of service requests to the system. Predicting the values of the performance metrics depends not only on the workload parameters but also on the system parameters.

Examples of workload parameters are:

- Average service demand of customers
- Average arrival rate of customers
- Average resource demands of the customers

Examples of system parameters are: customer queue size, number of server queues, server speed, total number and types of resources available in the system.

1.4.2 Performance Metrics

The main results of running a performance model are the values of the performance measures. The most common performance measures are:

- Average response times - the average period between an arrival of a customer and the instant that the customer has received service.
- Average throughput - the average number of customers serviced in some specified period.
- server utilization - the portion of total (simulation) time that the server carries out work (usual a percentage); usually, this is percentage of time that the server is not idle.

Other performance measures usually relevant in studying operating systems are:

- Average waiting time
- Availability
- Reliability
- Capacity
- Fairness
- Speedup

1.4.3 Additional Performance Concepts

Parameters that changed during a performance evaluation are called factors, for example, the number of users.

The general goal of most performance studies is one of the following:

- Compare different alternatives
- Find the optimal parameter value

The nominal capacity of a system is given by the maximum achievable throughput under ideal workload conditions. The usable capacity is the maximum throughput achievable under given constraints. The efficiency of a system is the ratio of usable capacity to nominal capacity.

The reliability of a system is measured by the probability of errors (or by the mean time between errors). The availability is given by the fraction of the time that the system is available for user requests. The interval during which the system is available is called the uptime. Often the mean uptime is called the mean time to failure (MTTF).

1.5 Modeling System Behavior

Dynamic and stochastic systems are systems whose behavior changes with time and that include some degree of uncertainty. The state of a *dynamic system* is usually expressed as a function of time (time dependent). An operation is a sequence of activities that may change the state of the system. An *event* is the occurrence at an instance of time.

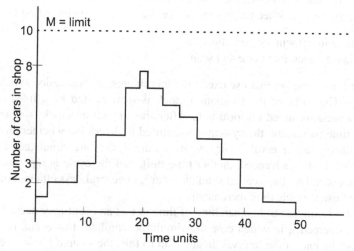

Fig. 1.4 Number of cars in the queue

The model of a simple carwash system is a discrete-event model; when an arrival event occurs, it causes a change in the state variable that represents the number of cars waiting to receive service from the machine (the server). This state variable and any other only change its value when an event occurs, i.e., at discrete instants. Figure 1.4 shows the changes in the number of cars in the model for the simple car-wash system.

The dynamic composition of a system can be described in terms of activities, events, and processes (active objects). An activity is the smallest unit of work; it has a finite interval of time to perform. A sequence of activities (an operation) is initiated when an event occurs. One or more activities transform the state of a system.

Processes are active components of a model and are used to represent the structure and all or part of the life of active entities in the real system.

1.6 Simulation Time

In addition to the components in a model, the simulation software has a *simulation clock*. This maintains the simulation time and is updated after every event in a *simulation run*.

The simulation time at which an event occurs is called its *event time*. The simulation executive, (i.e., the program that implements and controls the simulation) must include a means for carrying out a time change in the system and must keep track of the passage of simulation time. Increasing the value of the *simulation clock* achieves this. There are two basic techniques to change the time of the simulation clock:

- Fixed time increment, or periodic scan
- Variable time increment or event scan

Simulation executives that use fixed time increments are also called synchronous executives. The value of the simulation clock is incremented by a fixed amount, which is a predetermined uniform unit. After the simulation clock is adjusted by this fixed time increment, the system is examined to determine whether any events occurred during that interval. If any events occurred, they are simulated. The simulation clock is then advanced another time unit, and the cycle is repeated. These simulation executives (also called simulators) are, in general, less efficient than simulators that use variable time increments.

The main limitation of this handling of time is that an event may occur between two time increments, in which case the simulator simulates this event as if it had occurred at the end of the interval. In addition to this, the system needs to examine the simulation at fixed intervals, in some cases to find out that nothing has happened.

Variable time increment of the simulation clock is used by most discrete-event systems and offers the greatest flexibility. The simulation clock is incremented at the occurrence of the next imminent event. Thus, the simulation clock is incremented from one event time to the next event time, without regarding the interval that separates these event occurrences. After updating the simulation clock, the simulation system simulates the event (implements the resulting changes), and the whole cycle is repeated.

In a typical system, there may be several activities being carried out in parallel (simultaneously). The two approaches to handling time, periodic scan and event scan, are simple approaches to simulating parallelism.

1.7 Discrete-Event Simulation Approaches

There are three world views (approaches) for discrete-event simulation. The various simulation systems provide facilities for model implementation according to the world view. The three approaches are:

1. Activity scanning

2. Event scheduling
3. Process interaction

During a simulation run, the simulation executive (simulation control program) and the software model execute together. The software model (the program that implements the simulation model) is composed of a number of code segments whose structure depends on the simulation approach used.

1.7.1 The Activity World View

The activity is the basic building block of the activity world view. An activity sequence immediately follows a state change in the system. In the model program, each activity sequence is considered a segment of program waiting to be executed. An activity sequence is executed if and only if the corresponding conditions are satisfied. At the end of each activity sequence, control is returned to the simulation executive. If the conditions corresponding to an activity sequence are not satisfied, then control is returned to the simulation executive without performing the activity sequence. The system moves from event to event, and at each event, the conditions for each activity sequence are tested. The activity scanning approach provides locality of state; each activity routine in a model describes all the activities that must be performed due to the model assuming a particular state (i.e., because of a particular set of conditions becoming true).

1.7.2 The Event World View

The event is the building block for the event world view. The code segments of the software model are event routines. There is an event routine associated with each type of event, and it performs the operations required to handle that type of event. An event routine is invoked (or called) every time an event of that type occurs. An event routine is composed of the set of operations or activities that may follow from a state change in the model. The simulation executive uses the event list to find the next imminent event and then invokes the corresponding event routine.

1.7.3 The Process Interaction World View

The major components of a system are known as *entities*. There are two important categories of these entities, the first category are the *active* entities (i.e., they have a life of their own). These active entities are also known as *process*. The other category includes the *passive* entities.

A system is composed of active and passive components or entities. Active entities interact among themselves and with the *environment* to accomplish the system's goal. This interaction determines the behavior of the system. These active entities are known as processes.

In the process world view, the behavior of the system under study is represented by a set of interacting processes. A process performs a sequence of operations during its life within the system. The merging of the event sequences of these processes contains all events that occur in the system.

The *event list* used with this approach is composed of a sequence of event nodes (also called event notices), each of which contains the event time and the process (or pointer to the process) to which the event belongs. This sequence is ordered by non-decreasing values of the event times. Similar to the other approaches to discrete-event simulation, the simulation executive manages the processes in the event list. The simulation executive carries out the following tasks:

1. Placement of processes at particular points in time in the event list
2. Removal of processes from the event list
3. Rescheduling of processes (in the event list)

The simulation executive keeps track of simulation time with the clock, and from the event list, decides which process to activate next. The event time for this process (the current process) becomes the new value of the simulation clock. The operations of the current process are performed after the simulation executive advances the clock.

1.8 Simulation Software

Although all that is required for implementing a simulation model can be accomplished with a general-purpose high-level programming language, it is much easier and convenient to use some type of simulation software. The various levels of simulation support software are:

1. A general-purpose (object-oriented) programming language, such as C++ and Java
2. A simulation package or library, such as PsimJ2, Silk, and Simjava, Psim3. These are used with a general-purpose programming language
3. An object-oriented simulation language, such as OOSimL and Simscript III
4. An integrated simulation environment, such as Arena, FlexSim, Simul8, and Pro-Model.

Simulation software at levels 2 and 3 provide the most flexibility and power for implementing simulation models. The last level (level 4) provides the easiest and simplest way for developing simulation models but at the expense of flexibility and ability to implement fairly large and complex models. Most simulation software tools provide the following functions:

- Advancing the simulation clock when an event occurs
- Scheduling the events by their time of occurrence
- Providing simple and priority queues
- Providing standard mechanism for resource manipulation by processes
- Providing the general behavior for processes (active objects)
- Providing random number generators for various probability distributions

The following list includes several relevant software tools for discrete-event simulation.

SimPack and Sim++	GPSS	CSIM
FlexSim	SLAM	Simple++
Taylor II	SimPy	Arena
Extend	AweSim	iThink
Simul8	DESP	ProModel

The following list includes several software packages for discrete-event simulation for use with the Java programming language.

JavaSim	JSIM	DESMO-J
Simjava	Silk	PsimJ2

The following list includes several simulation languages for discrete-event simulation.

Simula/DEMOS	GPSS	Simscript 2.5
Modsim III	Simscript III	OOSimL

1.9 Simulation Study

A simulation study involves much more than developing a simulation model. This study consists of a sequence of stages that starts with the definition of the goals and is carried out in a possibly iterative manner. The simulation study is defined by the following general steps:

1. Definition of the *problem statement* for the simulation study. This statement must provide the description of the purpose for building the model, the questions it must help to answer, and the performance measures relevant to these questions.
2. *Data collection.* This stage includes tasks of gathering as much data as possible about the existing system under study, a similar system, and/or the environment where the new system will operate. The model parameters and input probabilities to be used in the model will be defined. Assumptions have to be taken on those aspects of the model for which no data is available.
3. Definition of the *conceptual model.* This is a description of what is to be accomplished with the simulation model to be constructed; ideally, the description should be clear, precise, complete, concise, and understandable. This description includes the list of relevant components, the interactions among the components, and the relationships among the components.
4. *Design of the model.* This stage describes the details of the data structures necessary to implement the components and the details of the algorithms for the relationships and dynamic behavior of the model.
5. *Implementation of the simulation Model.* This implementation can be carried out using a general-purpose high-level programming language, a simulation language, or an integrated software simulation environment. The main tasks in this phase are the coding, debugging, and testing the software model.
6. *Verification of the model.* From different runs of the implementation of the model (or the model program), this stage compares the output results with those that would have been produced by a correct implementation of the conceptual model.
7. *Validation of the model.* This stage compares the outputs of the verified model with the outputs of a real system. This stage compares the model with reality.
8. *Design of experiments.* This stage includes planning the experiments according to the goals of the simulation study.
9. *Analysis of results.* This stage involves statistical analysis and interpretation of the results and depends heavily on the previous stage.

The conceptual model of the system is usually described using the Unified Modeling Language (UML) and additional notation used in simulation modeling. UML is a standard set of graphical notational conventions used to describe various views about the structure and behavior of the system under study.

The conceptual model is formulated from the initial problem statement, informal user requirements, and data and knowledge gathered from analysis of previously developed models. Figure 1.5 illustrates the relationship between the conceptual model and the simulation model.

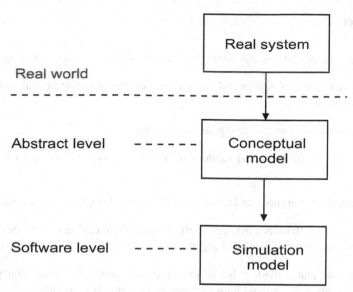

Fig. 1.5 Conceptual Model

1.10 Key Terms

simulation model	system	components
entities	environment	flow entities
servers	resources	queues
simulation run	trace	performance metric
random behavior	simulation study	verification
validation	simulation software	workload

1.11 Summary

A model is an abstract representation of a system. Simulation involves developing a simulation model of a system, carrying out experiments with the model, making inferences from the results of running the simulation model. A performance model is a model developed to study the performance of a system. The common types of simulation models are: continuous, discrete-event, deterministic, and stochastic. The performance evaluation of systems is often carried out with simulation models. Examples of performance measures are throughput, average response time, and server utilization.

Exercises

1.1. Write a list of systems that would have can modeled as single-server models.

1.2. Investigate the differences and similarities between a mathematical model and a simulation model.

1.3. Is a queue a resource? Investigate and discuss.

1.4. Why is it useful to model random behavior of a system? Give a reasonable answer.

1.5. Explain the differences and similarities between a flow item and a customer.

1.6. Explain the differences between verification and validation of a model. Which one is more important? Give good arguments.

1.7. Investigate and provide a list of examples of continuous simulation models. What are the main differences with discrete-event simulation models?

1.8. Explain the reasons why a conceptual model definition is necessary when developing a simulation model.

Chapter 2
Introduction to Arena

Arena is an easy-to-use, powerful modeling and simulation software tool that allows the user to construct a simulation model and run experiments on the model. The software generates several reports as a result of a simulation run.

2.1 The Arena Window

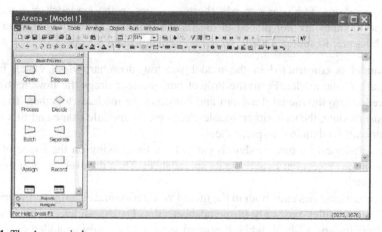

Fig. 2.1 The Arena window

After Arena starts, the computer screen shows the Arena window. Figure 2.1 shows what the Arena window typically looks like. This is the academic version 12.00.00. There are three main regions that can be identified in the main Arena window:

J.M. Garrido, *Object Oriented Simulation: A Modeling and Programming Perspective*,
DOI: 10.1007/978-1-4419-0516-1_2,
© Springer Science + Business Media, LLC 2009

- The *Project Bar*, located on the left side of the Arena window and below the tool bars. The project bar contains three panels: the *Basic Process* panel, the *Report* panel, and the *Navigate* panel. Every panel contains several modules that are used in constructing simulation models.
- The *Model window flowchart view*, located on the right side of the Arena window and below the tool bars. This view is actually the workspace for the simulation model. It will contain all the model graphics: the flowchart, animation, and other drawings of the model.
- The *Model window spreadsheet view*, located on the right-hand side and below the flowchart view. The spreadsheet view shows the model data.

2.2 Arena Modules

The construction of simulation models with Arena, involves using modeling shapes, called *modules*, from the Basic Process panel. These modules are used as the building blocks in constructing a simulation model. There are two types of modules on a panel:

- *Flowchart modules*. The user places flowchart modules in the model window and connects them to form a flowchart, which describes the logic of model. The most common flowchart modules are: Create, Process, Decide, Dispose, Batch, Separate, Assign, and Record.
- *Data modules*. The user can edit these modules in the spreadsheet interface. These modules are not placed in the model window. The most common data modules are: Resource, Queue, Variable, Schedule, and Set.

A model is constructed in the model window flowchart view, which is the workspace of the model. From the Project bar, the user drags the flowchart modules needed into the model flowchart and connects the modules together. To edit a flowchart module, the user either double-clicks on the module shape and fills in the form, or edits its data in the spreadsheet.

The definition of a data module is carried out by clicking on the shape of then module in the Project bar to activate its spreadsheet. Then the user can edit the data of the module.

Flowchart modules exist both in the model workspace and as a row in the spreadsheet. Data modules exist only in spreadsheet view. Data modules can be added or deleted via the spreadsheet, while flowchart modules can only be added or deleted by placing the object or removing the object from the model workspace.

2.3 Using Arena

To build a simulation model and to carry out simulation runs with Arena, a user performs the following steps:

1. Construction of a basic model. Arena provides the model window flowchart view, which is a flowchart-style environment for building a model. The user selects and drags the flowchart module shapes into the model window and connects them to define process flow of the model.
2. Adding data to the model parameters. The user adds actual data (e.g., processing times, resource demands, others) to the model. This is done by double-clicking on module icons and adding data.
3. Performing a simulation run of the model. The user runs the simulation and examines the results.
4. Analysis of the simulation results provided by the automatic reports of Arena. The user can expand the statistics.
5. Modifying and enhancing the model according to the user needs.

Arena provides a family of application solution templates (ASTs) built on the Arena simulation system.

2.4 A Simple Model of The Carwash System

Vehicles arrive into a carwash shop to get a simple wash and clean up. The Carwash system consists of a single wash machine, which provides the actual service to the vehicles. Arriving vehicles join a line to wait for service. The vehicle at the head of the line is the one that is next to be serviced by the carwash machine. After the vehicle wash is completed, the vehicle leaves the system. The vehicles are considered the customers of the system, as they are the entities requesting service by the server (the wash machine). Figure 2.2 shows a graphical view of the conceptual model of the Carwash system.

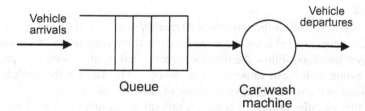

Fig. 2.2 Graphical view of the conceptual model of the Carwash system

The objects that flow through the system are the vehicles and in Arena, these objects are known as *entities*.

The first task in building the model is to define the flowchart of the model. To start the construction of a new model in Arena, the user activates the File menu and select New. A new model is given the name *Model1* by default.

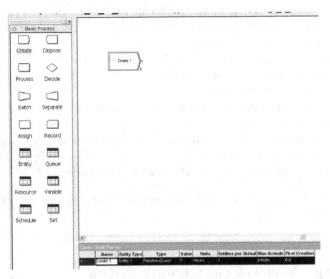

Fig. 2.3 Create module in model of the Carwash system

From the Project bar on the left-hand side of the Arena window, the user activates the Basic Process panel and drags the Create module into the flowchart view of the model window. Then the user drops the module shape in a convenient place, on the upper left-hand side of the flowchart view. Figure 2.3 shows the Create module in the flowchart view of the model window. This is the first module in constructing the model for the Carwash system. The figure shows only part of the Arena screen.

The Create module is the source of arriving vehicles into the system. To assign value to attributes or properties of the module, the user double-clicks on the module shape and enters the data requested in the small dialog window, as shown in Figure 2.4.

The name assigned to the module is *Arrival of vehicles*. The entity type is *Vehicles*. The arrival of vehicles occur randomly and the time between arrivals (the inter-arrival intervals) follow the behavior represented by an exponential probability distribution with mean value of 7.5 in minutes. The data for the module could also be filled in the spreadsheet view, below the model workspace.

The other modules needed to construct this simple simulation model are: a Process module and a Dispose module. As mentioned previously, these modules must be connected in such a manner as to represent the flow of entities through the system.

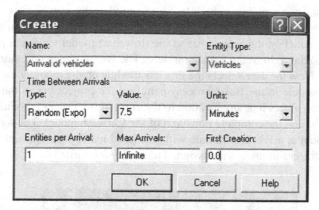

Fig. 2.4 Data in the properties of the Create module

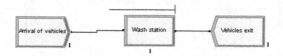

Fig. 2.5 Flowchart of the Carwash model

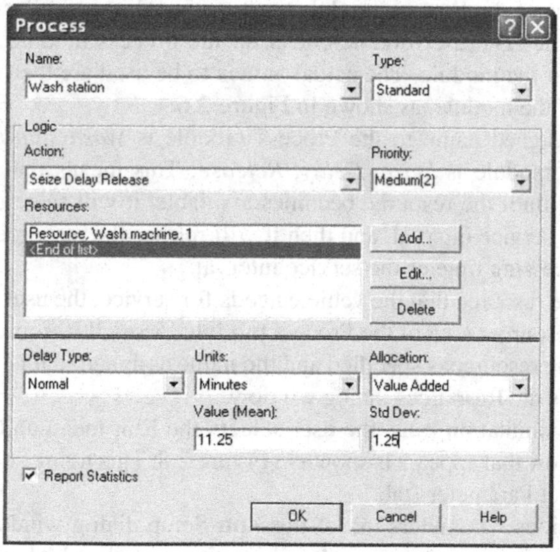

Fig. 2.6 Properties of the Process module of the Carwash model

To place the two remaining modules in the model, the user selects the Create module, which is on the model view. The user then drags the Process module in the Basic process panel on the project bar to the flowchart model view and places it at any location to the right of the Create module. The two modules will automatically be connected. Now the user selects the Process module on the model view and drags the Dispose module in the Basic process panel on the project bar to the flowchart model view and places it at any location to the right of the Process module.

Figure 2.5 shows the complete flowchart of the Carwash model. The second module in the model is a Process module with assigned name *Wash station*. The third module is a Dispose module with assigned name *Vehicles exit*.

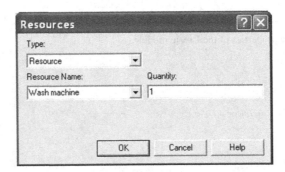

Fig. 2.7 The resources dialog window in the Carwash model

The properties of the Process module were assigned in a similar manner as for the Create module. The user double-clicks on the Process module and opens the dialog window of the module. The actual values to be used are then assigned to all the properties of the module, as shown in Figure 2.6.

The name assigned name to the Process module is *Wash station*. The Action selected for the module is *Seize, Delay, Release*. This means that a vehicle that arrives will wait until the resource becomes available, it will seize the resource, it will wait for the service interval, and then it will release the resource. The *Delay* is actually the processing time or the service interval.

To specify the resource that the vehicle needs for service, the user clicks the Add button on the Resources area of the Process module. A small Resources dialog window appears. The resource is specified and the name assigned to it is *Wash machine*. Figure 2.7 shows the Resources dialog window.

To setup the simulation runs, the user selects the Run menu and selects Setup. The dialog window that appears is shown in Figure 2.8. This figure shows the project title in the Project Parameters tab.

The Replications Parameters tab of the Run Setup dialog window is shown in Figure 2.9. The main parameter set is the replication Length, which is the simulation period.

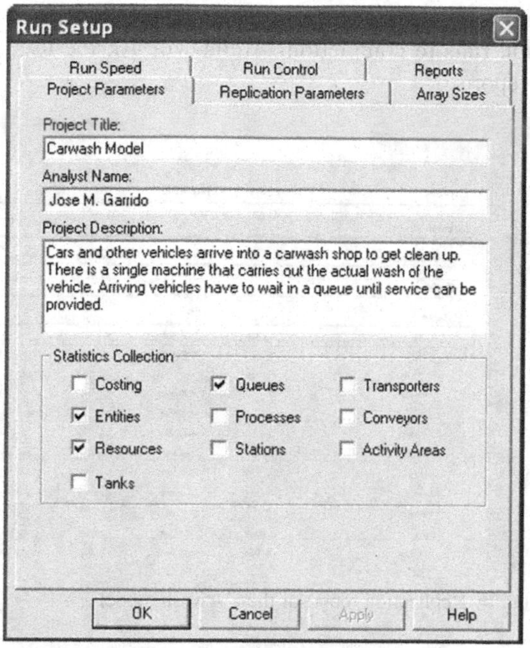

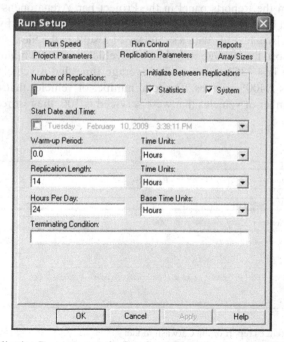

Fig. 2.8 The Project Parameters in the Run Setup dialog window of the Carwash model

Fig. 2.9 The Replication Parameters on the Run Setup dialog window of the Carwash model

To run the simulation, the user selects Go from the Run menu, or presses F5. After the simulation runs to completion, Arena will ask the user whether he/she needs to open the reports.

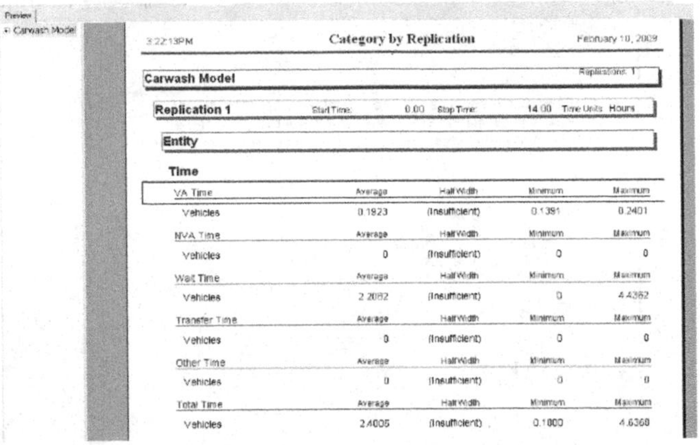

Fig. 2.10 The Category by Replication report of the Carwash model

The various reports produced by Arena after a simulation run can be accessed and opened from the Reports panel in the Project bar. Arena opens the Category Overview Report by default. Figure 2.10 shows part of the Category by Replications report. There is also a text file with a summary of results in the file `Carwash.out`.

From this report, the average wait time of a vehicle is 2.2082 minutes. The maximum wait time is 4.4362 minutes. The average time that a vehicle spent in the car wash shop is 2.4005 minutes. The total number of vehicles that arrived is 106 and the total number of vehicles that were serviced is 106, the rest remained in the system.

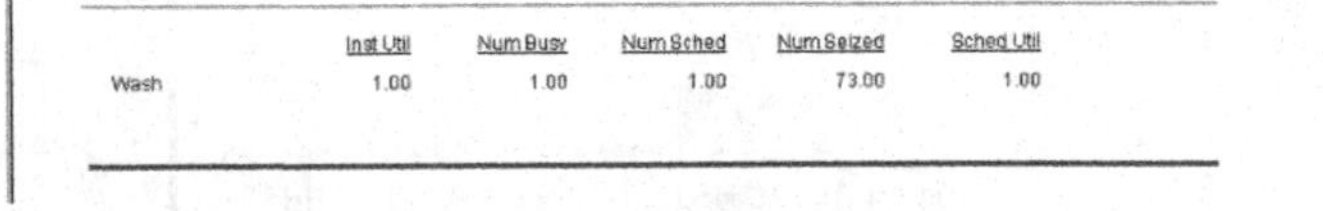

Fig. 2.11 The Resources report of the Carwash model

Figure 2.11 shows part of the Resources report produced after the simulation run. The resource (wash machine) *utilization* was 100%. The total number of times that the resource was seized was 73.

3:27:47PM		Queues				February 10, 2009
Carwash Model						Replications: 1
Replication 1	Start Time:	0.00	Stop Time:	14.00	Time Units:	Hours

Queue Detail Summary

Time

| Wash station.Queue | Waiting Time 2.24 |

Other

| Wash station.Queue | Number Waiting 16.85 |

Fig. 2.12 The Queues report of the Carwash model

Figure 2.12 shows part of the Queues report. The average time that a vehicle spent on the queue was 2.24 minutes. The average number of vehicles waiting in the queue was 16.85.

Changing the mean inter-arrival interval to 14.5 minutes, changes the output results as shown in Figure 2.13. The total number of vehicles serviced is 49. The average waiting time is 1.969 minutes. The resource utilization is 0.6738 or 67.38%.

The basic animation possible with Arena consists of showing with a small visual object the arrival of an entity and its accumulation in the queue. The default picture for an entity can be changed by editing the Entity data module.

The other animation consists of showing visually the states of the resource, Idle and Busy. To place a picture to indicate each state, the user edits a picture in the Resource Picture Placement dialog by clicking the Resource button in the Animate bar, which is the second tool bar at the top of the Arena window.

Arena provides a facility to generate or draw dynamic plots of a simulation run. To define a plot, the user clicks on the Plot button on the Animate bar and enters the data on the Plot dialog window that appears.

2.5 Summary

Arena is a very versatile integrated simulation development tool. Constructing a simulation model involves identifying one or more flow objects known as entities that flow through the system and then building a flowchart of the model using Arena's flowchart modules. The model is then enhanced by editing some of the data

Queue				

Time

Waiting Time	Average	Half Width	Minimum Value	Maximum Value
Wash station.Queue	0.1969	(Insufficient)	0.00	0.9194

Other

Number Waiting	Average	Half Width	Minimum Value	Maximum Value
Wash station.Queue	0.6892	(Insufficient)	0.00	5.0000

Resource				

Usage

Instantaneous Utilization	Average	Half Width	Minimum Value	Maximum Value
Wash machine	0.6738	(Insufficient)	0.00	1.0000

Number Busy	Average	Half Width	Minimum Value	Maximum Value
Wash machine	0.6738	(Insufficient)	0.00	1.0000

Number Scheduled	Average	Half Width	Minimum Value	Maximum Value
Wash machine	1.0000	(Insufficient)	1.0000	1.0000

Scheduled Utilization	Value
Wash machine	0.6738

Total Number Seized	Value
Wash machine	49.0000

Fig. 2.13 Partial report after modifying the input parameters

modules. Arena provides a simple method to setup the simulation parameters and the model input parameters. A variety of reports with the corresponding simulation results is produced.

Exercises

2.1. Write a list of systems that would have a similar model as the one for the Carwash system.

2.2. Increase the inter-arrival interval of the arriving vehicles in the Carwash model and perform one or more simulation models. Comment on the differences in results compared to the results from the original simulation run.

2.3. Decrease the inter-arrival interval of the arriving vehicles in the Carwash model and perform one or more simulation models. Comment on the differences in results compared to the results from the original simulation run.

2.4. Increase the average processing interval of the vehicles in the Carwash model and perform one or more simulation models. Comment on the differences in results compared to the results from the original simulation run.

2.5. Decrease the average processing interval of the vehicles in the Carwash model and perform one or more simulation models. Comment on the differences in results compared to the results from the original simulation run.

2.6. After reading the documentation on how to construct a plot for a simulation run, add a plot to the carwash model. This plot should show the number of vehicles in the system as the simulation time progresses.

2.7. After reading the documentation on how to animation in a simulation run, add animation that shows the state of the wash machine (Idle and Busy). Also include another picture for the vehicles that arrive and wait in the queue.

Chapter 3
Introduction to Flexsim

Flexsim is a powerful and easy-to-use modeling and simulation software tool that allows the user to construct a three-dimensional computer simulation model of a real-life system and run experiments on the model. Flexsim is a discrete-event simulation software tool that provides realistic graphical animation and extensive performance reports that enables the user to identify problems and evaluate alternative solutions in a short amount of time.

3.1 Modeling Concepts and Terms in Flexsim

A discrete-event simulation model will normally have dynamic objects known as *flowitems* that that move or flow through the model. A *process flow* is a series of processing, queuing and transportation stages in the model. Each stage of the process flow represents a task and may require one or more resources.

There are various types of resources and building blocks used in constructing a simulation model and are represented by *Flexsim objects*. Examples of these are: the Source object, the Queue object, the Processor object, and the Sink object. Flexsim objects are found in the Object Library grid panel, located on the left-hand side of the Flexsim window, as shown in Figure 3.1.

The Flexsim objects are connected to communicate with each other to define the process flow of the model. To connect the various Flexsim objects, each of these has a number of *ports*. There are three types of ports: input, output, and central. Input and output ports are used in the routing of flow items. Typically, the output port of one object is connected to an input port of another object.

J.M. Garrido, *Object Oriented Simulation: A Modeling and Programming Perspective*,
DOI: 10.1007/978-1-4419-0516-1_3,
© Springer Science + Business Media, LLC 2009

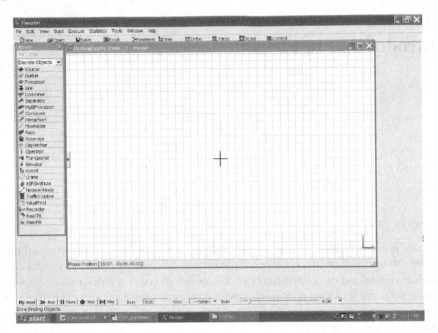

Fig. 3.1 The Flexsim window

3.1.1 The Flexsim Window

After starting Flexsim, the computer displays the Flexsim screen, which is shown in
Figure 3.1 and includes the Flexsim menu, toolbars, the Object Library, and Orthographic Model View window.

3.1.2 Flexsim Objects

The construction of simulation models with Flexsim, involves using modeling
blocks, known as *Flexsim objects*, from the Object Library panel. These are used
as the building blocks in constructing a simulation model.

A model is constructed in the Model View window, which is the workspace of
the model. From the Object Library panel, the user drags the Flexsim objects needed
into the model view window and connects the objects. Four of the most common
Flexsim objects are: the Source, the Queue, the Processor, and the Sink objects.

The *Source object* creates the items that flow through the model. These items are
known as flowitems. The *Queue object* is a temporary storage for items waiting for
the availability of a resource. The *Processor object* is a resource that simulates a
processing stage in the model's process flow. The *Sink object* is a terminating object
for the flow items in the model.

The user can set simulation parameters by double-clicking on the various objects and opening the objects' parameters windows.

3.2 Using Flexsim

To build a simulation model and to carry out simulation runs with Flexsim, a user performs the following steps:

1. Create the Flexsim objects of the model. The user selects and drags the Flexsim objects into the model view window of the model.
2. Connect the ports for the routing of flow items and define process flow. To connect an object's output ports to the input ports of another object, the user has to press and hold the A-key on the keyboard, then click and hold the left mouse button on the first object, drag the mouse to the next object, and release the mouse button.
3. Add data to the model parameters. The user adds actual data (e.g., processing times, resource demands, others) to the model. This is done by double-clicking on the Flexsim objects and adding data for the various parameters. Examples of these parameters are: the processor's operation time, the capacity of the queue, arrival rate, the routing logic, and so on.
4. Reset the model.
5. Perform a simulation run of the model. The user runs the simulation and examines the results.
6. Analyze the simulation results.
7. Modify and enhance the model according to the user needs.

3.3 A Simple Model of The Carwash System

Cars and other vehicles arrive into a carwash shop to get a simple wash and clean up. The Carwash system consists of a single wash machine, which provides the actual service to the vehicles. Arriving vehicles join a line to wait for service. This line is known as a queue. The vehicle at the head of the queue is the one that is next to be serviced by the carwash machine. After the vehicle wash is complete, the vehicle leaves the system.

Vehicles are considered the customers of the system, as they are the entities that arrive and request service from the carwash machine. These entities flow through the model and are known in Flexsim as the flowitems, which represent the vehicles in the system. Figure 3.2 shows a graphical view of the conceptual model of the Carwash system.

As mentioned previously, to build a simulation model in Flexsim the user defines the general structure of the model using Flexsim objects.

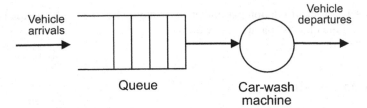

Fig. 3.2 Graphical view of the conceptual model of the Carwash system

To start constructing a new simulation model in Flexsim, the user activates the File menu and selects New. A new window of the orthographic view of the model is created.

From the Object Library on the left-hand side of the screen, the user drags the Source object into the Orthographic view of the model window and places it on the upper left-hand side of the model view. In the model of the Carwash system, the Source object represents the source of arriving vehicles into the system.

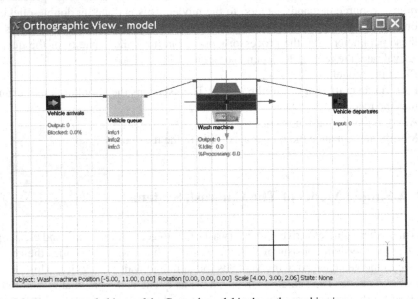

Fig. 3.3 The connected objects of the Carwash model in the orthographic view

The Source object has the default name Source1 since it is the first Source object in the model for the Carwash system. In a similar manner, the other three objects are created in the orthographic view. The default names of the objects are: Queue2, Processor3, and Sink4.

The four objects created to build the Carwash model now have to be connected. For this simple model, the method to connect one object to the next in the process flow of the model, is straightforward.

To create an output port of one object, an input port of another object, and connect the two objects, the user clicks on the first object and drag the mouse to the second object while holding down A-key on the keyboard. In this way, the Source object is connected to the Queue object, the Queue object is connected to the Processor object, and the Processor object is connected to the Sink object. Figure 3.3 shows the objects of the Carwash model connected and with the final names of the objects.

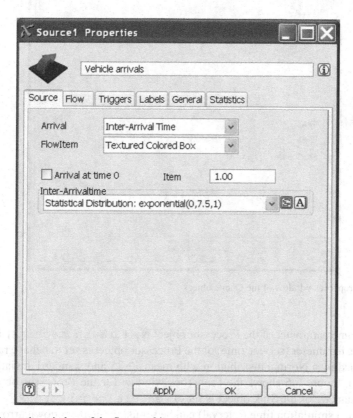

Fig. 3.4 Properties window of the Source object

To set value to the parameters of the Source object, the user double-clicks on the object and enters the data in the Properties window. Figure 3.4 shows the Properties window of the Source object.

The name parameter of the Source object is set to Vehicle arrivals. The arrivals of vehicles occur randomly and the inter-arrival intervals follow the behavior represented by an exponential probability distribution. The mean value for the inter-arrival period is set to 7.5 (minutes).

In a similar manner, the name parameter of the Queue object is set to Vehicle queue. The Maximum Content parameter is set to 10000. Figure 3.5 shows the Properties window of the Queue object.

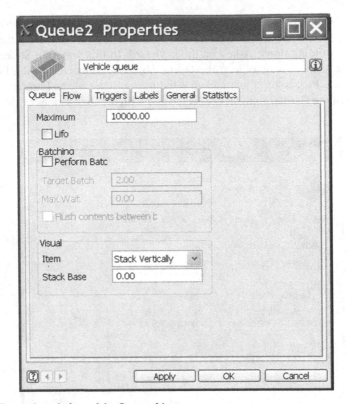

Fig. 3.5 Properties window of the Queue object

The name parameter of the Processor object is set to `Wash machine`. The Process Time parameter (service time) of the Processor object is set to behave randomly and defined by a Normal distribution with mean 11.25 and standard deviation 1.25 (minutes). Figure 3.6 shows the Properties window for the Processor object. The name parameter of the Sink object is set to `Vehicle departures`.

The total simulation time (interval) can be set using the drop-down arrow, entering the value of the simulation interval, and clicking the Set button. The simulation toolbar is the third bar from the top of the Flexsim screen, as shown in Figure 3.7. Note that the simulation time is set to 840.00 minutes.

To start a simulation run, press the Reset button then the Run button on the simulation tool bar. This could also be done from the Execute menu. The simulation run speed can also be adjusted using the slider located on the right of the simulation toolbar.

The simulation of the Carwash model runs for 840.00 minutes, and the results of the simulation can be collected by opening the various Flexsim objects and selecting the Statistics tab. Figure 3.8 shows the results of the Wash machine component. One of the performance metrics shown is the output *throughput*, which is the number of vehicles serviced during the simulation period and is 121.00 vehicles.

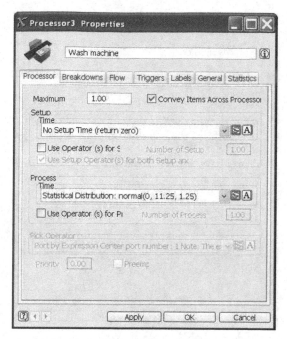

Fig. 3.6 The Properties window of the Wash machine of the Carwash model

Fig. 3.7 The simulation tool bar

The statistics of the state of the Wash machine is shown as a pie chart in Figure 3.9. This shows that the 33.4% of the total simulation time, the Wash machine was idle, and 66.6% of the time the machine was busy. This last metric is also known as the machine *utilization*.

The statistics of the Vehicle queue is shown in Figure 3.10. The utilization of the queue is shown in the pie chart shown in Figure 3.11.

Changing the mean inter-arrival interval to 14.5 minutes, changes the output results. This can be seen by opening the Vehicle queue statistics as shown in Figure 3.12. The total number of vehicles that have been enqueued is now 59. The average vehicle wait time is 1.5 minutes. The queue utilization is 9.4%, as shown in the chart of Figure 3.13.

Figure 3.14 shows the Statistics tab on the Properties window of the Wash machine. The output throughput is now 58 vehicles. The maximum service time is 27.96 minutes. Figure 3.15 shows the chart with the utilization of the Wash machine; it has a value of 27.5%.

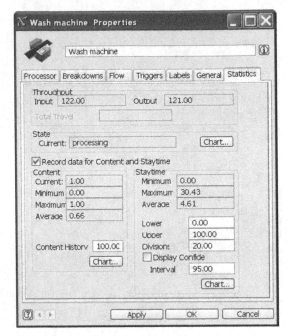

Fig. 3.8 The statistics of the Wash machine of the Carwash model

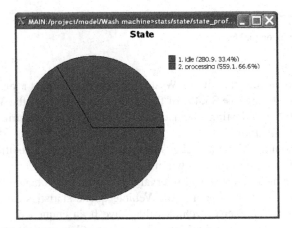

Fig. 3.9 The statistics of the state of the Wash machine of the Carwash model

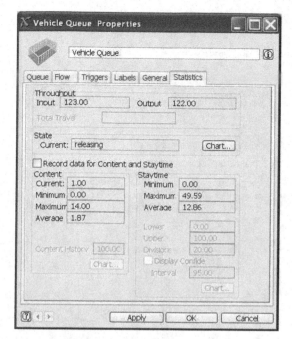

Fig. 3.10 The statistics of the Vehicle queue of the Carwash model

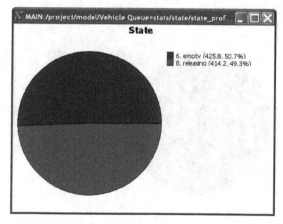

Fig. 3.11 The statistics of the state of the Vehicle queue of the Carwash model

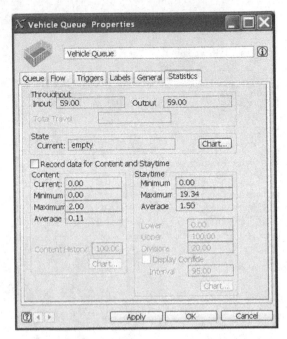

Fig. 3.12 The modified statistics of the Vehicle queue component of the Carwash model

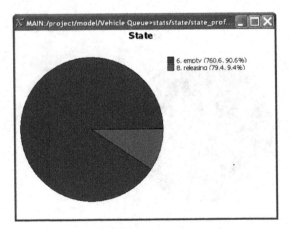

Fig. 3.13 The modified statistics of the state of the Vehicle queue of the Carwash model

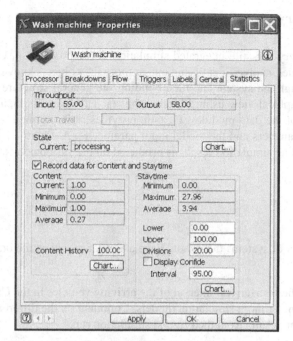

Fig. 3.14 The modified statistics of the Wash machine of the Carwash model

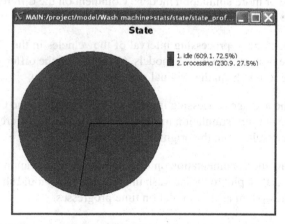

Fig. 3.15 The modified statistics of the state of the Wash machine of the Carwash model

3.4 Summary

Flexsim is a very versatile integrated simulation development tool. Constructing a simulation model involves identifying one or more flow objects known as flowitems that flow through the system and then building the general structure of the model in the orthographical view using Flexsim objects. The model is then enhanced by editing some of the data modules. Flexsim provides a simple method to setup the simulation parameters and the model input parameters. A variety of statistics with the corresponding simulation results is produced on the various objects.

Exercises

3.1. Write a list of systems that would have a similar model as the one for the Carwash system.

3.2. Increase the inter-arrival interval of the arriving vehicles in the Carwash model and perform one or more simulation models. Comment on the differences in results compared to the results from the original simulation run.

3.3. Decrease the inter-arrival interval of the arriving vehicles in the Carwash model and perform one or more simulation models. Comment on the differences in results compared to the results from the original simulation run.

3.4. Increase the average processing interval of the vehicles in the Carwash model and perform one or more simulation models. Comment on the differences in results compared to the results from the original simulation run.

3.5. Decrease the average processing interval of the vehicles in the Carwash model and perform one or more simulation models. Comment on the differences in results compared to the results from the original simulation run.

3.6. After reading the documentation on how to navigate in the animation views for a simulation run, add a plot to the carwash model. This plot should show the number of vehicles in the system as the simulation time progresses.

Part II
Object Oriented Programming with OOSimL

This part presents an overview of object orientation in modeling and implementation. The OOSimL simulation language is introduced.

Chapter 4
Programs and Software Development

4.1 Introduction

A program is a sequence of instructions together with data definitions. The computer executes the program by performing one instruction after the other in the specified order.

The first part of this chapter describes the general programming concepts, the second part of the chapter explains program compilation and program execution.

Developing programs involves following a software development process. This is essential to increase the quality of software produced at a reasonable cost. This chapter also presents the preliminary concepts of program development process.

4.1.1 Programs

The hardware in a computer system is driven and controlled by software, which consist of the set of programs that execute in the computer. These control, manage the hardware, and carry out system and user tasks.

A program consists of data descriptions and instructions to manipulate this data. The types of programs that carry out system tasks are known as *system programs* and control the activities and functions of the various hardware components. An example of system programs is the operating system, such as Unix, Windows, MacOS, OS/2, and others.

User programs, also known as *application programs*, carry out tasks that solve specific problems for the users. These programs execute under control of the system programs. Application programs are developed by individuals and organizations for solving specific problems.

J.M. Garrido, *Object Oriented Simulation: A Modeling and Programming Perspective*,
DOI: 10.1007/978-1-4419-0516-1_4,
© Springer Science + Business Media, LLC 2009

4.2 Programming Languages

A programming language is a set of syntax and semantic rules for writing programs. It is a formal notation that is used to write the data description and the instructions of a program. The programming language's syntax rules describe how to write sentences. The semantic rules describe the meaning of the sentences. These two types of rules must be consistent. There are several levels of computer programming languages, basically low-level and high-level languages.

4.2.1 Assembly Languages

The symbolic machine languages are also known as assembly languages and are low-level programming languages. In these languages, various mnemonic symbols represent operations and addresses in memory. These languages are hardware dependent; there is a different assembly language for every computer type. Assembly language is still used today for detailed control of hardware devices; it is also used when extremely efficient execution is required.

4.2.2 High-Level Programming Languages

A high-level programming language provides a programmer the facility to write instructions to the computer in the form of a program. A programming language must be expressive enough to help programmers in the writing of programs for a large family of problems.

High-level programming languages are hardware independent and more problem-oriented (for a given family of problems). These languages allow more readable programs, and are easier to write and maintain. Examples of these languages are Pascal, C, Cobol, FORTRAN, Algol, Ada, Smalltalk, C++, Eiffel, and Java.

Simula was the first object-oriented language developed in the mid-sixties and used to write simulation models. The original language was an extension of Algol. In a similar manner, C++ was developed as an extension to C in the early eighties.

Java was developed by Sun Microsystems in the mid-nineties and has far more capabilities than any other object-oriented programming language to date, unfortunately, it has a relatively low-level syntax.

Languages like C++ and Java can require considerable effort to learn and master. Several newer and experimental, higher-level, object-oriented programming languages have been developed. Each one has a particular goal. One such language is *OOSimL* (Object Oriented Simulation Language); its main purpose is to develop simulation models, make it easier to learn object-oriented programming principles, and help students transition to Java.

4.2.3 Compiling a Program

A program written in a programming language is compiled or translated to an equivalent program in machine language, which is the only programming language that the computer accepts for processing.

In addition to *compilation*, another step known as *linking* is required before a program can be executed. Programming languages like Java, require compilation and interpretation. This last step involves execution of the compiled program.

Two special programs are needed, the compiler and the interpreter. The Java compiler checks for syntax errors in the source program and translates it into *bytecode*, which is the program in an intermediate form. The Java bytecode is not dependent on any particular platform or computer system. To execute this bytecode, the Java Virtual Machine (JVM), carries out the interpretation of the bytecode.

4.2.4 Compiling OOSimL Programs

Programs written in OOSimL (an object-oriented language that is higher level than Java), are compiled with the OOSimL compiler. This is a translator that checks for syntax errors in the language, and translates the program from OOSimL to Java. This compiler is a special program that is freely available from the following Web page:

```
http://science.kennesaw.edu/~jgarrido/oosiml.html
```

The OOSimL compilation is illustrated in Figure 4.1. Appendix A explains in further detail how to use the OOSimL compiler.

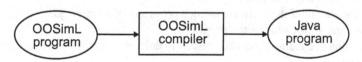

Fig. 4.1 OOSimL Compilation

4.3 Software Development

The main goal of software development is to solve a given real-world problem. This involves the following general tasks:

1. Understanding and describing the problem in a clear and unambiguous form

2. Designing a solution to the problem
3. Developing a computer solution to the problem.

4.3.1 Software Life Cycle

A software development process involves carrying out a sequence of activities. These activities represent the life of the software from birth to retirement. In most cases, the development process is also known as the *software life cycle*.

The software life cycle basically consists of the following phases:

1. Software development
2. Operational activities that applies the software in the problem environment
3. Maintenance activities that report defects in the software and the subsequent fixes and releases of new versions of the software
4. Software retirement when it can no longer be maintained.

The simplest model of the software life cycle is the *waterfall model*. This model represents the sequence of phases or activities to develop the software system through installation and maintenance of the software. In this model, the activity in a given phase cannot be started until the activity of the previous phase has been completed.

Figure 4.2 illustrates the sequence of activities or phases involved in the waterfall model of the software life cycle.

The various phases of the software life cycle are the following:

1. Analysis that results in documenting the problem description and what the problem solution is supposed to accomplish.
2. Design, which involves describing and documenting the detailed structure and behavior of the system model.
3. Implementation of the software using a programming language.
4. Testing and verification of the programs.
5. Installation and maintenance that results in delivery, installation and maintenance of the programs.

In practice, the waterfall model is argued by many to be very inconvenient and difficult to use, mainly because for any non-trivial project, to get one phase of a software product's lifecycle completed and correct before moving on to the next phases.

There are some variations proposed for the waterfall model of the life cycle. These include returning to the previous phase when necessary. Recent trends in system development have emphasized an iterative approach, in which previous stages can be revised and enhanced.

A more complete model of software life cycle is the *spiral model* that incorporates the construction of *prototypes* in the early stages. A prototype is an early

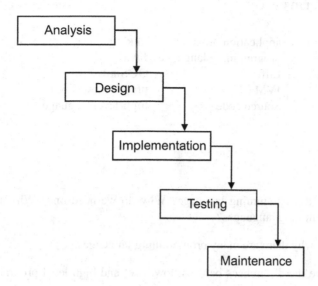

Fig. 4.2 The waterfall model

version of the application that does not have all the final characteristics. Other development approaches involve prototyping and rapid application development (RAD).

4.4 Summary

Application programs are programs that the user interacts with to solve particular problems. System programs are programs that control the hardware and the application programs.

There are several programming languages available. OOSimL is a language designed to facilitate writing simulation models and general programs. Compilation is the task of translating a program from its source language to an equivalent program in machine code.

The software development process is a well-defined sequence of tasks that are carried out to produce a program that is a computer solution to the given problem. It is strongly recommended to follow a software development process even for small programs.

4.5 Key Terms

system programs	application programs	linking
instructions	programming language	Java
C++	Eiffel	OOSimL
compilation	JVM	program execution
bytecode	Source code	high-level language

Exercises

4.1. What is a programming language? Why do we need one? Why are there so many programming languages?

4.2. Explain why there are many programming languages.

4.3. What are the differences between low-level and high-level programming languages?

4.4. Explain the purpose of compilation. How many compilers are necessary for a given application? What is the difference between program compilation and program execution? Explain.

4.5. What is the real purpose of developing a program? Can we just use a spreadsheet program such as MS Excel to solve numerical problems? Explain.

4.6. Find out the differences in compiling and linking Java and C++ programs.

4.7. Explain why OOSimL is a high-level programming language.

4.8. For developing small programs, is it still necessary to use a software development process? Explain. What are the main advantages in using a process? What are the disadvantages?

Chapter 5
Object Orientation

5.1 Introduction

This chapter presents the basic principles of object orientation. The concepts of objects, collection of objects, encapsulation, models, information hiding, and classes are explained.

The general structure of a class and instances of a class are explained in a simplified manner. Other preliminary concepts in object-oriented programming such as inheritance, reuse, abstraction, and modularization are also explained.

When developing software, a simplified representation of every problem is used to design and implement a computer solution. This representation is called a *model* of the problem. A model is composed of a set of the abstract representation of collections of objects, each one representing a real-world entity. Real-world applications consist of collections of real-world objects interacting with one another and with their surroundings.

5.2 Modules

For complex problems or systems, the general approach is to divide the problem into smaller problems that are easier to solve. The partitioning of a problem into smaller parts is known as *decomposition*. These small parts are known as modules, which are easier to manage.

System design usually emphasizes modular structuring, also called modular decomposition. A problem is divided into smaller problems (or subproblems), and a solution is designed for each subproblem. Therefore, the solution to a problem consists of several smaller solutions corresponding to each of the subproblems. This approach is called modular design. Object-oriented design enhances modular design by providing classes as the most important decomposition (modular) unit. A program structure is basically organized as an assembly of classes.

J.M. Garrido, *Object Oriented Simulation: A Modeling and Programming Perspective*,
DOI: 10.1007/978-1-4419-0516-1_5,
© Springer Science + Business Media, LLC 2009

5.3 Modeling Objects

Abstraction is used to model the objects in a problem domain. This involves the elimination of unessential characteristics. A model includes only the relevant aspects of the real-world system. Therefore, only the relevant objects and only the essential characteristics of these objects are included in the model.

Several levels of detail are needed to completely define objects and the collections of objects in a model. The activities in object-oriented modeling are:

1. Identifying the relevant objects for the model
2. Using abstraction to describe these objects
3. Defining collections of similar objects

An abstract representation is a simplified description and includes only the relevant or essential properties of part of a real system. A model is such an abstract representation of some part of the problem domain.

Real-world entities or real-world objects are the fundamental components of a real world system. Identifying and modeling real-world entities in the problem domain are the central focus of the object-oriented approach. A real-world entity has the responsibility of carrying out a specific task. Real-world entities identified in the real-world environment are modeled as objects.

Objects with similar characteristics are grouped into collections, and these are modeled as *classes*.

Objects and classes are described in a standard notation, the Unified Modeling Language (UML). This chapter and throughout the book simplified UML diagrams are employed when describing classes and objects.

5.3.1 Defining Classes

In modeling a real-world problem, collections of similar objects are identified. Classes are then defined as abstract descriptions of these collections of objects, which are objects with the same structure and behavior. A class defines the attributes, and behavior for all the objects of the class.

Figure 5.1 shows two collections of real-world objects and the modeling of the classes.

An object belongs to a collection or class, and any object of the class is an *instance* of the class.

A software implementation of class consists of:

- Data declarations that represent the attributes of the class
- Behavior representation as one or more operations (also known as functions and methods)

A class is represented graphically in UML as a simplified class diagram. The following is an example of a representation of class *Employee*, in a simplified UML

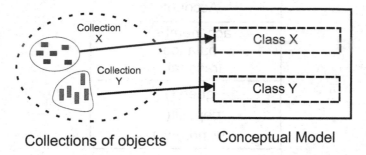

Collections of objects   **Conceptual Model**

Fig. 5.1 Collections of objects

diagram that shows the structure and behavior for all objects of this class. The attributes defined for this class are *salary*, *emp_number*, *name*, and *emp_date*. Figure 5.2 shows the diagram that describes class *Employee*.

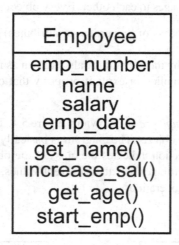

Fig. 5.2 Diagram of class *Employee*

Another example of a class is shown next. Figure 5.3 shows the diagram that describes class *Account*.

5.3.2 Describing Objects

Three basic categories of real-world objects can be identified:

• Physical objects such as persons, animals, cars, balls, traffic lights, and so on

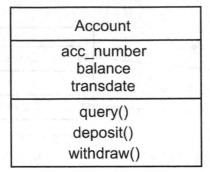

Fig. 5.3 Diagram of class *Account*

- Non-tangible objects such as contracts, accounts, and so on
- Conceptual objects that are used to represent part of the components or part of the behavior of the problem.

Objects exhibit independent behavior and interact with one another. Objects communicate by sending messages to each other. Every object has:

- State, represented by the set of properties (or attributes) and their associated values
- Behavior, represented by the operations, also known as methods, of the object
- Identity, which is an implicit or explicit property that can uniquely identify an object.

Two objects of class *Employee* are shown in Figure 5.4. This is the UML diagram that shows the state of the objects. The diagram is basically a rectangle divided into three sections. The top section indicates the class of the object, the middle section includes the list of the attributes and their current values, and the bottom section includes the list of object operations.

:Employee		:Employee
879156 "John Martin" 45000.00 7/08/2001		4651961 "Nancy Dow" 38766.50 10/5/2004
get_name() increase_sal() get_age() start_emp()		get_name() increase_sal() get_age() start_emp()

Fig. 5.4 Two objects of class *Employee*

The state of an object is defined by the values of its attributes. The two objects of class *Employee* have different states because their attributes have different values.

An object of class *Account* is shown in Figure 5.3. This object has three attributes, *acc_num*, *balance*, and *transdate*. The object also has and three operations, *deposit* and *withdraw*, and *query*. The values of these attributes are also shown. The behavior of this object is dependent on another object that can start any of these operations.

5.4 Object Interactions

Object interaction involves objects sending *messages* to each other. The object that sends the message is the requestor of a service that can be provided by the receiver object.

An object sends a message to request a service, which is provided by the object receiving the message. The sender object is known as the *client* of a service, and the receiver object is known as the *supplier* of the service. Passive objects perform operations in response to messages.

An object of class *Employee* interacts with an object of class *Account*, by invoking an operation of the object of class *Account*.

These interactions are object-specific; a message is always sent to a specific object. This is also known as *method invocation*. A message normally contains three parts:

- The operation to be invoked or started
- The input data required by the operation to perform
- The result of the operation

The standard UML diagram known as the *communication diagram* is used to describe the general interaction between two or more objects (the sending of messages between objects).

Figure 5.5 shows a simple communication diagram to describe the interaction between an object of class *Employee* with an object of class *Account*. In this example, the object of class *Employee* invokes the *deposit* operation of the object of class *Account*. The first object sends a message to the second object (of class *Account*). As a result of this message, the object of class *Account* performs its *deposit* operation.

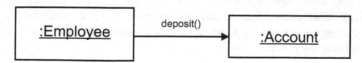

Fig. 5.5 Communication diagram with two objects

5.5 Other Concepts of Object Orientation

Object orientation provides enhanced modularity in developing software systems.
An application is basically a set of well-structured and related *modules*. The class
is the most basic module of a program, and is the main decomposition unit of a
program. In other words, a program is decomposed into a set of classes. The application is organized as an assembly of classes. Figure 5.6 illustrates the notion of an
assembly of classes.

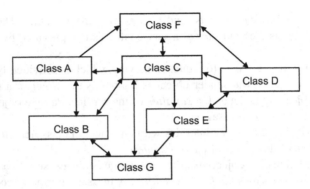

Fig. 5.6 An assembly of classes

This is the *static view* of a program (that implements an application). The *dynamic view* of the application is a set of objects performing their behavior and interacting among themselves.

5.5.1 Encapsulation

The encapsulation principle describes an object as the integration of its attributes
and behavior in a single unit. There is an imaginary protecting wall surrounding
the object. This is considered a protection mechanism. To protect the features of an
object, an access mode is specified for every feature.

The access mode specifies which features of the object can be accessed from
other objects. If access to a feature (attribute or operation) is not allowed, the access
mode of the feature is specified to be *private*. If a feature of an object is *public*, it is
accessible from any other objects.

5.5.2 Information Hiding

As mentioned previously, an object that provides a set of services to other objects is known as a *provider* object, and all other objects that request these services by sending messages are known as *client* objects. An object can be a service provider for some services, and it can also be a client for services that it requests from other (provider) objects.

The principle of information hiding provides the description of a class only to show the services the objects of the class provide to other objects and hiding all implementation details. In this manner, a class description presents two views:

1. The *external view* of the objects of a class. This view consists of the list of services (or operations) that other objects can invoke. The list of services can be used as a service contract between the provider object and the client objects.
2. The *internal view* of the objects of the class. This view describes the implementation details of the data and the operations of the objects in a class. This information is hidden from other objects.

These two views of an object are described at two different levels of abstraction. The external view is at a higher level of abstraction. The external view is often known as the *class specification*, and the internal view as the *class implementation*.

With the external view, information about an object is limited to that only necessary for the object's features to be invoked by other objects. The rest of the knowledge about the object is not revealed.

In general, the external view of the objects should be kept separate from the internal view. The internal view of properties and operations of an object are hidden from other objects. The object presents its external view to other objects and shows what features (operations and attributes) are accessible.

5.6 Summary

One of the first tasks in modeling object-oriented applications is to identify the objects and collections of similar objects in the problem domain. An object has properties and behaviors. The class is a definition of objects with the same characteristics.

A model is an abstract representation of a real system. Modeling involves selecting relevant objects and relevant characteristics of these objects.

Objects collaborate by sending messages to each other. A message is a request by an object to carry out a certain operation on another object, or on the same object. Information hiding emphasizes the separation of the list of operations that an object offers to other objects from the implementation details that are hidden to other objects.

5.7 Key Terms

models	abstraction	objects
collections	real-world entities	object state
object behavior	messages	attributes
operations	methods	functions
UML diagram	interactions	method invocation
classes	encapsulation	information hiding
private	public	class specification
class implementation	collaboration	

Exercises

5.1. What are the differences between classes and objects? Why an object is considered a dynamic concept? Why the class is considered a static concept? Explain.

5.2. Explain the differences and similarities of the UML class and object diagrams. What do these diagrams actually describe about an object and about a class? Explain.

5.3. Is object interaction the same as object behavior? Explain and give examples. What UML diagram describes this?

5.4. Briefly explain the differences between encapsulation and information hiding. How are these two concepts related? Explain.

5.5. Are the external view and internal view of a class at different levels of abstraction? Explain. Is this considered important in software development? Explain.

5.6. Identify the type and number of objects involved in an automobile rental office. For every type of object, list the properties and operations. Draw the class and object diagrams for this problem.

5.7. Describe the object interactions necessary for the objects in the automobile rental office. Draw the corresponding communication diagrams.

5.8. Identify the various objects in a supermarket. How many objects of each type are there? List the properties and the necessary operations of the objects. Draw the corresponding UML diagrams for this problem.

5.9. List the private and public characteristics (properties and operations) for every type of object in the two the previous Exercises. Why do you need to make this distinction? Explain.

Chapter 6
Object-Oriented Programs

6.1 Introduction

As mentioned in the previous chapter, object-orientation enhances the decomposition of a problem. Classes are the principal decomposition units, therefore, a class is considered a module and a decomposition unit. A class is also a type for objects.

This chapter presents and explains the basic structure of a class. An introduction to data descriptions and the general structure of a function is discussed. The construction of simple object-oriented programs is presented in the last part of this chapter.

6.2 Programs

An object-oriented program is an implementation of the classes that were modeled in the analysis and design phase of the software development process. This is the static view of a program that describes the structure of the program composed of one or more modules known as *classes*.

When the program executes, objects of these classes are created and made to interact among them. This is the dynamic view of a program, which describes the behavior of the program while it executes. This behavior consists of the set of *objects*, each one exhibiting individual behavior and interacting with other objects.

6.3 Definition of Classes

A class defines the structure and the behavior of the objects in that class. The software definition of a class consists of:

- The attribute declarations of the class

J.M. Garrido, *Object Oriented Simulation: A Modeling and Programming Perspective*,
DOI: 10.1007/978-1-4419-0516-1_6,
© Springer Science + Business Media, LLC 2009

• Descriptions of the operations, known as methods or functions of the class

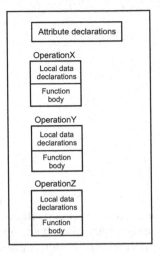

Fig. 6.1 Structure of a typical class

The attributes in a class are defined as data declarations declarations of the class. The behavior of the objects of the class is represented by the descriptions of the operations of the class.

The general structure of a class is shown in Figure 6.1 that illustrates the declarations of the attributes and the definitions of three operations: *OperationX*, *OperationY*, and *OperationZ*. Each of these operations consists of local data declarations and its instructions.

The smallest modular unit is an operation, also known as a function or method; it carries out a single task. It is not standalone unit because every function belongs to a class; a function is an internal decomposition unit.

6.4 Implementation of Programs

The software implementation of a program is carried out writing the code in a suitable programming language. Detailed design is often written in pseudo-code, which is a high-level notation at the level between the modeling diagrams and the programming language.

6.4.1 Programming Languages

Programming languages have well-defined syntax and semantic rules. The syntax is defined by a set of grammar rules and a vocabulary (a set of words). The legal sentences are constructed using sentences in the form of *statements*. There are two groups of words: *reserved words* and *identifiers*.

Reserved words are the keywords of the language and have a predefined purpose in the language. These are used in most statements with precise meaning, for example, **class**, **inherits**, **variables**, **while**, **if**, and others.

Identifiers are names for variables, constants, functions, and classes that the programmer chooses, for example, *emp_number*, *employee_name*, *salary*, *emp_date*, and on.

The main variable declarations in a class are the attributes. The other data declarations are the ones inside a function and are known as *local* variable declarations. The structure of object-oriented programs includes the following kinds of statements:

- Class definitions
- Declaration of data constants
- Declaration of simple variables
- Declaration of object references
- Definition of methods or functions

Within the body of function definitions, language instructions are included to create objects and to manipulate the objects created.

6.4.2 Implementing Classes

A class definition is implemented with a class header and additional statements; these are:

1. The **description** statement, which may be used to include a textual documentation or description of the class. This section ends with a start-slash (*/).
2. The **class** statement is used for the class header. This includes assigning a name to the class and other information related to the class.
3. The **private** keyword starts the section for the declarations of the private attributes of the class or definitions of the private operations.
4. The **protected** keyword starts the section for the declaration of protected attributes of the class or definitions of the projected operations.
5. The **public** keyword starts section for the declarations of the private attributes or the definition of the public operations of the class.
6. The **endclass** statement ends the class definition.

With OOSimL, the general syntactic definition of a class is:

description
    . . .
class ⟨ *class_name* ⟩ **is**
  private
      . . . [data declarations]
  protected
      . . . [data declarations]
  public
      . . . [data declarations]
  private
   [definitions of private operations]
  protected
   [definitions of private operations]
  public
   [definitions of public operations]
endclass ⟨ *class_name* ⟩

6.5 Data Declaration

Data descriptions are the data declarations that define the class attributes. Three groups of data attributes can be defined in a class: constants, variables, and object references.

      constants
       . . .
      variables
       . . .
      object references
       . . .

Each data declaration consists of:

- A unique name to identify the data item
- An optional initial value
- The type of the data item

The name of a data item is an identifier and is given by the programmer; it must be different from any keyword in OOSimL (or in Java).

6.5.1 Data Names

Text symbols are used in all algorithm description and in the source program. The special symbols that indicate essential parts of an algorithm are called *keywords*. These are reserved words and cannot be used for any other purpose. The symbols used for uniquely identifying the data items and are called *identifiers* and are defined by the programmer. For example, *x, y, z, s*, and *area*.

The data items normally change their values when they are manipulated by the instructions in the various operations. These data items are known as *variables* because their values change when instructions are applied on them. Those data items that do not change their values are called *constants*. These data items are given an initial value that will never change.

6.5.2 Data Types

Data types can be of two groups: *elementary* (also known as primitive) data types and classes.

Elementary types are classified into the three following categories:

- Numeric
- Text
- Boolean

There are three groups of numeric types: **integer**, **float**, and **double**. The non-integer types are also known as real (or fractional), which means that the numerical values have a fractional part.

Integer values are countable to a finite value, for example, age, number of automobiles, number of pages in a book, and so on. Real values (of type **float**) have a decimal point; for example, cost amount of an item, the height of a building, current temperature in a room, a time interval (period). These values cannot be expressed as integers. Values of type **double** provide more precision than type **float**.

There are of two basic types of text data items: **character** and type **string**. Data items of type **string** consist of a sequence of characters. The values for these two types of data items are textual values.

Another data type is the one in which the values of the variables can take a truth-value (true or false); these variables are of type **boolean**.

Complex types are the classes and are used as types for object reference variables in all object-oriented programs. Values of these variables are references to objects.

6.5.3 Data Declarations in OOSimL

Each data description includes the name or identifier for variable or constant and its type. The initial value of a variable or constant is optional. There are two general categories of variables:

- Variables of elementary or primitive type
- Object reference variables

In object-oriented programming languages, the programmer defines classes as types for object reference variables, then creating objects of these classes.

6.5.3.1 Variables of Elementary Types

The OOSimL statement for the declaration of variables of elementary types has the following form:

define ⟨ variable_name ⟩ **of type** ⟨ elementary_type ⟩

Examples of data declarations in OOSimL of two constants of types **integer** and **double**, and three variables of type **integer**, **float**, and **boolean**.

```
constants
    define MAX_PERIOD = 24 of type integer
    define PI = 3.1416 of type double
variables
    define number_elements of type integer
    define salary of type float
    define act_flag of type boolean
```

6.5.3.2 Object References

An object reference variable can refer to an object. The following OOSimL statement declares object references variables and has the structure:

define ⟨ object_ref_name ⟩ **of class** ⟨ class_name ⟩

The following statements declare an object reference variable called *server_obj* of class *Server*, and an object reference variable *car1* of class *Car*.

```
object references
    define serverobj of class Server
    define car1 of class Car
```

6.5.4 Temporal and Spatial Properties

Additional properties of data items declared are important to fully understand identifying data items in software development, these concepts are:

- The *scope* of a data item is that portion of a program in which statements can reference that data item. Variables and constants declared as attributes of the class can be accessed from anywhere in the class. Instructions in any functioned of the class can use these data items. Local declarations define data items that can only be used by instructions in the function in which they have been declared.
- The *persistence* of a data item is the interval of time that the data item exists—the lifetime of the data item. The lifetime of a variable declared as an attribute of a class, exists during the complete life of an object of the class. Data items declared locally will normally have a life time only during which the function executes.

6.6 Functions

Classes consist of attribute declarations and definitions of functions (or methods).

A function carries out a specific task of a class. Figure 6.2 illustrates the general structure of a function. The definition of a function consists of two basic parts:

- Local data declarations
- The sequence of statements with instructions that manipulate the data

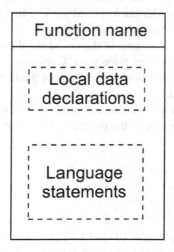

Fig. 6.2 Structure of a function

The body of a function is composed of data declaration and instructions that manipulate the data. The scope of the data declared in the function is *local* to the function. The data in a function only exists during execution of the function; their persistence is limited to the lifetime of the function.

The brief documentation about the purpose of the function is described in the paragraph that starts with the keyword **description** and ends with a star-slash (*/). Other comments can be included at any point in the function to clarify and/or document the function. Line comments start with a double forward slash (//) and end with the line.

The name of the function is declared in the **function** statement. This name is used when the function is called or invoked by some other function. In OOSimL, the basic form of a function definition is as follows.

> **description**
>
>   .   .   .
>
> **function** ⟨ *function_name* ⟩ **is**
>   **constants**
>
>   .   .   .
>
>   **variables**
>
>   .   .   .
>
>   **object references**
>
>   .   .   .
>
>   **begin**
>   .   .   . [instructions]
> **endfun** ⟨ *function_name* ⟩

The keyword **function** starts the header followed by the name of the function; the body of the function starts with the keyword **is**. The function definition ends with the **endfun** keyword and the name of the function.

Similarly to the data declarations in the class, the data declarations are divided into constant, variable, and object references. Constant, variable, and object declarations are optional. The instructions in the body of the function appear between the keywords **begin** and **endfun**.

The special function, *main*, starts and terminates the execution of the entire program; it is the control function of the program. One of the classes of the program must include this function.

6.7 Summary

A program consists of an assembly of classes. This is the static view of a program. A class is a decomposition unit—a basic modular unit; a problem can be decomposed into smaller subproblems.

A class is a collection of objects with similar characteristics. It is also a type for object reference variables. A class is a reusable unit; it can be reused in other applications.

The structure of a class consists of data definitions and function definitions. Data declarations in the class define the attributes of the class; data declarations also appear in the functions to define the function's local data. A function includes data definitions and instructions.

Data definitions consist of the declarations of constants, variables of simple types, and object reference variables.

The implementation of classes in OOSimL and other object-oriented programming languages is accomplished by writing the program using the language statements and structuring the program according to the language syntax.

6.8 Key Terms

static view	dynamic view	decomposition
modules	units	class reuse
package	devices	data declaration
variables	constants	simple types
primitive types	class structure	object references
class description	local data	initial value
data types	scope	persistence

Exercises

6.1. Is a class an appropriate decomposition unit? What other units are possible to consider?

6.2. What is the purpose of a control function such as *main*?.

6.3. The software implementation for a problem is decomposed into classes and functions. Explain this decomposition structure. What is the purpose of decomposing a problem into subproblems?

6.4. Is it convenient to include public attribute definitions in classes? What are the advantages and disadvantages? *Hint*: review the concepts of encapsulation and information hiding.

6.5. When a program executes, the objects of the program interact collaborating to accomplish the overall solution to the problem. This is a dynamic view of a program. Where and when are these objects created and started? Explain.

Chapter 7
Functions

7.1 Introduction

A function carries out a specific task in a class. A function is an internal decomposition unit because every function belongs to a class. Object orientation promotes the reuse of class, which means that a class can be used in another application.

A function can receive input data from another function when invoked; the input data passed from another function is called a parameter. The function can also return output data when it completes execution.

This chapter describes class and function decomposition. The chapter also discusses the basic mechanisms for data transfer between two functions; several examples are included.

7.2 Function Implementation

A program is normally decomposed into classes, and classes are divided into methods or functions.

As mentioned previously, data declared within a function is known only to that function—the scope of the data is *local* to the function. The data in a function has a limited lifetime, it only exists during execution of the function.

The name of the function is used when it is called or invoked by some other function. The relevant documentation of the function is described in the **description** paragraph, which ends with a star-slash (*/). The OOSimL statements for defining a function are:

>   **description**
>
>   . . .
>
>   */
>   **function** ⟨ *function_name* ⟩ **is**

J.M. Garrido, *Object Oriented Simulation: A Modeling and Programming Perspective*,
DOI: 10.1007/978-1-4419-0516-1_7,
© Springer Science + Business Media, LLC 2009

constants
. . .
variables
. . .
object references
. . .
begin
. . . [instructions]
endfun ⟨ *function_name* ⟩

The data declarations are divided into constant declarations, variable declarations, and object declarations. This is similar to the data declarations that appear in the class. These declarations define local data in the function and are optional. The instructions of the function appear between the keywords **begin** and **endfun**. The following OOSimL code shows a simple function for displaying a text message on the screen.

```
description
    This function displays a message
    on the screen. */
function show_message is
begin
    display "Computing data"
endfun show_message
```

7.3 Function Calls

A function starts executing when it is called by another function. A function *call* is also known as *method invocation*. The function that calls another function is known as the calling function; the second function is known as the called function. When a function calls or invokes another function, the flow of control is altered and the second function starts execution. When the called function completes execution, the flow of control is transferred back (returned) to the calling function. This function continues execution from the point after it called the second function.

After completion, the called function may or may not return a value to the calling function. From the data transfer point of view, there are three general categories of functions:

1. *Simple functions* are functions that do not return any value when they are invoked. The previous example, function *show_message*, is a simple (or void) function because it does not return any value to the function that invoked it.
2. *Value-returning* functions that return a single value after completion.
3. Functions with *parameters* are functions that require one or more data items as input values when invoked.

Functions that combine the last two categories —functions that return a value and that have parameters are also grouped in two categories, according to their purpose:

- Functions that return the value of an attribute of the object and do not change the value of any attribute(s) of the object. These are known as *accessor* functions.
- Functions that change the state of the object in some way by altering the value of one or more attributes in the object. Normally, these functions do not return any value. These are known as *mutator* functions.

Good programming practice recommends defining the functions in a class as being either accessor or mutator.

7.3.1 Calling Simple Functions

Simple functions do not return a value to the calling function. An example of this kind of function is *show_message*, discussed previously. There is no data transfer to or from the function. In OOSimL, the statement that calls or invokes a simple function that is referenced by an object reference variable is:

call ⟨ *function_name* ⟩ **of** ⟨ *object_reference* ⟩

In the following example, function *show_message* that belongs to an object referenced by *carobj*, is invoked from function *main*, the call statement is:

call show_message **of** carobj

Figure 7.1 shows the calling function and the called function, *show_message*. After completing its execution, the called function returns the flow of control to the calling function.

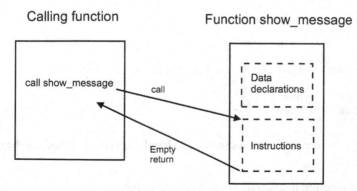

Fig. 7.1 The calling and called functions

Data can be transferred between the calling and the called function. This data transfer may occur from the calling function to the called function, from the called function to the calling function, or in both directions.

7.3.2 Value-Returning Functions

Value-returning functions transfer data from the called function to the calling function. In these functions, a single value is calculated or assigned to a variable and is returned to the calling function.

The called function is defined with a type, which is the type of the return value. The function *return type* may be a simple type or a class. After the execution of the called function completes, control is returned to the calling function with a single value. The OOSimL statements that define the form of a value-returning function are:

description

     .   .   .

    */

function ⟨ *function_name* ⟩ **of type** ⟨ *return_type* ⟩ **is**

     .   .   .

       return ⟨ *return_value* ⟩

   endfun ⟨ *function_name* ⟩

The value in the return statement can be any valid expression, following the **return** keyword. The expression can include constants, variables, object references, or a combination of these.

The following example defines a function, *get_name* that returns the value of the attribute *emp_name* of an object of class Employee. This value is returned to the calling function. In the header of the function, the type of the value returned is indicated as **string**. The code for this function definition is:

```
description
   This function returns the name of the employee object.
   */
function get_name return type string is
begin
    return name
endfun get_name
```

The value-returning function can be called and the value returned can be used in several ways:

- Call the function in a simple assignment statement
- Call the function in an assignment with an arithmetic expression

- Call the function in a more complete *call* statement

The value returned by the called function is used by the calling function by assigning this returned value to another variable. The following example shows a function calling function *get_salary*. The calling function assigns the value returned to variable *sal*. There are several ways to write this code and the statements are:

```
set sal = call get_salary
call get_salary return value to sal
set sal = get_salary()
```

The value returned can be used in an assignment with an arithmetic expression after calling a function. For example, after calling function *get_salary*, the value returned is assigned to variable *sal*. This variable is then used in an arithmetic expression that multiplies *sal* by variable *percent*. The value that results from evaluating this expression is assigned to variable *upd_sal*. This assignment statement is:

```
set upd_sal = sal * percent
```

7.3.3 Function Calls with Arguments

The called function can receive data values when called from another function. The functions definition for functions to be called should include data definitions known as *parameter declarations*. These parameter definitions are similar to local data declarations and have local scope and persistence. The called function may return a value, although it is not recommended to define the called function for this.

The data values sent to the called function by calling function are known as *arguments* and can be actual values (constants) or names of data items. When there are two or more argument values in the function call, the argument list consists of the data items separated by commas. The argument list should appear after the keyword **using** in the **call** statement. The OOSimL **call** statement for a function call with arguments is:

call ⟨ *function_name* ⟩ **of** ⟨ *object_ref* ⟩
using ⟨ *argument_list* ⟩

The following example is a call to function *cal_area* that belongs to an object referenced by *myobj*. The function calculates and displays the area of a triangle given two arguments *x* and *y*. This **call** statement is:

```
call cal_area of myobj using x, y
```

The declaration of parameters in a function defines for every parameter a type and a parameter name. The general structure of a function with parameter declaration is:

description

    . . .
    */
function ⟨ *function_name* ⟩
parameters ⟨ *parameter_list* ⟩
is

    . . .

endfun ⟨ *function_name* ⟩

In the following example, function *cal_area* computes the area of a triangle given the base and altitude. The code for the function in OOSimL is:

```
description
   This function calculates the area of
    A triangle given the base b and the height h
    it then prints the result on the screen.
    */
function cal_area
parameters b of type float,
           h of type float
is
variables
   define area of type float    // local variable
begin
   set area = b * h * 0.5
   display "Area of triangle is: ", area
   return                        // empty return
endfun cal_area
```

In the example, function *cal_area* declares the parameters *b* and *h*. The parameters are used as placeholders for the corresponding argument values transferred from the calling function. Figure 7.2 illustrates the call of function *cal_area* with argument values from the calling function.

7.4 Constructors

One or more *constructors* functions, also known as *initializer* functions, will normally appear in a class definition. These are special functions that are called when creating objects of the enclosing class. The main purpose of an initializer function is to set the object created to an appropriate initial state. The attributes of the corresponding object are assigned to some initial values.

In the following example, class *Employee* include the attribute declaration and the definition of the initializer function.

```
class Employee is
```

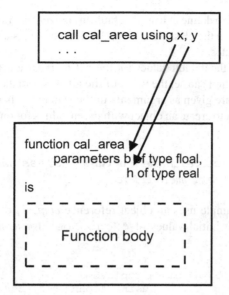

Fig. 7.2 Using arguments in a function call

```
private
variables
    define salary of type double
    define age of type integer
    define name of type string
    define sal_increase of type double
object references
    define employ_date of class EmpDate
public
description
  This is the constructor, it initializes an Employee
  object on creation.     */
function initializer
parameters iname of type string,
           isalary of type double,
           iage of type integer
is
begin
  set salary = isalary
  set age = iage
  set name = iname
  set sal_increase = 0.0
  set employ_date = null
endfun initializer
. . . [other functions in the class]
endclass Employee
```

It is recommended to define at least a default initializer function. When no initializer function appears in the class definition, the default values are (zero and empty)
assigned to the attributes.

In class *Employee* the default values for the *sal_increase* attribute is set to 0.0.

An initializer function can set the value of the attributes to the values given when
called. These values are given as arguments in the statement that creates the object.
The general statement to create an object with given values for one or more attributes
is:

> **create** ⟨ *object_ref_name* ⟩ **of class** ⟨ *class_name* ⟩
> **using** ⟨ *argument_list* ⟩

The following example uses an object reference *emp_obj* of class *Employee* to
create an object with initial values of "John Doe" for *name*, 35876.00 for
salary, and 45 for *age*.

```
create emp_obj of class Employee
                    using "John Doe", 35876.00, 45
```

Overloading is the programming facility of defining two or more functions with
the same name. This facility of the programming language allows any function in
a class to be overloaded. These functions are defined with the same name, but with
a different number of and types of parameters. In this way, there is more than one
way to initialize an object of the class.

7.5 Complete Sample Program

The following example is a complete program that consists of two classes: class
Employeem and class *Comp_salary*. The definition of class *Employee* is as follows:

```
description
   This program computes the salary increase for an employee;
   if his/her salary is greater than $45,000 the salary
   increase  is 4.5%, otherwise the salary increase is 5%.
   This is the class for employees. The main attributes are
      salary, age, and name.  */
class Employeem is
   private
   variables                        // variable data declarations
      define salary of type float
      define age of type integer
      define obj_name of type string
      define salincrease of type float   // salary increase
   public
   description
      This is the constructor, it initializes an object on
```

```
      creation.        */
   function initializer
   parameters iname of type string,
             isalary of type float,
             iage of type integer
   is
   begin
     set salary = isalary
     set age = iage
     set obj_name = iname
   endfun initializer
   description
     This funtion gets the salary of the employee object. */
   function get_salary return type float is
     begin
       return salary
   endfun get_salary
   description
     This function returns the name of the employee object. */
   function get_name return type string is
     begin
       return obj_name
   endfun get_name
   description
       This function computes the salary increase and
       updates the salary of an employee.         */
   function sal_increase is
     constants    // constant data declarations
       define percent1 = 0.045 of type float
       define percent2 = 0.050 of type float
     begin                   // body of function starts here
       if salary > 45000.00 then
          set salincrease = salary * percent1
       else
          set salincrease = salary * percent2
       endif
       add salincrease to salary    // update salary
   endfun sal_increase
   description
     This function returns the salary increase for
     the object. */
   function get_increase return type float is
    begin
       return salincrease
   endfun get_increase
 endclass Employeem
```

The other class, *Comp_salary*, includes function *main* that starts and controls the execution of the entire program. The following code is the implementation of class *Comp_salary*.

```
 description
   This program computes the salary increase for an employee;
```

```
    if his/her salary is greater than $45,000 the salary
    increase is 4.5%, otherwise the salary increase is 5%.
    This class creates and manipulates the objects of
    class Employeem. */
class Comp_salary is
  public
  description
      This is the main function of the application.
      */
  function main is
    variables
      define increase of type float
      define salary of type float
      define age of type integer
      define empname of type string
    object references
      define emp_obj of class Employeem
    begin
      display "Enter salary: "
      read salary
      display "Enter age: "
      read age
      display "Enter employee name: "
      read empname
      create emp_obj of class Employeem using
                            empname, salary, age
      call sal_increase of emp_obj
      set increase = call get_increase of emp_obj
      set salary = get_salary() of emp_obj // updated salary
      display "Employee name: ", empname
      display "increase: ", increase, " new salary: ",
                                                    salary
    endfun main
  endclass Comp_salary
```

7.6 Static Features

Functions or attributes in a class may not be associated with any object of the class. These features are known as *static* features and do not belong to an object, although they are defined in a class. To access these features, the class name followed by a dot and then the name of the feature is used. The following example invokes method *cos* of class *Math*:

```
set angle = Math.cos(x) * delta
```

To define a static function, the keyword **static** is written before the name of the function. The following example is the header for the definition of method *compute_h*:

```
function static compute_h is
 . . .
endfun compute_h
```

In a similar manner, the declaration of a static attribute is written with the keyword **static** before the variable declaration. These variables should normally be private and should be accessed by (public) accessor functions. When the program executes, for every declaration of a static variable, there is only one copy of its value shared by all objects of the class. Often, static variables are also known as class variables, and static methods as class methods.

The following example declares a static variable named *count_pins* and initializes it to value 20.

```
static integer count_pins = 20
```

7.7 Summary

Functions are internal modular units in a class. Classes are modular units that can be reused in other applications. Invoking functions involves several mechanisms for data transfer. Calling simple functions do not involve data transfer between the calling function and the called function. Value-returning functions return a value to the calling function. Calling functions that define one or more parameters involve values sent by the calling function and used as input in the called function.

Functions can also be grouped as accessor and mutator functions. The first group of functions access and return the value of some attribute of the object. The second group changes some of the attributes of the object.

Constructor functions are special functions that set the attributes of a class to appropriate values when an object is created. These functions are known as initializer functions.

Static features are associated with the class that defined them and not with its objects. The value of a static variable is shared by all objects of the class.

7.8 Key Terms

methods	functions	method invocation
function call	messages	object reference
object creation	object manipulation	local declaration
return value	assignment	parameters
arguments	local data	default values
static features	initializer	constructor

Exercises

7.1. Why is a function a decomposition unit? Explain.

7.2. What is the purpose of function *main*?

7.3. Explain the data transfer among functions.

7.4. Explain the reasons why it is good programming practice to separate the role of a function as being either an accessor or a mutator function.

7.5. Define a function that includes one or more parameters.

7.6. Explain why more than one initializer function definition may appear in a class.

7.7. Add two attributes, *emp_date* and *emp_address* to class *Employeem*, also add any necessary functions.

Chapter 8
Design and Program Structures

8.1 Introduction

The purpose of programming is designing a computer solution to a problem. An *algorithm* and the appropriate data structures have to be designed that will carry out the problem solution. An algorithm is a detailed and precise sequence of activities that accomplishes a solution to a problem.

A programming language is used to implement an algorithm and data descriptions that represent the solution to a problem. This chapter explains the general design structures of an algorithm. These are explained using informal, more general, and higher-level notations: *flowcharts* and *pseudo-code*.

8.2 Design Notations

Designing a solution to a problem involves design of an algorithm, which will be as general as possible to solve a family or group of similar problems. To describe an algorithm, several notations are used, such as informal English, flowcharts, and pseudo-code.

An algorithm can be described at several levels of abstraction. Starting from a very high-level and general level of description of a preliminary design, to a much lower-level that has more detailed description of the design.

A notation is a more informal and higher level than a programming language. It is set of rules used for the informal description of an algorithm. Two widely-used design notations are:

- Flowcharts
- Pseudo-code

J.M. Garrido, *Object Oriented Simulation: A Modeling and Programming Perspective*,
DOI: 10.1007/978-1-4419-0516-1_8,
© Springer Science + Business Media, LLC 2009

8.2.1 *Flowcharts*

Flowcharts consist of a set of symbol blocks connected by arrows. A flowchart is a visual representation for describing a sequence of design or action steps of the solution to a problem. The arrows that connect the blocks show the order in which the action steps are to be carried out. The arrows also show the flow of data.

Several simple flowchart blocks are shown in Figure 8.1. A flowchart always begins with a *start* symbol, which has an arrow pointing from it. A flowchart ends with a *stop* symbol, which has one arrow pointing to it.

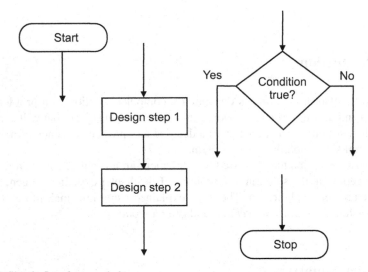

Fig. 8.1 Simple flowchart symbols

The *process* symbol or *transformation* symbol is the most common and general symbol; it represents a design step. The symbol is shown as a rectangular box and represents any computation or sequence of computations carried out on some data. There is one arrow pointing to it and one arrow point from it.

Another flowchart symbol has the shape of a vertical diamond, and it represents a selection of alternate paths in the sequence of design steps. This symbol is also shown in Figure 8.1. This symbol is known as a decision block or a conditional block because the sequence of instructions can take one of two directions in the flowchart.

The flowchart symbol for a data input or output operation is shown in Figure 8.2. There is one arrow pointing into the block and one arrow pointing out from the block.

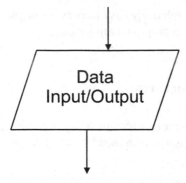

Fig. 8.2 Flowchart data input/output symbol

For larger or more complex algorithms, flowcharts are used for the high-level description of the algorithms.

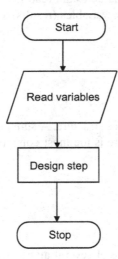

Fig. 8.3 A simple flowchart

A simple flowchart with several basic symbols is shown in Figure 8.3.

8.2.2 Pseudo-code

Pseudo-code is a notation that uses English description for describing the algorithm that defines a problem solution. It can be used to describe relatively large and complex algorithms. Pseudo-code is much easier to understand and use than any programming language. It is relatively easy to convert the pseudo-code description of an algorithm to a high-level programming language.

8.3 Algorithmic Structures

There are four design structures with which any algorithm can be described. These can be used with flowcharts and with pseudo-code notations. The basic design structures are:

- *Sequence*, any task can be broken down into a sequence of steps.
- *Selection*, part of the algorithm takes a decision and select one of several alternate paths of flow of actions. This structure is also known as alternation or conditional branch.
- *Repetition*, this part pf the algorithm has a set of steps that are to be executed zero, one, or more times. This structure is also known as looping.
- *Input-output*, the values of variables are read from an input device (such as the keyword) or the values of the variables (results) are written to an output device (such as the screen)

8.3.1 Sequence

Figure 8.3 illustrates the sequence structure. A simple sequence of flowchart blocks is shown. The sequence structure is the most common and basic structure used in algorithmic design.

8.3.2 Selection

With the selection structure, one of several alternate paths will be followed based on the evaluation of a condition. Figure 8.4 illustrates the selection structure. In the figure, the actions in *Action step1* are executed when the condition is true. The instructions in *Action step2* are executed when the condition is false.

A flowchart example of the selection structure is shown in Figure 8.5. The condition of the selection structure is $X > 0$ and when this condition evaluates to true, the block with the action `increment  j` will execute. Otherwise, the block with the action `decrement  j` is executed.

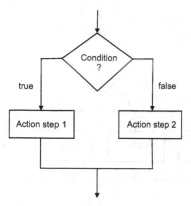

Fig. 8.4 Selection structure in flowchart form

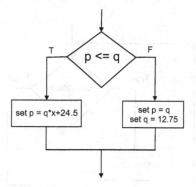

Fig. 8.5 An example of the selection structure

A variation of the selection structure has multiple alternate paths, each one depends on the value of a variable. This structure is known as the *case* construct. Figure 8.6 illustrates this construct.

8.3.3 Repetition

The repetition structure will cause a set of action steps to be repeated several times. Figure 8.7 shows this structure. The execution of the actions in *Action step1* are repeated while the condition is true. This structure is also known as the *while loop*.

A variation of the repetition structure is shown in Figure 8.8. The actions in *Action step1* are repeated until the condition becomes true. This structure is also known as the *repeat-until* loop.

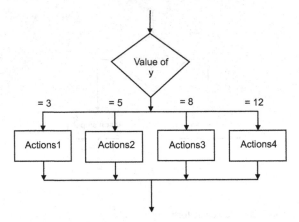

Fig. 8.6 The *case* construct

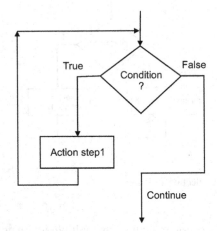

Fig. 8.7 Repetition structure in flowchart form

8.4 Programming Statements

Programming languages are used to implement the solution that has been designed; this includes the data descriptions and the algorithm. A programming language has language *statements* that are used for data declarations and for writing the instructions.

This section mainly deals with simple OOSimL statements, such as the assignment and I/O statements.

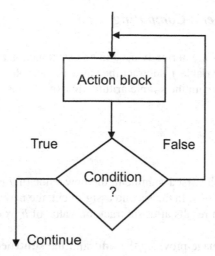

Fig. 8.8 Repeat-until loop of the repetition structure

8.4.1 Assignment and Arithmetic Expressions

The most used statement is the *assignment* statement and is used to assign a value to a variable. The statement is written with the keyword **set**. This variable must be written on the left-hand side of the equal sign, which is the assignment operator.

The value to assign can be directly copied from another variable, from a constant value, or from the value that results after evaluating an expression.

In the following example, the constant value 1435.5 is assigned to variable h and the value 100 to variable j.

```
variables
    float h
    float p
    float q
    integer j
begin
    . . .
    set h = 1435.5
    set j = 100
    set p = q + 14.5 * h
```

The third assignment statement in the example, variable p is assigned the result of evaluating the expression, $q + 14.5 * h$.

8.4.2 Simple Numeric Computing

Arithmetic expressions are normally used in an assignment statement. For example add 5 to the value of variable j, subtract the value of variable h from variable p, the assignment statements with the simple arithmetic expressions are:

```
set  j = j + 5
set  p = p - h
```

In the example, in the first assignment, the new value of j is assigned by adding 5 to the previous value of j. In the second assignment, the new value of variable p is assigned the value that results after subtract the value of h from the previous value of p.

The OOSimL language provides the **add** and the **subtract** statements that are equivalent to the assignments of in the example. The following two statements show the same computation.

```
add 5 to j
subtract h from p
```

To add or subtract 1, the language provides the **increment** and the **decrement** statement. For example, `increment  j`, adds the constant 1 to the value of variable j. `decrement  k` subtracts the constant value 1 from the value of variable k.

The arithmetic expression used in the assignment statements discussed previously were very simple; only basic arithmetic operations appeared in the expressions. These are addition, subtraction, multiplication, and division.

To carry out more complex calculations, the language class library provides various numerical functions. Most of these functions are static, so to use a particular function of the *Math* library class, the name of the class must appear followed by a dot and then the name of the particular function invoked. Class *Math* is part of the class library supplied with the Java compiler. This class provides several mathematical functions, such as square root, exponentiation, trigonometric.

For example, consider the value of the expression $\cos x + y$ assigned to variable z and $\sqrt{t}$ - p

The expression in the assignment statement use the mathematical functions *cos* and *sqrt* in class `Math`. The OOSimL statements are:

```
set  z = Math.cos(x) + y
set  y = Math.sqrt(t) - p
```

The value of the mathematical expression b^2 assigned to variable *area*, is coded as:

```
set area = Math.pow(b, 2)
```

8.4.3 Console I/O

The programming language OOSimL provides two basic statements for console input/output. The input statement reads a value of a variable from the input device (e.g., the keyboard). This statement is written with the keywords **read**, for input of a single variable. The output statement can be used for the output of a list of variables and literals, it is written with the keyword **display**. The general form of the input statement is:

```
read ⟨ variable_name ⟩
```

The following example uses the **read** statement to read a value of variable *h*:

```
read h
```

The input statement implies an assignment statement for the variable *h*, because the variable changes its value to the new value that is read from the input device.

The output statement writes the value of one or more variables to the output device. The variable does not change their values. The general form of the output statement is:

```
display ⟨ data_list ⟩
```

With the output statement, a list of data items can be displayed on the console. The following example displays on the console: a string literal, followed by the value of variable *h*, followed by another string literal, and followed by the value of variable *q*.

```
display "value of h: ", h, " value of q: ", q
```

8.5 Computing Area and Circumference

This problem computes the area and circumference of a circle, given its radius. The high-level algorithm description in informal pseudo-code notation is:

1. Read the value of the radius of a circle, from the input device.
2. Compute the area of the circle.
3. Compute the circumference of the circle.
4. Print or display the value of the area of the circle to the output device.
5. Print or display the value of the circumference of the circle to the output device.

A more detailed algorithm description follows:

1. Read the value of the radius r of a circle, from the input device.
2. Establish the constant π with value 3.14159.
3. Compute the area of the circle, $area = \pi \times r^2$.
4. Compute the circumference of the circle $cir = 2 \times \pi \times r$.
5. Print or display the value of $area$ of the circle to the output device.
6. Print or display the value of cir of the circle to the output device.

The following OOSimL program implements the data description and the algo-rithm for calculating the area of a circle. The example has a single class that includes function *main*. This class calls a function, *pow* of the library class, *Math*.

```
description
    This class computes the area and circumference of
    A circle, given its radius. This value is read
    using console I/O.
    */
class Circle_comp is
 public
 function main is
    // data descriptions
 constants
    define PI = 3.14159 of type double
 variables
    define r of type float
    define area of type double
    define cir of type double
 begin
    // instructions starts here
    display "enter value of radius: "
    read r
    // compute area of circle
    set area = PI * Math.pow(r, 2)
    // compute circumference of circle
    set cir = 2.0 * PI * r
    // now print the results
    display "Area of circle is: ", area
    display "Circumference of circle is: ", cir
 endfun main
endclass Circle_comp
```

After compiling the program is executed and produces the following results on the console:

```
Enter value of radius: 2.75
Area of circle is: 23.758274375
Circumference of circle is: 17.278745
```

8.6 Summary

A computer program is the implementation of the computer solution to a problem. It is written in an appropriate programming language. The program includes the data descriptions and the algorithm. Data descriptions involve identifying, assigning a name, and assigning a type to every data item used in the problem solution. Data items are variables and constants.

The precise, detailed, and complete description of a solution to a problem is known as an algorithm. The notations to describe algorithms are flowcharts and pseudo-code. Flowcharts are a visual representation of the execution flow of the various instructions in the algorithm. Pseudo-code is an English-like notation to describe algorithms.

The design structures are sequence, selection, repetition, and input-output. These are used to describe any algorithm.

8.7 Key Terms

algorithm	flowcharts	pseudo-code
variables	constants	declarations
structure	sequence	action step
selection	repetition	Input/Output
statements	data type	identifier

Exercises

8.1. Write the algorithm and data descriptions for computing the area of a triangle. Use flowcharts.

8.2. Write the algorithm and data descriptions for computing the area of a triangle. Use pseudo-code.

8.3. Write a complete OOSimL program for computing the area of a triangle. Use two classes.

8.4. Write the algorithm and data descriptions for computing the perimeter of a triangle. Use pseudo-code.

8.5. Write the algorithm and data descriptions for computing the perimeter of a triangle. Use flowcharts.

8.6. Write a complete OOSimL program for computing the perimeter of a triangle. Use two classes.

8.7. Write the data and algorithm descriptions in flowchart and in pseudo-code to compute the conversion from a temperature reading in degrees Fahrenheit to Centigrade. The algorithm should also compute the conversion from Centigrade to Fahrenheit.

8.8. Implement the OOSimL program to compute the conversion from a temperature reading in degrees Fahrenheit to Centigrade. The program should also compute the conversion from Centigrade to Fahrenheit.

8.9. Write an algorithm and data descriptions in flowchart and pseudo-code to compute the conversion from inches to centimeters and from centimeters to inches.

8.10. Implement the OOSimL program to compute the conversion from inches to centimeters and from centimeters to inches.

Chapter 9
Selection

9.1 Introduction

To fully describe algorithms, four design structures are used: sequence, selection, repetition, and input/output. This chapter explains two selection statements in the OOSimL language. The statements are the **if** and the **case** statements.

Conditions are used in the selection statements. Conditions are expressions of type **Boolean** that evaluate to a truth-value (true or false). Simple conditions are formed with relational operators for comparing two data items. Compound conditions are formed by joining two or more simple conditions with the *logical* operators.

For examples of applying the selection statements, two problems are discussed: the solution of a quadratic equation and the solution to of the salary problem.

9.2 Selection Structure

The selection design structure is also known as alternation, because alternate paths are considered based on a condition.

9.2.1 Flowchart of Selection Structure

The selection structure provides the capability for decision-making. Because the selection design structure is better understood using a flowchart, Figure 9.1 is repeated here. The figure shows two possible paths for the execution flow. The condition is evaluated, and one of the paths is selected. If the condition is true, then the left path is selected and *Action step1* is performed. If the condition is false, the other path is selected and *Action step2* is performed.

J.M. Garrido, *Object Oriented Simulation: A Modeling and Programming Perspective*,
DOI: 10.1007/978-1-4419-0516-1_9,
© Springer Science + Business Media, LLC 2009

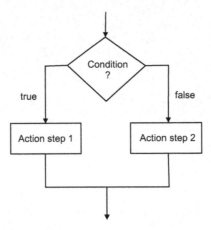

Fig. 9.1 Flowchart of the Selection structure

9.2.2 IF Statement

The selection structure is written with an **if** statement, also known as an if-then-else statement. This statement includes three sections: the condition, the then-section, and the else-section. The else-section is optional. Several keywords are used in this statement: **if, then, else**, and **endif**. The general form of the **if** statement is:

> **if** ⟨ *condition* ⟩
>   **then**
>   ⟨ *first sequence of statements* ⟩
>   **else**
>   ⟨ *alternate sequence of statements* ⟩
> **endif**

The **if** statement that corresponds to the selection structure in Figure 9.1 is:

> **if** condition is true
>   **then**
>   perform instructions in Action step1
>   **else**
>   perform instructions in Action step2
> **endif**

When the **if** statement executes, the condition is evaluated and only one of the two alternatives will be carried out: the one with the statements in *Action step1* or the one with the statements in *Action step2*.

9.2.3 Boolean Expressions

Boolean expressions are written to form conditions. A condition consists of an expression that evaluates to a truth-value, **true** or **false**.

A simple Boolean expression can be formed with the values of two data items and a relational operator. The following list of relational operators can appear in a Boolean expression:

- Less than, <
- Less or equal to, <=
- Greater than, >
- Greater or equal to, >=
- Equal, ==
- Not equal, !=

Examples of simple conditions are:

```
height > 23.75
a <= b
p == q
```

OOSimL supports not only conditions with the syntax in the previous example, but also provides additional keywords can be used for the relational operators. For example, the previous Boolean expressions can also be written as:

```
height greater than 23.75
a less or equal to b
p equal to q
```

9.2.4 Example of Selection

In this example, the condition to be evaluated is: $p \leq q$, and a decision is taken on how to update variable p. Figure 9.2 shows the flowchart for part of the algorithm that includes this selection structure.

The OOSimL code for this example is:

```
if p <= q
then
    set p = q * x + 24.5
else
    set p = q
```

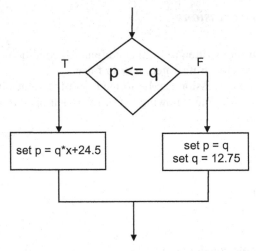

Fig. 9.2 Example of selection structure

        set q = 12.75
    endif

9.3 Example Program

This example computes the gross pay, taxes, and net pay of employees, given the hours worked and the hourly rate.

9.3.1 High-level Design

The overall description of the data and algorithm is shown in Figure 9.3. The flow of control in the selection structure depends on the condition: *gpay* **greater than** *TAXB*.

The high-level description of algorithm in pseudo-code follows:

1. Read values of employee name, employee number, hours worked, and hourly rate.
2. Compute gross pay: hours worked × hourly rate
3. if gross pay > tax bracket then
   Compute tax amount: (gross pay − tax bracket) × tax rate
   Compute net pay: gross pay − tax amount
   else compute net pay = gross pay
4. Display employee name, tax amount, net pay

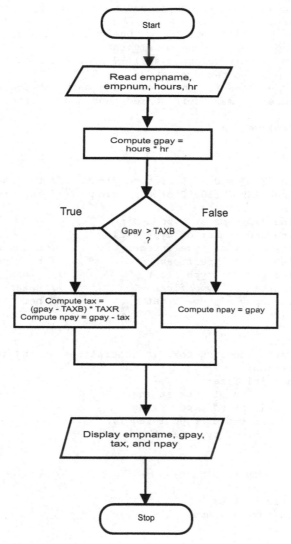

Fig. 9.3 General problem description

9.3.2 Implementation

The implementation of the employee payment problem consists of two classes:
PayEmployee and *Comp_pay*. The most interesting part of the solution for this prob-
lem includes the selection statement and is found in function *compute_pay* of class
PayEmployee.

```
description
```

```
    This program computes the amount to pay an employee weekly
    after deducting taxes.
    The gross pay is computed from the number of hours worked
    by the employee, and the hourly rate.
    The income tax is computed as 14.75% of the amount earned
    that exceeds the tax bracket, $110.00
    This is the class for employees. The main attributes are
       emp_number, name, hours worked, and hourly rate.
    */
class PayEmployee is
  private
  constants

      define TAXR = 0.1475 of type float    // tax rate
      define TAXB = 110.00 of type float    // tax bracket
  variables
      define emp_name of type string
      define emp_number of type string
      define hours of type integer          // hours worked
      define hr of type float               // hourly rate
      define gpay of type float             // gross pay
      define tax of type float              // taxes
      define npay of type float             // net pay
  public
      //
  description
     This is the constructor, it initializes an object
     on creation.     */
  function initializer
  parameters iname of type string,
             inumb of type string,
             ihours of type integer,
             ihr of type float
    is
    begin
      set emp_number = inumb
      set hr = ihr
      set hours = ihours
      set emp_name = iname
    endfun initializer
    //
    description
      This funtion gets the tax amount paid by the
      employee object.     */
    function get_tax return type float is
      begin
         return tax
    endfun get_tax
    //
    description
      This function returns the name of the employee object.
      */
    function get_name return type string is
      begin
```

```
      return emp_name
   endfun get_name
   //
   description
      This function computes the gross pay, the taxes,
      and the net pay of an employee.
      */
   function compute_pay is
     begin
       // compute gross pay
       set gpay = hours * hr
       //
       // compute tax and net pay
       if gpay > TAXB then
          set tax = (gpay - TAXB) * TAXR
          set npay = gpay - tax   // net pay
       else
          set npay = gpay
       endif
   endfun compute_pay
   //
   description
      This function returns the net pay for the
      PayEmployee object.      */
   function get_npay return type float is
    begin
      return npay
   endfun get_npay
endclass PayEmployee
//
```

The following class, *Comp_pay* includes the function *main*, which creates and manipulates objects of class *PayEmployee*.

```
description
   This program computes the gross pay, tax amount,
   and net pay an employee;
   */
class Comp_pay is
  public

  description
     This is the main function of the application.
     */
  function main is
    variables
      define net_pay of type float
      define taxes of type float
      define empname of type string
      define empnum of type string
      define hours of type integer
      define hrate of type float
    object references
```

```
        define emp_obj of class PayEmployee
      begin

        display "Enter employee name: "
        read empname
        display "Enter employee number: "
        read empnum
        display "Enter hours worked: "
        read hours
        display "Enter hourly rate: "
        read hrate
        create emp_obj of class PayEmployee using empname,
                empnum, hours, hrate
        call compute_pay of emp_obj
        set net_pay = call get_npay of emp_obj
        set taxes = get_tax() of emp_obj // get tax amount paid
        display "Employee name: ", empname, " Net pay: ",
                net_pay, " Tax amount: ", taxes
      endfun main
  endclass Comp_pay
```

9.4 If Statement with Multiple Paths

The **if** statement with multiple paths is used to implement decisions involving more than two alternatives. The additional **elseif** clause is used to expand the number of alternatives. The general form of the *if* statement with *k* alternatives is:

```
   if ⟨ condition ⟩
      then
         ⟨ sequence1 of statements ⟩
      elseif ⟨ condition2 ⟩
      then
         ⟨ sequence2 of statements ⟩
      elseif ⟨ condition3 ⟩
      then
         ⟨ sequence3 of statements ⟩
         . . .
      else
         ⟨ sequencek of statements ⟩
   endif
```

The conditions in a multiple-path **if** statement are evaluated from top to bottom until one of the conditions evaluates to true. The following example applies the **if** statement with four paths.

```
if height > 6.30
then increment group1
elseif height > 6.15
then increment group2
elseif height > 5.85
then increment group3
elseif height > 5.60
then increment group4
else increment group5
endif
```

9.5 Using Logical Operators

With the logical operators, complex Boolean expressions can be constructed. The logical operators are: **and**, **or**, and **not**. These logical operators help to construct complex (or compound) conditions from simpler conditions. The general form of a complex conditions using the **or** operator and two simple conditions, *cond1* and *cond2*, is:

```
cond1 and cond2
cond1 or cond2
 not cond1
```

The following example includes the **and** logical operator:

if x >= y **and** p == q
then
    ⟨ *statements_1* ⟩
else
    ⟨ *statements_2* ⟩
endif

The condition can also be written in the following manner:

if x **greater or equal to** y **and** p **is equal to** q
   . . .

The following example applies the **not** operator:

not (p > q)

9.6 The Case Statement

The case structure is a simplified version of the selection structure with multiple paths. The **case** statement evaluates the value of a single variable or simple expression of type **integer** or of type **character** and selects the appropriate path. The case statement also supports compound statements, that is, multiple statements instead of a single statement in one or more of the selection options. The general form of this statement is:

```
case ⟨ selector_variable ⟩ of
   value  variable_value : ⟨ statements ⟩
     . . .
endcase
```

In the following example, the temperature status of a boiler is monitored and the temperature status is stored in variable *temp_status*. The following case statement first evaluates the temperature status in variable *temp_status* and then assigns an appropriate string literal to variable *mess*, finally this variable is displayed on the console.

The example assumes that the variables involved have an appropriate declaration, such as:

```
variables
    define temp_status of type character
    define mess of type string
    . . .
    case temp_status of
        value 'E' : mess = "Extremely dangerous"
        value 'D' : mess = "Dangerous"
        value 'H' : mess = "High"
        value 'N' : mess = "Normal"
        value 'B' : mess = "Below normal"
    endcase
      . . .
    display "Temperature status: ", mess
```

The default option of the **case** statement can also be used by writing the keywords **default** or **otherwise** in the last case of the selector variable. For example, the previous example can be enhanced by including the default option in the case statement:

```
    case temp_status of
        value 'E' : mess = "Extremely dangerous"
        value 'D' : mess = "Dangerous"
        value 'H' : mess = "High"
```

```
        value 'N': mess = "Normal"
        value 'B': mess = "Below normal"
        otherwise
              mess = "Temp rising"
   endcase
        . . .
      display "Temperature status: ", mess
```

9.7 Summary

The selection design structure evaluates a condition then takes one of two (or more) paths. This structure is also known as alternation. The two selection statements in pseudo-code explained are the **if** and **case** statements. The first one is applied when there are two or more possible paths in the algorithm, depending on how the condition evaluates. The case statement is applied when the value of a single variable or expression is evaluated, and there are multiple possible values.

The condition in the **if** statement consists of a Boolean expression, which evaluates to a truth-value (true or false). Relational operators and logical operators are used to form Boolean expressions.

9.8 Key Terms

selection	alternation	condition
if statement	case statement	relational operators
logical operators	truth-value	then
else	endif	endcase
otherwise	default	elseif

Exercises

9.1. Write the flowchart and develop a program that finds and display the largest of four numbers, which are read from console.

9.2. Write a flowchart and develop a program that finds and display the smallest of four numbers, which are read from console.

9.3. Write a complete design in flowchart and a program that computes the solution to a quadratic equation. The program must include complex roots, in addition real roots.

9.4. Develop a modification to the Employee Pay program presented in this chapter. When the number of hours is greater than 40, the (overtime) hourly rate is 40% higher.

9.5. Develop a program for computing the distance between two points. A point is defined by a pair of values (x, y). The distance, d, between two points, $P_1(x_1, y_1)$ and $P_2(x_2, y_2)$ is defined by:

$$d = \sqrt{(x_2 - x_1)^2 + (y_2 - y_1)^2}$$

9.6. Write a flowchart design and a complete program to compute the total amount to pay for movie rental. The movie rental store charges $4.50 per day for every DVD movie. For every additional period of 12 hours, the customer must pay $0.50.

9.7. Develop a design in flowchart and a program that computes the fare in a ferry transport passengers with motor vehicles. Passengers pay an extra fare based on the vehicle's weight. Use the following data: vehicles with weight up to 780 lb pay $80.00, up to 1100 lb pay $127.50, and up to 2200 lb pay $210.50.

9.8. Develop a design in flowchart and a program that computes the average student grades. The input data are the four letter grades.

Chapter 10
Repetition

10.1 Introduction

A repeat structure is a structure that allows a block of code to be executed repeatedly based on a given boolean condition. There are three forms of the repetition structure: the *while* loop, the *repeat-until* loop, and the *for* loop.

The first construct, the *while* loop, is the most general one. The other two repetition constructs can be expressed with the *while* loop.

10.2 The While Loop Structure

The *while* loop structure consists of a block of code and a condition. The condition is first evaluated – if the condition is true the code within the block is then executed. This repeats until the condition evaluates to false. The while-loop structure checks the condition before the block of code is executed

10.2.1 While-Loop Flowchart

A flowchart with the *while* loop structure is shown in Figure 10.1. The block of code consists of a sequence of actions.

The actions in the code block are performed while the condition is true. After the actions are performed, the condition is again evaluated, and the actions are again performed if the condition is still true. This continues until the condition changes to false, at which point the loop terminates.

The condition is tested first, and then the block of code is performed. If this condition is initially false, the actions in the code block are not performed.

J.M. Garrido, *Object Oriented Simulation: A Modeling and Programming Perspective*,
DOI: 10.1007/978-1-4419-0516-1_10,
© Springer Science + Business Media, LLC 2009

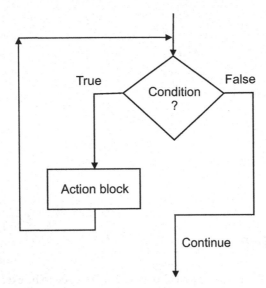

Fig. 10.1 A flowchart of the while-loop

The number of times that the loop is performed is normally a finite integer value. A well-defined loop will eventually terminate. The condition is sometimes called the *loop condition*, and it determines when the loop terminates. A non-terminating loop is defined in special cases and will repeat the actions forever.

A counter variable has the purpose of storing the number of times (iterations) that the actions are repeated. The counter variable is of type integer and is incremented (or decremented) on each repetition. The counter variable must be initialized to a given value.

10.2.2 The While Statement

The **while** statement includes the condition (a Boolean expression), the statements in the code block, and the keywords **while**, **do**, and **endwhile**. The code block is placed after the **do** keyword and before the **endwhile** keyword. The following lines of code show the general form of the while-loop statement that corresponds to the portion of flowchart shown in Figure 10.1.

```
while ⟨ condition ⟩ do
     ⟨ statements in code block ⟩
endwhile
```

In the following example, a **while** statement appears with a counter variable, *j*. This counter variable is used to control the number of times the repeat group will be performed.

```
constants
  define MAX_NUM = 15 of type integer   // maximum number
                                        // of times through the loop
variables
  define j of type integer    // loop counter
  define sum of type float
  ...
begin
  set j = 1   // initial value
  while j <= MAX_NUM do
     set sum = sum + 12.5
     increment j
  endwhile
  display "Value of sum: ", sum
  ...
```

10.3 Employee Pay Problem with Repetition

This problem uses repetition to compute the gross pay and net pay to a given number of employees, *num*, which is read from the console. The processing for each employee has been discussed previously.

In the flowchart, the actions performed to compute gross and net pay for every employee is included in the code block and placed in a while loop. In the program, the **while** statement is used. The condition compares the loop counter, *j* with the given number of employees read, *num*. The condition for the repetition (loop) is: $j <= Num$.

The value of variable *num* represents the number of employees to process. Figure 10.2 shows the flowchart for the algorithm for the problem with repetition.

The following class includes the modified function *main*, which has the while loop. The other class, *PayEmployee*, has not been changed.

```
description
  This program processes the net pay for a given
  number of employees. For every employee,
  it computes the gross pay, tax amount, and net
  pay an employee.
  */
class Comp_pay is
  public
  description
```

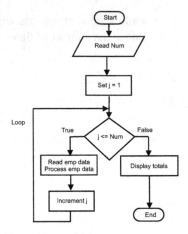

Fig. 10.2 Employee pay problem with repetition

```
        This is the main function of the application.
        */
function main is
  variables
    define num of type integer
    define j of type integer
    //
    define net_pay of type float
    define taxes of type float
    define empname of type string
    define empnum of type string
    define hours of type integer
    define hrate of type float
    define total_taxes of type float
    define total_npay of type float
  object references
    define emp_obj of class PayEmployee
  begin
    display "Enter number of employees to process"
    read num
    set j = 1
    set total_taxes = 0.0
    set total_npay = 0.0
    while j <= num do
        display "Enter employee name: "
        read empname
        display "Enter employee number: "
        read empnum
        display "Enter hours worked: "
        read hours
        display "Enter hourly rate: "
        read hrate
        create emp_obj of class PayEmployee
            using empname, empnum, hours, hrate
```

```
              call compute_pay of emp_obj
              set net_pay = call get_npay of emp_obj
              set taxes = get_tax() of emp_obj    // get tax amount
              display "Employee name: ", empname,
                    " Net pay: ", net_pay, " Tax amount: ", taxes
              increment j
              add taxes to total_taxes
              add net_pay to total_npay
          endwhile
          display "Total taxes: ", total_taxes
          display "total net pay: ", total_npay
      endfun main
  endclass Comp_pay
```

Variables *total_taxes* and *total_npay* accumulate on every iteration in the while loop, the tax amount and the net pay respectively. These variables are often known as accumulator variables.

10.4 Loop Until

The loop *until* structure is a control flow statement that allows code to be executed repeatedly based on a given condition. The structure consists of a block of code and the condition.

The actions within the block are executed first, and then the condition is evaluated. If the condition is not true the actions within the block are executed again. This repeats until the condition becomes true.

Loop until structures check the condition after the block is executed, this is an important difference with while loop, which tests the condition before the actions within the block are executed. Figure 10.3 shows the flowchart for the loop-until structure.

The OOSimL statement of the loop-until structure, corresponds directly with the flowchart in Figure 10.3 and uses the keywords **repeat, until,** and **endrepeat.** The following portion of code shows the general form of the loop-until statement.

repeat
    ⟨ *statements in Action block* ⟩
until ⟨ *condition* ⟩
endrepeat

The following example shows the code of a loop until statement for the pay employee problem.

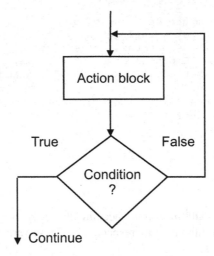

Fig. 10.3 Loop-until structure

```
set j = 0
repeat
    display "Enter employee name: "
    read empname
    display "Enter employee number: "
    read empnum
    display "Enter hours worked: "
    read hours
    display "Enter hourly rate: "
    read hrate
    create emp_obj of class PayEmployee
         using empname, empnum, hours, hrate
    call compute_pay of emp_obj
    set net_pay = call get_npay of emp_obj
    set taxes = get_tax() of emp_obj    // get tax amount
    display "Employee name: ", empname,
         " Net pay: ", net_pay, " Tax amount: ", taxes
    increment j
    add taxes to total_taxes
    add net_pay to total_npay
until j > num
endrepeat
```

10.5 For Loop Structure

The third type of loop structure is the *for* loop. It explicitly uses a loop counter; the
initial value and the final value of the loop counter have to be indicated. The *for*

loop is most useful when the number of times that the loop is carried out is known in advance. The **for** statement has the keywords: **for, to, downto, do,** and **endfor**. The **for** statement has the general form:

> **for** ⟨ *counter* ⟩ = ⟨ *initial_value* ⟩ **to** ⟨ *final_value* ⟩
> **do**
>   Action block
> **endfor**

On every iteration, the loop counter is automatically incremented. The last time through the loop, the loop counter has its final value allowed. In other words, when the loop counter reaches its final value, the loop terminates. The *for* loop is similar to the *while* loop in that the condition is evaluated before carrying out the operations in the repeat loop.

The following portion of code uses a **for** statement for the repetition part of the employee pay problem.

```
for j = 1 to num do
    display "Enter employee name: "
    read empname
    display "Enter employee number: "
    read empnum
    display "Enter hours worked: "
    read hours
    display "Enter hourly rate: "
    read hrate
    create emp_obj of class PayEmployee
        using empname, empnum, hours, hrate
    call compute_pay of emp_obj
    set net_pay = call get_npay of emp_obj
    set taxes = get_tax() of emp_obj    // get tax amount
    display "Employee name: ", empname,
        " Net pay: ", net_pay, " Tax amount: ", taxes
    increment j
    add taxes to total_taxes
    add net_pay to total_npay
endfor
```

10.6 Summary

With the repetition structures, a group of instructions in the action block of the statement in the loop is carried out repeatedly. The number of times the repetition group is carried out depends on the condition of the loop.

There are three types of loop structures: *while loop*, *loop until*, and *for loop*. In the *while* and *for* loops, the loop condition is tested first, and then the repetition group is carried out if the condition is true. The loop terminates when the condition is false. In the *loop-until* construct, the repetition group is carried out first, and then the loop condition is tested. If the loop condition is true, the loop terminates; otherwise the repetition group is executed again.

10.7 Key Terms

repetition	loop	while
loop condition	do	endrepeat
repeat group	loop termination	loop counter
endwhile	accumulator	repeat-until
for	to	downto
endfor		

Exercises

10.1. Develop a program that computes the average of a set of input values. Use a while loop.

10.2. Develop a program that computes the average of a set of input values. Use a for loop.

10.3. Develop a program that computes the average of a set of input values. Use a repeat-until loop.

10.4. Develop a program that computes the maximum value from a set of input numbers. Use a while loop.

10.5. Develop a program that computes the maximum value from a set of input numbers. Use a for loop.

10.6. Develop a program that computes the maximum value from a set of input numbers. Use a repeat-until loop.

10.7. Develop a program that finds the minimum value from a set of input values. Use a while loop.

10.8. Develop a program that finds the minimum value from a set of input values. Use a *for* loop.

10.9. Develop a program that finds the minimum value from a set of input values. Use a repeat-until loop.

10.10. Develop a program that computes the student group average, maximum, and minimum grade. The program uses the input grade for every student. Use a while loop.

10.11. Develop a program that computes the student group average, maximum, and minimum grade. The program uses the input grade for every student. Use a *for* loop.

10.12. Develop a program that reads rainfall data in inches for yearly quarters from the last five years. The program computes the average rainfall per quarter, the average rainfall per year, and the maximum rainfall per quarter and for each year.

10.13. Develop a program that computes the total inventory value amount and total per item. The program reads item code, cost, and description for each item. The number of items to process is not known.

Chapter 11
Arrays

11.1 Introduction

An array is a static data structure that can store multiple values of the same type. These values are stored using contiguous memory locations with the same name. The values in the array are known as *elements*. Arrays can be used to store and manipulate a large number of values of the same type. This mechanism provides the ability to handle large number of values in a single collection and to refer to each value with an index.

An integer value or variable known as *index* is used to access a particular element of the array. The values of the index start from zero and it represents the relative position of the element in the array. Figure 11.1 shows an array with 10 elements.

An array is a static data structure because once the array is declared (and created), its size or capacity cannot change. An array is declared to hold 50 elements cannot be changed to hold a larger number of elements. The programmer will normally carry out the following sequence of steps to use an array:

1. Declaring the array with appropriate name and type
2. Optionally assigning initial values to the array elements
3. Manipulating the individual elements of the array

11.2 Array Declaration

To declare an array, an identifier is used for the name of the array. The type of the array is a simple (primitive) type or a class. The general statement for declaring an array of a simple type is:

define ⟨ *array_name* ⟩ **array** [ ] **of type** ⟨ *array_type* ⟩

J.M. Garrido, *Object Oriented Simulation: A Modeling and Programming Perspective*, 115
DOI: 10.1007/978-1-4419-0516-1_11,
© Springer Science + Business Media, LLC 2009

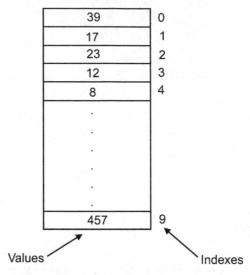

Fig. 11.1 An array with 10 elements

Arrays of simple types must be declared in the *variables* section of data definitions. In the following example an array *width* of type *float* is declared.

```
variables
     define width array [] of type float
     . . .
```

The statement for declaring an array of object references has the general form:

define ⟨ *array_name* ⟩ **array** [ ] **of class** ⟨ *class_name* ⟩

Arrays of these types are declared in the *object references* section of data declarations. The following example declares an array *points* of class *Point*.

```
object references
     define points array [] of class Point
     . . .
```

11.3 Creating Arrays

After an array has been declared, it must be created with an appropriate capacity or
size, and then values can be assigned to specific elements. The capacity of the array

is the number of elements it can hold. The general form of the statement for creating
an array is:

> **create** ⟨ *array_name* ⟩ **array** [⟨ *capacity* ⟩]
> **of type** ⟨ *array_type* ⟩

The following statement creates array, *width*, with capacity of 50 elements. This
array was already declared.

```
create temp array [50] of type float
. . .
```

The general form of the statement to create an array of object references is:

> **create** ⟨ *array_name* ⟩ **array** [⟨ *capacity* ⟩]
> **of class** ⟨ *class_name* ⟩

An identifier constant is normally used to specify the capacity of the array. For
example, given the constant *MAX_NUM* has a value 50 and *NUM_OBJECTS* a value
of 25, the statements for declaring and creating the array *width* and array *points* are:

```
constants
    define MAX_NUM = 50 of type integer
    define NUM_OBJECTS = 25 of type integer
variables
    define width array [] of type float
object references
    define points array [] of class Point
. . .
begin
. . .
    create width array [MAX_NUM] of type float
    create points array [NUM_OBJETS] of class Point
```

The actual number of elements in the array is usually less than the total number
or capacity of the array. For example, an array is declared with a capacity of 50
elements but only the first 20 elements of the array are used. An array is a static data
structure, therefore elements cannot be inserted or deleted from the array.

11.4 Manipulating an Array

Manipulating an array involve accessing the individual elements of the array and
performing some computing. To access an individual element of an array, an integer
value, known as the *index*, is used with the name of the array. The range of index
values is 0 to the capacity of the array minus 1.

To access a particular element of an array a statement uses the name of the array followed by the index value in rectangular brackets. The following **set** statement assigns a value of 33.55 to element 3 of array *width*.

```
set width[2] = 33.55
```

The index value used is an integer constant, a constant identifier, or an integer variable. The following statement uses a reference to element 3 of array *width* with variable *j* as the index.

```
constants
   define MAX_NUM = 50 of type integer
variables
   define width array [] of type float
   define j of type integer
   . . .
   create width array [MAX_NUM] of type float
   set j = 2
   set temp[j] = 33.55
```

An array of object references is not an array of objects since the objects are stored elsewhere in memory. The following statement creates an object of class Point and assigns this to element with index *j* of array *points* (of class Point):

```
create points[j] of class Point
```

Element *j* of array *points* now refers to the newly created object of class Point. To invoke a public function of an object referenced in an element of an array, the call statement is used followed by the name of the array and the index value enclosed in brackets.

The following statement is used to invoke function *get_xcoord* of the object referenced by element with index *j* of array *points*.

```
variables
   define x of type float
   define j of type integer
   . . .
begin
   . . .
   set x = call get_xcoord of points[j]
```

11.5 Array Parameters

An array may be defined as a parameter in the header of a function definition. When invoking this function, an array of the same or similar type can then be passed as argument. A reference to the array is passed in the function call.

A function with an array parameter declares the array in the header of the function definition after the **parameters** keyword. The general form of a function header with a parameter definition is:

> **description**
>
>   . . .
>
>   */
>
> **function** ⟨ *function_name* ⟩
> **parameters** ⟨ *parameter_list* ⟩ **is**
>
>   . . .
>
> **endfun** ⟨ *function_name* ⟩

The data declarations in *parameter_list* section of the function header may have zero or more array declarations. The general form of these parameter declarations is:

> ⟨ *array_name* ⟩   **array** [ ]
>   **of type** ⟨ *simple type or class* ⟩

The following example defines a function that finds the maximum value in an array of type *float*. The function defines the array parameter and an integer parameter. This second parameter is the number of elements in the array. The function returns the maximum value found.

```
description
   This function calculates the maximum value of
   an array parameter myarray, it then returns the
   result.
   */
function maximum return type float
parameters myarray array [] of type float,
           num of type integer is
variables
   define max of type float        // local variable
   define j of type integer
begin
   set max = myarray[0]
   for j = 1 to num - 1 do
       if max < myarray[j] then

           set max = myarray[j]
       endif
   endfor
```

```
      return max
endfun maximum
```

In the call to a function and passing an array as an argument, only the name of the array is used. The following code calls function *maximum* and pass array *marr* and constant *NUM* as arguments.

```
constants
    define NUM = 100 of type integer
variables
    define marr array [] of type float
    define maxval of type float
    . . .
    create marr array [NUM] of type float
    . . .
    set maxval = call maximum using marr, NUM
    . . .
```

A function may also return the reference to an array. In the following example, a function creates an array *h* then returns a reference to this array.

```
    create h array [NUM] of type float
    . . .
    return h
```

11.6 Array Return Types

The return type of a function can be specified to be of an array of a simple type or an array of a class. The following statement defines the general form of the return type in a class header.

function ⟨ *function_name* ⟩
    return ⟨ *type_class* ⟩ **array** [] ⟨ *type_class name* ⟩

In the following examples, two function definitions appear. The first example defines the return type of a function as an array of integer and the second example defines the return type of a function as an array of class Person.

```
function arrayfun1 return type array [] integer
parameters myarray array [] of class Person,
           num of type integer
is
. . .
endfun arrayfun1
```

```
function arrayfun2 return class array [] Person
parameters myarray array [] of class Point
is
. . .
endfun arrayfun2
```

11.7 Arrays with Multiple Dimensions

More than one dimension can be defined with arrays. Two-dimension arrays, also known as matrices, are mathematical structures with values arranged in columns and rows. Two index values are required, one for the rows and one for the columns.

With two-dimensional arrays, two numbers are defined each in a pair of brackets. The first number defines the range of values for the first index (for rows) and the second number defines the range of values for the second index (for the columns).

The following statements declare and create a two-dimensional array named *tmatrix* with capacity 50 rows and 15 columns.

```
constants
   define ROWS = 50 of type integer
   define COLS = 15 of type integer
variables
   define tmatrix array [][] of type float
   . . .
   create tmatrix array [ROWS][COLS] of type float
```

Two indexes are required to reference the elements of a two-dimensional array. The following statements assign all the elements of array *tmatrix* to 0.0:

```
for j = 0 to COLS - 1 do
   for i = 0 to ROWS - 1 do
      set tmatrix [i][j] = 0.0
   endfor
endfor
```

Two loop definitions are needed, an outer loop and an inner loop (this is also known nested loops). The inner loop varies the row index and outer loop varies the row index. The assignment statement sets the value 0.0 to the element at row i and column j.

11.8 Examples with Arrays

In this section, several simple applications of arrays are discussed. These find the maximum, minimum, average values, others to carry out search and sorting in arrays.

11.8.1 Finding Maximum and Minimum Values in an Array

Finding the minimum and/or maximum values stored in an array, involve accessing all the elements of the array. The algorithm for finding the maximum value in pseudo-code is:

1. Assign the current largest value found to be the value of the first element of the array.
2. Assign value zero to the index value of the first element.
3. Perform the following steps for each of the other elements of the array

   a. Access the next element in the array.
   b. Examine its value, if the value of the current element is greater than the largest value so far, update the value found so far with this element value and save the index of the element.

4. The index value of the element value found to be the largest in the array is the result.

The algorithm described is implemented in function *maxf*. The function uses array *myarr* of type *float* that has *num* elements. The function returns the index value with the largest value found.

```
description
   This function of the element with the maximum
   value in the array and returns its index.
   */
function maxf return type integer
parameters num of type integer,
        myarr array [] of type float
is
   variables
      define j of type integer        // index variable
      // index of element with largest value
      define k of type integer
      define max_val of type float    // largest value
   begin
      set k = 0                  // index first element
      set max_val = myarr[0] // max value so far
      for j = 1 to num - 1 do
         if myarr[j] > max_val
```

```
        then
            set k = j

            set max_val = myarr[j]
        endif
      endfor
    return k                          // result
  endfun maxf
```

11.8.2 The Average Value in an Array

To compute the average value in an array, all the elements have to be added to an accumulator variable, *sum*. The algorithm for computing the average value in pseudo-code is:

1. Assign the accumulator variable, *sum*, to the value of the first element of the array.
2. For each of the other elements of the array, add the value of the next element in the array to the accumulator variable.
3. Divide the value of the accumulator variable by the number of elements in the array. This is the result value calculated.

An accumulator variable is used to store the summation of the element values in the array. In an array x with n elements. The summation of x with index j starting with $j = 1$ to $j = n$ is expressed mathematically as:

$$sum = \sum_{j=1}^{n} x_j.$$

Function *averagef* implements the algorithm. The function uses array *myarr*, which is declared as an array of type *float* and has *num* elements. The function returns the average value calculated.

```
  description
      This function calculates the average of the
      elements in array myarr.
      */
  function averagef return type float
  parameters myarr array of type float,
             num of type integer
  is
      variables
        define sum of type float     // variable for summation
        define avg of type float     // average value
        define j of type integer
      begin
```

```
      set sum = 0
      for j = 0 to num - 1 do
         add myarr[j] to sum
      endfor
      set avg = sum / num
      return avg
   endfun averagef
```

11.8.3 Searching

Searching involves examining the elements of an array for an element with particular value. Not all the elements of the array need to be examined, the search ends
when and if an element of the array has a value equal to the requested value. There
are two general techniques for searching: linear search and binary search.

11.8.3.1 Linear Search

Linear search finds the element with a specified value. The algorithm starts to compare the requested value with the value in the first element of the array and if not
found, compare with the next element and so on until the last element of the array
is compared with the requested value.

The result of this search is the index of the element in the array that is equal to
the requested value. If the requested value is not found, the result is a negative value.
The algorithm description in informal pseudo-code is:

1. Repeat for every element of the array:

   a. Compare the current element with the requested value. If the values are equal,
      store the value of the index as the result and search no more.
   b. If values are not equal, continue search.

2. If the value requested is not found, set the result to value -1.

Function *searcht* searches the array for an element with the requested temperature value, *t_val*. For the result, the function assigns to *t* the index value of the
element with the value requested. If the requested value is not found, the function
assigns a negative integer value to *t*.

```
   description
      This function carries out a linear search of
      the array of temperature for the temperature
      value in parameter t_val. It sets the index
      value of the element found, or -1 if not found.
      */
   function searcht return type integer
```

```
parameters t_val of type float,
          myarr array [] of type float,
          num of type integer
is
   variables
      define j of type integer
      define found = false of type boolean
   begin
     set j = 0
     while j < num and found not equal true do
       if myarr [j] == t_val
       then
           set t = j
           set found = true
       else
           increment j
       endif
     endwhile
     if found not equal true
     then
         set t = -1
     endif
     return t
endfun searcht
```

11.8.3.2 Binary Search

In this type of search technique, the values to be searched have to be sorted in some given ascending order. The part of the array elements to include in the search is split into two partitions of about the same size. The middle element is compared with the requested value. If the value is not found, the search is continues on only one partition. This partition is again split into two smaller partitions until the element is found or until no more splits are possible (not found). The binary search technique applied to a sorted array.

Binary search is a very efficient search technique compared to linear search because the number of comparisons is smaller. The efficiency of a search algorithm is determined by the number of relevant operations in proportion to the size of the array to search. The significant operations in this case are the comparisons of the element values with the requested value.

For an array with N elements, the average number of comparisons with linear search is $N/2$, and if the requested value is not found, the number of comparisons is N. With binary search, the number of comparisons is $\log_2 N$. The description of the algorithm in pseudo-code is:

1. Set up the lower and upper bounds of the array.
2. Repeat the search while the lower index value is less than the upper index value.

   a. Split the array into two partitions. Compare the middle element with the requested value.

   b. If the value of the middle element is the search value, the result is the index of this element, search no more.

   c. If the search value is less than the middle element, change the upper bound to the index of the middle element minus 1. The search will continue on the lower partition.

   d. If the search value is greater or equal to the middle element, change the lower bound to the index of the middle element plus 1. The search will continue on the upper partition.

3. If the search value is not found, the result is -1.

Function *bsearcht* implements the binary search algorithm using array parameter *myarr*.

```
description
     This function implements a binary search of
     the myarr array using search value in
     parameter t_val. It sets the index
     value of the element found, or -1 if not found.
     */
function bsearcht return type integer
parameters t_val of type float
           myarr array [] of type float
           num of type integer
is
variables
     define t of type integer
     define found = false of type boolean
     define lower of type integer // index lower bound
     define upper of type integer    // index upper bound
     define middle of type integer   // index of middle
begin
     set lower = 0
     set upper = num
     while lower < upper and found not equal true
     do
       set middle = (lower + upper) / 2
       if t_val == myarr[middle]
       then
          set found = true
          set t =   middle
       else
         if t_val < myarr[middle]
         then
            set upper = middle -1
         else
            set lower = middle + 1
         endif
       endif
     endwhile
```

```
            if found not equal true
            then
                set t = -1
            endif
            return t
    endfun searcht
```

11.8.4 Sorting

Sorting is a technique that consists of rearranging the elements of the array in specified some order. If the values of the array to be sorted are numerical, then the two possible orders are ascending and descending. If the values of array are strings, then alphabetical order is the most practical. Some of the most widely known sorting algorithms are:

- Selection sort
- Insertion sort
- Bubble sort
- Shell sort
- Merge sort
- Quick sort

Selection sort is a very simple sorting algorithm. Given an array of a numerical type of size N, the algorithm performs several steps. First, it finds the index value of the smallest element value in the array. Second, it swaps this element with the element with index 0 (the first element. This step actually places the smallest element to the first position. Third, the first step is repeated for the part of the array with index 1 to $N - 1$, this excludes the element with index 0, which is at the proper position. The smallest element found is swapped with the element at position with index 1. This is repeated until all the elements are located in ascending order. The algorithm description in pseudo-code is:

1. Repeat the following steps for all elements with index J = 0 to N-2
2. Search for the smallest element from index J to N-1.
3. Swap the smallest element found with element with index J, if the smallest element is not the one with index J.

The following function *selectionsort* implements the algorithm for the selection sort.

```
    description
      This function implements a selection sort of
      the array.
      */
    function selectionsort
```

```
parameters myarr array [] of type float,
          num of type integer
is
   variables
      define N of type integer      // elements in array
      define Jmin of type integer   // smallest element
      define j of type integer
      define k of type integer
      define t_val of type float    // intermediate value
   begin
      set N = num
      for j = 0 to N - 2 do
         // search for the smallest element
         // in the index range from j to N-1
         set Jmin = j
         for k = j+1 to N - 1 do
            if myarr[k] < myarr[Jmin]
            then
                set Jmin = k
            endif
         endfor
         if Jmin != j
         then
             // swap elements with index J and Jmin
             set t_val = myarr[j]
             set myarr[j] = myarr[Jmin]
             set myarr[Jmin] = t_val
         endif
      endfor
   endfun selectionsort
```

The efficiency of the algorithm is formally expressed as $O(N^2)$. The number of element comparisons with an array size of N is $N^2/2 - N/2$. The first term $(N^2/2)$ in this expression is the dominant one; the order of growth of this algorithm is N^2.

11.9 Summary

Arrays are static data structures for storing a number of different values of the same type. Each of these values is known as an element. Once the array has been declared the capacity of the array cannot be changed. The type of an array can be a simple type or a class. To refer to an individual element, an integer value, known as the index, is used to indicate the relative position of the element in the array.

Searching involves finding an element in the array with a target value. Two important search algorithms are linear search and binary search. Sorting involves rearranging the elements of an array in some particular order of their values.

11.10 Key Terms

array declaration	creating arrays	accessing elements
static structure	array capacity	index
array element	element reference	searching
Linear search	Binary search	algorithm efficiency
sorting	Selection sort	matrix

Exercises

11.1. Implement a function that finds the minimum value element in an array and returns the index value of the element found.

11.2. Develop a function that sorts an array using the Insertion sort technique. This sort algorithm divides the array into two parts. The first is initially empty, it is the part of the array with the elements in order. The second part of the array has the elements in the array that still need to be sorted. The algorithm takes the element from the second part and determines the position for it in the first part. To insert this element in a particular position of the first part, the elements to right of this position need to be shifted one position to the right.

11.3. Develop a function that sorts an array using the Bubble sort technique. Investigate the algorithm for this sort technique.

11.4. Develop a function that sorts an array using the Merge sort technique. Investigate the algorithm for this sort technique.

11.5. Develop a function that sorts an array using the Quick sort technique. Investigate the algorithm for this sort technique.

11.6. Develop a function that computes the standard deviation of values in array. The standard deviation measures the spread, or dispersion, of the values in the array with respect to the average value. The standard deviation of array X with N elements is defined as:

$$std = \sqrt{\frac{sqdif}{N-1}},$$

where

$$sqdif = \sum_{j=0}^{N-1} (X_j - Avg)^2.$$

11.7. Develop a program that inputs and processes the rainfall data for the last five years. For every year, four quarters of rainfall are provided measured in inches. Hint: use a matrix to store these values. The attributes are: the precipitation (in inches), the year, and the quarter. The program must compute the average, minimum, and maximum rainfall per year and per quarter (for the last five years).

Chapter 12
Inheritance

12.1 Introduction

Inheritance is a class relationship among classes. The other basic class relationship is composition, which is a stronger form of association. These relationships are easily modeled in UML diagrams. Composition is a horizontal relationship and inheritance is a vertical relationship.

Inheritance is a facility provided by an object-oriented language for defining new classes from existing classes. The basic inheritance relationships and their applications are explained in some detail. Inheritance enhances class reuse, that is, the use of a class in more than one application.

12.2 Modeling Classes

A class is defined as a group of objects with common characteristics. Some classes of an application are completely independent because they do not have any relationship with other classes. The other classes in an application are related in some manner and they form a hierarchy of classes, therefore, class relationships must also be identified.

To help describe a class hierarchy, the most general class is placed at the top. This is known as the *parent* class and is also known as the *super* class (or the *base* class). A *subclass* inherits the (all attributes and operations) of its parent class. These characteristics of a class are also known as features.

A subclass can be further inherited to lower-level classes. In the UML class diagram, an arrow with an empty head points from a subclass (the derived class) to its base class to show that it is inheriting the features of its base class.

From UML diagram description of this type of class relationship, inheritance is seen as a vertical relationship between two classes. Figure 12.1 illustrates this class

J.M. Garrido, *Object Oriented Simulation: A Modeling and Programming Perspective*, DOI: 10.1007/978-1-4419-0516-1_12,
© Springer Science + Business Media, LLC 2009

relationship. Class *Motor Vehicle* is the base class, the other three classes inherit the features of this base class.

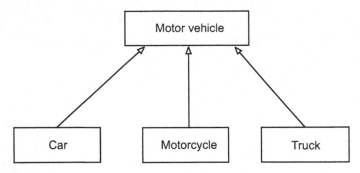

Fig. 12.1 Class inheritance

The terminology varies somewhat in different software environments. In UML, the term *generalization* is used instead of inheritance. In the Java programming language, the term *extends* is used for a class that inherits features from a base class.

12.3 Inheritance

In defining a new class using inheritance, the newly defined class acquires all the non-private features of an existing parent class. This mechanism is provided by most object-oriented programming languages. The parent class is also known as the *base* class, or the *super* class. The new class being defined is known as a *derived* class or *subclass*.

The base class is a more general class than its subclasses. A derived class can be defined by adding more features or modifying some of the inherited features. Therefore, a subclass can be defined as:

- An extension of the base class, if in addition to the inherited features, it includes its own attributes and operations.
- A specialized version of the base class, if it overrides (redefines) one or more of the features inherited from its parent class
- A combination of an extension and a specialization of the base class

Using UML, the term *generalization* is defined as the association between a general class and a more specialized class or extended class. This association is also known as *inheritance*, and it is an important relationship between two classes. In the UML class diagram, the arrow that represents this relationship points from a class (the derived class) to its parent class.

The purpose of inheritance is to define a new class from an existing class and to shorten the time compared to the development of a class from scratch. Inheritance also enhances class reuse.

The ability of a class to inherit the characteristics from more than one parent class is known as *multiple inheritance*. Most object-oriented programming languages support multiple inheritance. The OOSimL and Java languages only support single inheritance.

A simple class hierarchy with inheritance is shown in Figure 12.1. The base class is *Motorvehicle* and the subclasses are: *Car*, *Motorcycle*, and *Truck*.

All objects of class *Truck* in Figure 12.1 are also objects of class *Motorvehicle*, because this is the base class for the other classes. On the contrary, not all objects of class *Motorvehicle* are objects of class *Truck*.

12.3.1 Defining Subclasses with OOSimL

As mentioned previously, the public features of the base class are inherited by the subclass. Protected features are inherited by the subclass, but the access is limited to classes in the same package.

The definition of a subclass in OOSimL must include the keyword **inherits** followed by the name of the base class. The general form of the OOSimL statement for the header in the definition of a subclass is:

> **description**
>   . . .
> **class** ⟨ *class_name* ⟩ **inherits** ⟨ *base_class_name* ⟩ **is**
>   **private**
>   . . .
>   **protected**
>   . . .
>   **public**
>   . . .
> **endclass** ⟨ *class_name* ⟩

In UML class diagrams, a feature of the class is indicated with a plus (+) sign if it is public, with a minus (-) sign if it is private, and with a pound (#) sign if it is protected.

12.3.2 Inheritance and Initializer Functions

The initializer functions of a base class are the only public features that are not inherited by the subclasses. An initializer function of a subclass should initialize its own attributes (variables and object references) as well as the attributes defined in the base class. Therefore, when defining an initializer function of a subclass, it will normally invoke the initializer function of the base class.

The special name given to the initializer function of the base class is *super*. This call must be the first statement in the initializer function of the subclass. Calling function *super* may require arguments, and these must correspond to the parameters defined in the initializer function of the base class.

The statement to call or invoke an initializer function of the base class from the subclass is:

call super ⟨ **using** `argument_list` ⟩

If the argument list is absent in the call, the initializer function invoked is the default initializer of the base class.

In the following example, a new class, *Student*, is defined that inherits the features of an existing (base) class *Person*. The attributes of class *Person* are *pnumber*, *age*, *name*, and *address*. The initializer function of class *Person* sets initial values to these attributes.

The subclass *Student* has two other attribute, *major* and *gpa*. The initializer function of this class invokes the initializer function of the base class and sets initial values to its two attributes, *major* and *gpa*. The following code shows this part of class *Student*.

```
class Student inherits Person is
  private
  variables
      define major of type integer
      define gpa of type float
  public
  description
    This is the constructor, it initializes a Student
    Object on creation.
    */
  function initializer
  parameters
            imajor of type integer,
            igpa of type float,
            iname of type string,
            ipnum of type long,
            iage of type integer,
            iaddress of type string
  is
  begin
    // invoke the initializer of the base class
    call super using iname, ipnum, iage, iaddress
    set major = imajor
    set gpa = igpa
  endfun initializer
  . . .
  endclass Student
```

The attributes of a class are usually private, so the only way to set the initial values for the attributes of the base class is to invoke its initializer function of the base class.

In the previous code, this is accomplished with the statement:

```
call super using iname, ipnum, iage, iaddress
```

12.3.3 Complete Example with Inheritance

The following source code shows the implementation of the base class, *Person*. The attributes of class *Person* are *pnumber*, *age*, *name*, and *address*. The initializer function of class *Person* sets initial values to these attributes.

```
description
   This class represents person data. The attributes are
     ID number, age, address, and name.
   */
class Person is
   private
   variables
       define pnumber of type long
       define age of type integer
       define name of type string
       define address of type string
   public
   description
     This is the constructor, it initializes a Person object
     on creation.
     */
   function initializer
   parameters iname of type string,
             ipnum of type long,
             iage of type integer,
             iaddress of type string
   is
   begin
     //
     set pnumber = ipnum
     set age = iage
     set name = iname
     set address = iaddress
   endfun initializer
   //
   description
     This funtion gets the person mumber of the
 Person object.    */
   function get_pnum return type long is
   begin
       return pnumber
```

```
   endfun get_pnum
   //
   description
     This function returns the name of the employee object.
     */
   function get_name return type string is
     begin
       return name
   endfun get_name
   //
   description
       This function returns the address increase for the object.
       */
   function get_address return type string is
   begin
       return address
   endfun get_address
   //
   description
       This function displays the attributes of the Person object
       */
   function display_data is
   begin
       display name, " ", age, " ", address
   endfun display_data
 endclass Person
```

The following code shows the implementation of class *Student*, which is a sub-class of class *Person*.

```
description
   This class represents student objects. The attributes are
     major and GPA. The major is coded to an integer number.
     This class inherits class Person.
   */
class Student inherits Person is
   private
   variables
       define major of type integer
       define gpa of type float
   public
   description
     This is the constructor, it initializes a Student
     on creation.
     */
   function initializer
   parameters
             imajor of type integer,
             igpa of type float,
             iname of type string,
             ipnum of type long,
             iage of type integer,
             iaddress of type string
```

```
    is
    begin
        // invoke the initializer of the base class
        call super using iname, ipnum, iage, iaddress
        set major = imajor
        set gpa = igpa
    endfun initializer
    //
    description
      This funtion gets the student major of the
    object.
    */
    function get_major return type integer is
    begin
        return major
    endfun get_major
    //
    description
      This funtion sets the student major of the
object.      */
    function set_major parameters pmajor of type integer is
    begin
        set major = pmajor
    endfun set_major
    //
    description
      This function returns the GPA of the student object.
      */
    function get_gpa return type float is
    begin
        return gpa
    endfun get_gpa
    //
    description
      This function sets the GPA of the student object.
      */
    function set_gpa parameters pgpa of type float is
    begin
        set gpa = pgpa
    endfun set_gpa
    //
    description
      This function displays the attributes of the
      student object. it overrides the function of
      the base class
      */
    function display_data is
    begin
        call super.display_data
        display major, " ", gpa
    endfun display_data
endclass Student
```

12.3.4 Function Overriding

A subclass is a *specialization* of the base class if one or more functions of the base class are *redefined* (or overridden) in the subclass. The subclass is said to reimplement one or more functions of the base class.

In class *Student*, which was shown previously, function *display_data* is a redefinition of the function with the same name in the base class. Class *Student* inherits class *Person* and overrides function *display_data*. Therefore, class *Student* is an extension and also a specialized version of class *Person*.

12.4 Summary

Inheritance is a mechanism supported by most object-oriented languages. A subclass (derived class) inherits all the features of its base (parent) class. Inheritance is a vertical relationship among classes and enhances class reuse. Only the public and protected features of the base class can directly be accessed by a subclass. The initializer (constructor) functions of the base class are not inherited.

Using inheritance, a subclass can be an extension and/or a specialization of the base class. If a subclass defines new features in addition to the ones that it inherits from the base class, then the subclass is said to be an extension to the base class. If a subclass redefines (overrides) one or more functions of the base class, then the subclass is said to be a specialization of the base class.

12.5 Key Terms

classification	parent class	super class
base class	subclass	derived class
horizontal relationship	vertical relationship	class hierarchy
inherit	extension	specialization
class reuse	association	generalization
inheritance	reuse	overiding

Exercises

12.1. Explain how inheritance enhances class reuse. Why is class reuse important?

12.2. Explain the differences between horizontal and vertical relationships. How can these be illustrated in UML diagrams?

12.3. With inheritance, explain the limitations in dealing with private attributes.

12.4. Define one or two additional redefined functions in class *Student.*

12.5. Define one or two additional functions in extending class *Student.*

12.6. Define a different class that will inherit class *Person.* This new class should include features that would extend and provide a specialization of the base class, *Person.* Draw the corresponding UML diagrams.

12.7. Explain how class reuse is being applied in the previous problem, Exercise 12.6.

12.8. Design and implement the four classes in Figure 12.1. Include sufficient features in the base and subclasses to facilitate the testing of the complete application.

12.9. Define and implement a class to test the classers developed in the previous problem, Exercise 12.8.

12.10. Define two additional classes to include in the class hierarchy of Exercise 12.8.

12.11. Design and implement a program for manipulating complex numbers. A complex number has two attributes, the real part and the imaginary part of the number. The basic operations on complex numbers are: complex addition, complex subtraction, complex multiplication, and complex division. *Hint*: in addition to the rectangular representation of complex numbers (x,y), it might be helpful to include attributes for the polar representation of complex numbers (module, angle).

12.12. Define and implement and additional class to the problem in Exercise 12.8. Include class *Sport_car* in the class hierarchy as a subclass of *Car.* Design and implement a program with all these classes. Include attributes such as horse power, maximum speed, passenger capacity, load capacity, and weight. Include the relevant functions.

Chapter 13
Advanced Object Oriented Concepts

13.1 Introduction

Three important concepts in object orientation are introduced in this chapter: abstract classes, interfaces, and polymorphism. These are directly related to the concept of inheritance.

An *abstract* class has one or more functions that are not implemented, only their headers are defined. Abstract classes help improve the object-oriented model of the problem by providing only the specifications.

An *interface* is similar to an abstract class and allows the introduction to pure specifications, which involves the complete separation between specification and implementation.

Polymorphism is a mechanism that allows more flexibility in the design. It also provides generic programming. With generics, the more general classes are separated from the more specific or concrete classes. This separation helps to enhance reuse of the more general definitions in modeling and in programming.

13.2 Abstract Classes

An abstract class has one or more *abstract functions*. An abstract function has only its declaration (also called its specification) and no implementation is included. A pure abstract class has all its functions declared as abstract.

Because an abstract class has one or more functions without their implementations, the class cannot be instantiated and it is generally used as a base class. The subclasses override the abstract functions inherited from the abstract base class and provide implementation for these functions.

J.M. Garrido, *Object Oriented Simulation: A Modeling and Programming Perspective*,   141
DOI: 10.1007/978-1-4419-0516-1_13,
© Springer Science + Business Media, LLC 2009

13.2.1 Definition of Abstract Classes

In OOSimL, the keyword **abstract** is used before the keyword **class** when defining an abstract class. The definitions of abstract functions are also preceded by the keyword **abstract**. The OOSimL statements for abstract class definition has the following general form:

> **description**
>   . . .
> **abstract class** ⟨ *class_name* ⟩ **is**
>   **private**
>   . . .
>   **protected**
>   . . .
>   **public**
>   . . .
> **endclass** ⟨ *class_name* ⟩

As mentioned previously, an abstract class is normally defined as a base class. Base classes provide single general descriptions for the common functionality and structure of its subclasses. Therefore, an abstract class is a foundation on which to define subclasses. Classes that are not abstract classes are known as *concrete classes*.

For example, a class that represents basic geometric figures is defined as an abstract class. Two functions *area* and *perimeter* are declared in the class. These fucntions compute the area and the perimeter of a figure. Class *Genfig* is defined in the following code:

```
description
   This is an abstract class that defines a generic
   geometric figure
   */
abstract class Genfig is
public
   // compute are of geometric figure
   abstract function area return type double
   //
   // compute perimeter of geometric figure
   abstract function perimeter return type double
endclass Genfig
```

The base class *Genfig* is defined as an abstract class because it does not provide the implementation of the functions *area* and *perimeter*.

Figure 13.1 shows the class hierarchy with base class *Genfig* and three subclasses: *Rectangle*, *Triangle*, and *Circle*. The calculations of area and perimeter are different in each of these subclasses and the base class *Genfig* cannot include the

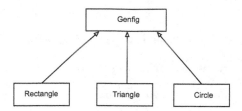

Fig. 13.1 A class hierarchy of geometric figures

implementations for these functions. The base class only provides the declaration (prototypes) for these functions.

Because the abstract class *Genfig* does not include the implementation body of the functions *area* and *perimeter*, objects of this class cannot be created. In other words, class *Genfig* cannot be instantiated.

13.2.2 Inheriting Abstract Classes

Because an abstract base class does not provide an implementation to one or more of its functions, the subclasses that inherit an abstract base class have to override (redefine) the functions that are defined as abstract functions in the abstract base class. The subclass, *Triangle*, for example, inherits class *Genfig* and includes the specific implementation of the functions *area*, *perimeter*, and the relevant attributes. The following code implements class *Triangle*.

```
description
     This class computes the area and perimeter
     of a triangle, given its three sides.
     */
class Triangle inherits Genfig is
  private
  variables
     define x of type double    // first side
     define y of type double    // second side
     define z of type double    // third side
  public
  description
     This function sets values for the three
     sides of the triangle.       */
function initializer parameters a of type double,
              b of type double, c of type double is
  begin
     set x = a
     set y = b
     set z = c
```

```
endfun initializer
//
  description
    This function computes the perimeter of a
    triangle. */
  function perimeter return type double is
  variables
      define lperim of type double
  begin
      set lperim = x + y + z
      return lperim
endfun perimeter
//
  description
    This function computes the area of a
    triangle.    */
  function area return type double is
  variables
      define s of type double     // intermediate result
      define r of type double
      define larea of type double
  begin
      set s = 0.5 * (x + y + z)
      set r = s * (s - x)*(s - y)*(s - z)
      set larea = call Math.sqrt using r
      return larea
  endfun area
endclass Triangle
```

13.3 Interfaces

An interface does not include constructors and cannot be instantiated. However, none of the functions of an interface include implementation, does not include attribute definitions although constant definitions are allowed. An interface is similar to a pure abstract class.

13.3.1 Interface Definition

The keyword **interface** is used followed by the name of the interface, in defining an interface. For the functions, the keyword **abstract** is not needed because all the functions are abstract functions. All features of an interface are implicitly public. The definition of an interface in OOSimL has the following general structure:

description

```
      . . .
interface ⟨ interface_name ⟩ is
   public
   constants
      . . .
   // public functions
      . . .
endinterface ⟨ interface_name ⟩
```

An interface, *IGenfig*, is shown in the following code. It defines the specification for the behavior of objects of any class that implements this interface. Note that the form of the interface is very similar to that of a pure abstract class.

```
description
   This is an interface that defines a generic
   geometric figure
   */
interface IGenfig is
 public
   // compute are of geometric figure
   function area return type double
   //
   // compute perimeter of geometric figure
   function perimeter return type double
endinterface IGenfig
```

13.3.2 Implementing an Interface

All methods declared in the interface must be implemented in the class that implements it. This class can define additional features. The header of the class that implements an interface has the keyword **implements** followed by the name of the interface. The class header has the general form:

description
      . . .
class ⟨ cls_name ⟩ **implements** ⟨ interface_name ⟩ **is**
      . . .
endclass ⟨ cls_name ⟩

Two additional and important differences between an interface and an abstract class is that multiple interfaces can be implemented by a class, whereas only one abstract base class can be inherited by a subclass, and it is mandatory for a class that implements an interface to implement all the functions defined in the interface.

13.4 Object Types

Abstract classes and interfaces can be used as *super types* for object references. Although they cannot be instantiated, interfaces and abstract classes are useful for declaring object references.

In the example of geometric figures, class *Genfig* is an abstract class and the other classes are subclasses. An object reference can be declared of type `Genfig`. Objects of the subclasses can be declared of each of their classes. The subclasses are considered subtypes of type *Genfig*. The following lines of code declare four object references, *gfigure*, *triangle_obj*, *circle_obj*, and *rect_obj*.

```
define gfigure of class Genfig
define triangle_obj of class Triangle
define circle_obj of class Circle
define rect_obj of class Rectangle
```

The types of these object references declared are considered subtypes in the problem domain because of the original class hierarchy represented in Figure 13.1.

The object reference *triangle_obj* is declared of type *Triangle*, but is also of type *Genfig* and any object reference of type *Triangle* is also of type *Genfig*.

The principle holds going upward in the class hierarchy, the opposite is not true; any object reference of type *Genfig* is not also of type *Rectangle*.

An interface can also be used as a super type, and all the classes that implement the interface are subtypes.

13.5 Polymorphism

Polymorphism is a runtime mechanism of an object-oriented language. This mechanism selects the appropriate version of a function to be executed depending on the actual type of the object. This function selection is based on *late binding* that occurs at execution time.

The typing principle explained previously allows an object reference of a super type to reference an object of a subtype. The following code creates objects for the object references *triangle_obj*, *circle_obj*, and *rect_obj*.

```
create triangle_obj of class Triangle using x, y, z
create circle_obj of class Circle using r
create rect_obj of class Rectangle using x, y
```

An object reference *gfigure* of class *Genfig* can be assigned to refer to any of the object of a subtype. The following code implements such an assignment.

```
set gfigure = triangle_obj
```

In this assignment, the type of object reference *triangle_obj* is a subtype of the type of object *gfigure*. It is legal to invoke a function of the abstract class *Genfig* that is implemented differently in the subclasses. The following code invokes function *perimeter*:

```
call perimeter of gfigure
```

The actual function invoked is the one implemented in class *Triangle*, because it is the actual type of the object reference *triangle_obj*. Another similar assignment can be included at some other point in the program.

The following code assigns the object reference *circle_obj* to the object reference *gfigure* and the call to function *perimeter* is the same as before, because the three subtypes represented by the three subclasses *Rectangle*, *Circle*, and *Triangle* each implement function *perimeter*.

```
set gfigure = circle_obj
call perimeter of gfigure
```

Because the implementation for function *perimeter* is different in the three classes, the runtime language system selects the right version of the function to call.

13.6 Summary

An abstract class has at least one abstract function. An abstract function is only a function declaration also known as the function specification and does not include its implementation. These classes cannot be instantiated; they can only be used as base classes. The subclasses redefine (override) the functions that are abstract in the base class. A pure abstract class has only abstract functions.

An interface is similar to a pure abstract class, but it cannot include data declarations. An interface may include constant declarations and may inherit another interface. A class can implement several interfaces.

An abstract class can be used as a type of an object variable (object reference); it can be used as a supertype, and the subclasses as subtypes. An object reference of a supertype can be assigned an object reference of a subtype. It is then possible to invoke a function of an object variable of a subtype. Polymorphism is a language mechanism that selects the appropriate function to execute. This selection is based on late binding. Polymorphism uses the actual type of the object reference.

13.7 Key Terms

abstract class	concrete class	abstract method
function overriding	pure abstract class	interface
supertype	subtype	polymorphism
late binding	generic programming	interface implementation

Exercises

13.1. Develop a program with appropriate classes for the following problem. A list of objects is required to store geometric figures and to calculate the perimeter and area of each figure when selected from the list. The geometric figures are circles, triangles, and rectangles.

The list is designed as an array of objects of class *Genfig*. Each element of the array is an object reference of a concrete class, *Circle*, *Triangle*, or *Rectangle*. The solution to this problem is generic by using this abstract class, the base class for all the other classes. The type of the array is *Genfig*, this class was discussed in this chapter. The capacity of the array is set with constant MAX_GEOM.

13.2. List and explain the differences and similarities between interfaces and abstract classes. Illustrate with two examples.

13.3. List and explain the differences and similarities between polymorphism and overloading. Include two examples.

13.4. List and explain the differences between implementing an interface and overriding the methods of an abstract class. Illustrate with two examples.

13.5. List and explain the differences between function overriding and polymorphism. Illustrate with two examples.

13.6. Is it possible to override one or more functions without using polymorphism? Explain and illustrate with an example.

13.7. Is it possible to define an abstract base class and one or more subclasses without using polymorphism? Explain and illustrate with an example.

13.8. OOSimL and Java support only single inheritance. Which is the most straightforward way to overcome this limitation? Include an example.

13.9. Modify the program discussed in Exercise 13.1 that uses base class *Genfig*. Add the ability of the geometric figures to draw themselves on the screen using dots and dashes. Define an interface at the top of the hierarchy.

13.10. Develop a complete program for the following problem. A corporation has several types of employees: executives, managers, regular staff, hourly paid staff, and others. A division of the corporation needs to maintain the data for all employees in a list. The solution to this problem will use a heterogeneous array of employee objects. Use an abstract base class and apply polymorphism to process the list (array).

13.11. Change the program in Exercise 13.10 by defining an interface instead of an abstract base class. Compare the two solutions to the problem.

13.12. Develop a complete program for the following problem. In a hierarchy of motor vehicles, find some behavior in all vehicles that is carried out in different manners. Define the top-level category with an abstract base class and one or more interfaces. Define and implement the subclasses.

Chapter 14
Introduction to Graphical Interfaces

14.1 Introduction

Programs with graphical interfaces provide a more convenient and effective manner for a user to interact with the application.

Using graphical user interfaces (GUIs), users can interact with graphical elements, such as buttons, menus, dialog boxes, and other graphical components. This chapter discusses the design and construction of simple GUIs using the two graphical libraries.

OOSimL depends on the underlying language Java that provides two graphical libraries (or packages) of classes. The first library of classes is called the abstract windows toolkit (*AWT*). The second library is called *Swing*. Programs that include GUIs, will access these two library packages using the following lines of code.

```
import all java.awt
import all javax.swing
```

14.2 Graphical Components

Users manipulate the various graphical components of a program to: view data of the program, enter data to the program, point, and click, thus to effectively interact with the program in execution. The most useful graphical components that form part of a graphical user interface are:

- Containers
- Simple components
- Events
- Listeners

J.M. Garrido, *Object Oriented Simulation: A Modeling and Programming Perspective*,
DOI: 10.1007/978-1-4419-0516-1_14,
© Springer Science + Business Media, LLC 2009

14.3 Containers

A basic GUI has only containers and simple components. A *container* is an object that can store graphical components and smaller containers. Examples of container objects are *frames* and *panels*.

A *simple component* is a small graphical object that displays data, allows the user to enter data, or simply indicates some condition to the user. Component objects are usually placed with other components in a container object. Layout managers are objects used to arrange contained objects in a container.

The size of graphical objects is normally measured in pixels. A pixel is the smallest unit of space that can be displayed on the video screen. The total number of pixels on the screen defines the *resolution* of the screen. High-resolution screens have a larger number of pixels and the pixels are much smaller.

Examples of component objects are buttons, labels, and text fields. Figure 14.1 shows the basic structure of a simple graphical user interface. The frame container has two panels, and each panel contains several graphical components.

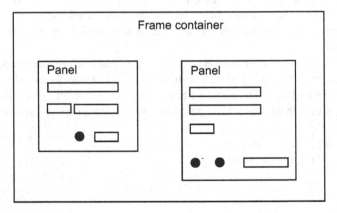

Fig. 14.1 A simple GUI

14.4 Frames

A *frame* is the largest type of container and can be created as an object of class *JFrame*. An empty frame window can be constructed by creating an object of class *JFrame* with a specified title, color, and size. Figure 14.2 shows an empty frame (window).

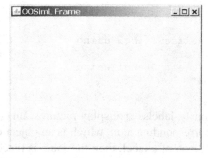

Fig. 14.2 An empty frame

The following lines of code implement function *const_frame* that constructs an empty frame with title "OOSimL Frame" and size of 400 by 300 pixels. The title is set by invoking the constructor of class *JFrame*, and the size is set by invoking the function *setSize* of object *frobj*. Function *setVisible* is invoked to make the frame window visible.

```
description
    This function constructs an empty frame.
    */
function const_frame is
  constants
    define WIDTH = 400 of type integer
    define HEIGHT = 300 of type integer
  object references
    define frobj of class JFrame
  begin
    create frobj of class JFrame using
            "OOSimL Frame"
    call setSize of frobj using WIDTH, HEIGHT
    call setVisible of frobj using true
  endfun const_frame
```

14.4.1 Simple Components

Text labels are components that display their text titles when they appear on a container of a window. Other labels can display images. A text label is defined as an object of class *JLabel*. When the objects of class *JLabel* are created, their text titles are defined.

The following lines of code include statements that declare two text labels and create the two text labels.

```
define flabel of class JLabel   // text label
```

```
object slabel of class JLabel
. . .
create flabel of class JLabel using
             "OOSimL"
create slabel of class JLabel using
             "DES"
```

As mentioned previously, labels can display pictures. Image labels display a picture by indicating the corresponding icon, which is an object of class *ImageIcon*. A picture is set up into an icon of a label, then the label is placed in a container. The pictures are normally in a standard format, such as *JPEG* or *GIF*.

In the following lines of code, the first two statements declare an object variable of class *ImageIcon* and an object of class *JLabel*. Another statement creates the icon object *imageobj* with a picture in the file *oosiml.gif*. The following statement creates the label object with the icon object *imageobj*.

```
define imageobj of class ImageIcon    // image
define labelobj of class JLabel       // for image
. . .
create imageobj of class ImageIcon using
             "oosiml.gif"
create labelobj of class JLabel using imageobj
```

14.4.2 Placing Components in a Frame

To place components into a frame, a special container called the *content pane*, an object of class *Container*, defines the working area for the frame window. All the graphical elements, components, and smaller container are added to the content pane.

The type of arrangement of graphical elements in the content pane is defined by the layout manager. There are six layout managers provided:

- Border, which arranges the components in the north, east, west, center, and south positions in the container
- Flow, which arranges the components in the container from left to right
- Grid, which arranges the components in a matrix with row and column positions
- Box, which arranges the components in a single row or single column
- Card, which arranges the components in a similar manner as the stack of cards
- Gridbag, which arranges the components in a similar manner as the grid but with variable size cells

The positioning of components using the border layout manager is illustrated in Figure 14.3.

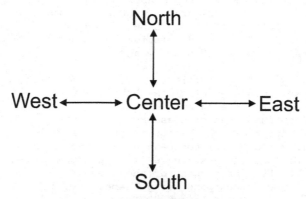

Fig. 14.3 The border layout manager positioning options

To manipulate the content pane object, a reference to this object is accessed by invoking method *getContentPane* of the frame object. Before adding the various graphical elements to the content pane, the layout must be set by invoking the method *setLayout*. The following lines of code define class *Contsample* that sets up an object of class *JFrame* with three components: two text labels and an image label.

```
import all javax.swing        // Library for graphics
import all java.awt
description
    A frame object is defined and displayed
    with an image and two text labels.    */
class Contsample is
  public
  description
    The main function in the program */
  function main is
  constants
      define WIDTH = 400 of type integer
      define HEIGHT = 300 of type integer
  object references
      define frobj of class JFrame // window
      // content pane
      define contpane of class Container
      define flabel of class JLabel  // text label
      define slabel of class JLabel
      define imageobj of class ImageIcon // image
      define imaglabel of class JLabel // for image
      define layoutman of class BorderLayout
  begin
      create frobj of class JFrame using
              "OOSimL"
```

```
        create flabel of class JLabel using
                  "     Discrete Event Simulation"
        create slabel of class JLabel using
                  "          Simulation Language"
        create imageobj of class ImageIcon using

                  "oosimls.gif"
        create imaglabel of class JLabel using
                  imageobj
        create layoutman of class BorderLayout
        set contpane = call getContentPane of frobj
        call setLayout of contpane using layoutman
        // Now add the text image label and text label
        // to the content pane of the window
        call add of contpane using flabel,
                  BorderLayout.NORTH
        //
        call add of contpane using imaglabel,
                  BorderLayout.CENTER
        //
        call add of contpane using slabel,
                  BorderLayout.SOUTH
        call setSize of frobj using WIDTH, HEIGHT
        call setVisible of frobj using true
    endfun main
  endclass Contsample
```

Figure 14.4 shows the window that is displayed on the screen when the program with class *Contsample* executes.

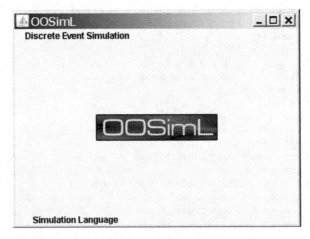

Fig. 14.4 The frame and its components

The components can be arranged using any layout manager. For the arrangement of components on the frame with a grid layout manager, the layout is a grid of rows and columns, and the components are of the same size. For example, the content pane can be divided into five rows and two columns. The following statements declare an object variable for a grid layout manager, create the object with five rows and two columns, and set the content pane of the window with the layout manager.

```
// layout manager
define gridman of class GridLayout
...
create gridman of class GridLayout using 5, 2
...
call setLayout of contpane using gridman
```

The title of a frame object can be set at any time by invoking method *setTitle* with a string argument. The size of the frame object is normally set before displaying it on the screen. The size is set by invoking method *setSize* with the values in pixels for width and height of the frame object.

The color is another attribute of a frame object. This attribute is normally set to a container in the frame, such as the content pane of the frame or the panels defined and contained in the content pane. The most common way to set the color of a container is invoking *setBackground*, which is defined in class *JFrame*. The argument is normally a predefined constant in class *Color*, which is available in the *AWT* package. These constants represent various colors to apply as background color to the container.

The following code includes a statement that sets the background color to green in frame object *frobj* and *contpane* is its content pane.

```
call setBackground of contpane using Color.green
```

14.5 Event-Driven Programs with GUIs

A program that responds to events while it executes is called event-driven, because the behavior of the program depends on the events generated by user actions. An *event* is a special non-visible object that represents an occurrence, usually as a result of some user action. Examples of GUI user actions that originate events are the click of the mouse, starting of mouse movement, a keystroke on the keyboard, and other actions. Each of these actions generates a specific type of event.

A *listener* is an object that handles an event; it waits for a specific event to occur and that responds to the event in some manner. Each listener has a relationship with an event or with a group of similar events. Listener objects must be carefully designed to respond to its type of events.

14.5.1 Event Components

Events are originated by various graphical components. Examples of these are buttons and text fields that generate events resulting from user actions. When the user clicks on the button, the listener object detects the event and responds.

The event-driven program declares and creates a button (as an object of class *JButton*). The program also declares and creates the corresponding listener object of a listener class.

A button is an object of class *JButton*. The following statements declare an object variable of class *JButton*. The button object is created with a title "Exit".

```
define mbutton of class JButton
. . .
create mbutton of class JButton using "Exit"
```

The type of event generated by the click of a button is called an *action event*. There is a direct relationship among the button object, the action event, and the listener object. Creating the action event and invoking the appropriate function of the listener object to handle the event is done automatically.

The listener object must be set to respond to an event generated by the button object—this is known as registering the listener object with the button object. When the event occurs, the action event generated is sent automatically to the corresponding listener object that responds to the event. In addition to creating a button object, the program must:

1. Define the class that implements the behavior of the listener object.
2. Declare the listener object reference for the button.
3. Create the listener object that will respond to the action event generated by the button.
4. Register the listener object for the button.

The graphical library packages (*AWT* and *Swing*) include several classes and interfaces for defining listener objects. For action events, the interface *ActionListener* must be implemented by the class that defines the behavior of the listener object.

The button object generates an action event and it sends to the listener object by invoking method *actionPerformed*. The interaction among these objects occurs automatically.

14.5.2 Registering a Listener Object

In order for a listener object to respond to an event, the listener object must be declared and created. The actual behavior of the listener object is defined in a class defined by the programmer. The following lines of code include statements that declare and create the listener object (of class *Bhandler*).

```
object bhandler of class Bhandler
...
create bhandler of class Bhandler
```

The listener object now has to be registered as the listener to the button object. In the following lines of code, the first statement invokes function *addActionListener* of the button to register its listener object, *bhandler*. Function *addActionListener* is defined in class *JButton*. The following statement adds the button defined previously to the content pane of the window with the south position. The content pane uses the border layout manager.

```
call addActionListener of mbutton using bhandler
call add of cpane using mbutton, BorderLayout.SOUTH
```

There is a different type of listener object for every type of event object, and the class definition that implements the behavior of listener objects depends on the type of events that these objects can handle (or respond to).

The class definition for action events must implement interface *ActionListener*, which is included in package *AWT*. The only method specified in the interface is *actionPerformed*, and has to be implemented in the class defined for action listener objects.

Class *Frbutton* is included in the CD that accompanies this book, it implements a frame window with three graphical components: a text label, a label with an icon, and a button. An object listener is defined for the button. The listener object terminates the program when the user clicks the button. Class *Bhandler* is also included in the CD, it defines the behavior of the object listener for the button used in class *Frbutton*.

14.5.3 Text Fields

A text field is a component that can display data can also be used for entering data to an application. For entering data, this component can generate an action event and send it to an action listener. An action listener object must be created and registered to the text field object.

After a user enters data in a text field and presses the Enter key, the text field object generates an action event and sends it to an action listener object. The text field is an object of class *JTextField*, which can be created with a given size and default text.

The following lines of code include two statements that declare an object reference and create the corresponding object of class *JTextField* of size 25 characters.

```
define mtext of class JTextField
. . .
create mtext of class JTextField using 25
```

A listener object has to be registered with a text field in a similar manner to registering a listener object to a button. The following statements declare and create a listener object, register an action event listener object with the text field object *mtext*, and include the text field in the content pane.

```
define tflistener of class Tlistener
define tflistener of class Tlistener
. . .
call addActionListener of mtext using tflistener
call add of cpane using mtext
```

Data is normally entered and displayed in string form, this requires proper conversion for entering and displaying numerical data. To get string data entered by a user into a text field, method *getText* of the text field object is used. To display string data in a text field, the method *setText* is used with the string as the argument.

The following statement gets the string data entered by the user in the text field *mtext*, and assigns the string value to variable *mstring*.

```
define mstring of type string
. . .
set mstring = call getText of mtext
```

Method *Double.parseDouble* is used with the string value to numeric of type **double**. This is actually a static method in class *Double*, which is a Java library class. The following statement converts the string *mstring* to a numeric variable *dlength* of type **double**.

```
define dlength of type double
. . .
set dlength = call Double.parseDouble using mstring
```

Before outputting numeric data (of type *double*) to a text field, it must be converted to a string value with method *String.valueOf*. The following statement converts variable *dlength* of type *double* to a string and assigns it to string variable *mstring*.

```
set mstring = call String.valueOf using dlength
```

14.5.4 Output Formatting

The formatting of non-integer numeric values must be done with an appropriate number of decimal digits. Using a decimal formatter produces a string that represents the number in one of several formats.

In the following lines of code, the two numeric variables of type *double*: *dlength* and *darea*, are formatted with the same pattern, which allows only two decimal digits (after the decimal point). The resulting numeric value is normally rounded to the specified decimal digits. The statements declare an object reference of class *DecimalFormat* (a Java library class), create the formatter object using a formatting pattern, and invoke function *format* of the formatter object using the numeric value to format.

```
define mft of class DecimalFormat
...

// for formatting output numeric data
create mft of class DecimalFormat
                    using "###,###.##"
...
set fdlength = call format of mft
                    using dlength
set farea = call format of myformat
                    using darea
```

14.6 Panels

In addition to objects of class *Frame*, smaller containers can be defined as objects of class *JPanel*. These objects can contain components such as labels, buttons, text fields, and other components. With panels (objects of class *JPanel*), a GUI can be organized in a hierarchical manner. All the panels and other components are placed in the content pane of the frame.

The following lines of code include statements that declare two panel objects, create the panels, and set the layout manager for each panel.

```
define apan of class JPanel
define bpan of class JPanel
. . .
create apan of class JPanel
create bpan of class JPanel
. . .
call setLayout of apan using gridmanager
call setLayout of bpan using flowmanager
```

The various components can be added to each panel, and the panels can be added to the content pane of the frame.

For example, a frame can be defined with two panels that are placed in the content pane of the frame using border layout. The first panel contains the labels and text fields using the grid layout. The second panel contains the two buttons using flow layout. The following lines of code show the implementation.

```
call add of cpane using
        apan, BorderLayout.CENTER
call add of cpane using
        bpan, BorderLayout.SOUTH
```

14.7 Applets

Applets are not standalone programs, because they require a Web browser to run. The code of the compiled class for an applet is placed in an HTML file with the appropriate tags. When a user uses his Web browser to start an applet, the compiled classes of the applet in the HTML file are downloaded from the server and executed.

The following lines of code show the tags in the HTML file with the compiled class *OOsimlapplet*.

```
<applet
code = "OOsimlapplet.class" width=300 height=400>
</applet>
```

A Web browser displays the complete Web page, including the GUI for the applet. A small and more complete HTML file with an applet embedded in it is shown next.

```
tt
<HTML>
  <HEAD>
     <TITLE> A sample Applet </TITLE>
  </HEAD>
<BODY BGCOLOR=blue TEXT=white>
  This is a simple applet that displays an OOSimL image.
  Any text included here in the HTML document.
  <CENTER>
    <H1> The KJP Applet </H1>
    <P>
       <APPLET CODE="OOsimlimag.class"
       WIDTH=250 HEIGHT=150>
       </APPLET>

  </CENTER>
</BODY>
</HTML>
```

The class definition of an applet must inherit class *JApplet* from the Swing library, or class *Applet* from the AWT library. Because applets are not standalone programs, so function *main* is not used. Instead, function *init* is included. A frame for a window is not defined because the applet automatically constructs a window.

The size of the applet window is set in the HTML file. The Web browser makes the applet visible.

In the following example, class *OOsimlimag* defines an applet that displays an OOSimL image and two text labels.

```
import all javax.swing  // Library for graphics
import all java.awt
description
    This applet creates and displays a frame window
    with an image and two text labels.    */
class OOsimlimag inherits JApplet is
  public
  description
    This is the function of the applet. */
  function init is
  object references
      // content pane
      define contpane of class Container
      define flabel of class JLabel  // text label
      define slabel of class JLabel
      define imageobj of class ImageIcon // image
      define imaglabel of class JLabel // for image
      define layoutman of class BorderLayout
  begin
      create flabel of class JLabel using
              "     Discrete Event Simulation"
      create slabel of class JLabel using
              "         Simulation Language"
      create imageobj of class ImageIcon using
              "oosimls.gif"
      create imaglabel of class JLabel using
              imageobj
      create layoutman of class BorderLayout
      set contpane = call getContentPane
      //
      call setLayout of contpane using layoutman
      // Now add the text image label and text label
      // to the content pane of the window
      call add of contpane using flabel,
              BorderLayout.NORTH
      //
      call add of contpane using imaglabel,
              BorderLayout.CENTER
      //
      call add of contpane using slabel,
              BorderLayout.SOUTH
    endfun init
  endclass OOsimlimag
```

14.8 Drawing Objects

To draw or paint, a graphics context is defined. This is carried by overriding method *paintComponent* in a subclass of class *JPanel*. An object of class *Graphics* is then used for drawing and painting.

The *coordinate system* used in drawing objects places the *origin* of the drawing area in its upper-left corner. All measures involved in drawing use pixels as the basic unit. The position of a visible dot is measured in the number of pixels to the right of the origin and the number of pixels below the origin. This gives the position using the coordinates (x, y). Figure 14.5 shows the coordinate system to represent the *position* of a point in the drawing area of the container.

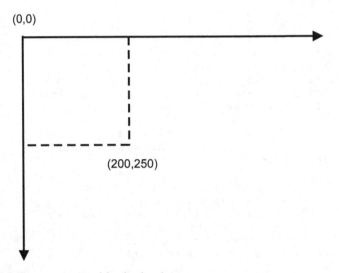

Fig. 14.5 Coordinate system used for the drawing area

14.8.1 Functions for Drawing

Another technique for drawing graphics objects is to define a class that inherits class *JComponent* and redefine function *paint*. An object is created, and its reference can then be added to a frame.

Function *paint* is defined with one parameter, an object reference of class *Graphics*, which is a class in the AWT package. Function *paint* is invoked automatically, so there is no need to explicitly call this function. The functions for drawing lines, circles, polygons, and so on, are features of the parameter of class *Graphics*.

Function *drawLine* draws a line on the drawing area, from point P1 to point P2, is invoked with the coordinates of the two points as arguments. The following statement draws a line from point P1(120, 50) to point P2(175, 65), using the object reference, *gobj*, of class *Graphics*.

```
call drawLine of gobj using 120, 50, 175, 65
```

All drawing statements must appear in function *paint*. The following statement draws a rectangle whose upper-left corner is located at point (100, 150), and with 50 pixels for width and 100 pixels for height.

```
call drawRect of gobj using 100, 150, 50, 100
```

In the following lines of code, an arc is drawn. The arc is part of an oval that is specified by an enclosing rectangle with the upper-left corner located in (x, y), and the size given by *width* and *height*. The portion of the arc to draw is specified by the starting angle and the final angle (in degrees).

```
int x = 20
int y = 50
width = 35
height = 25
startang = 0
finalang = 45
...
call drawArc of gobj using
          x, y, width, height, sang, fang
```

Several drawing functions defined in class *Graphics* are listed in Table 14.1.

Table 14.1 Drawing functions in class *Graphics*

drawOval	Draws the outline of an oval
draw2DRect	Draws a highlighted outline of a rectangle
drawPolygon	Draws a closed polygon
drawRoundRect	Draws a round-cornered rectangle
fillArc	Fills a portion of an oval with color
fillOval	Fills an oval with color
fillPolygon	Fills a polygon with color
fillRect	Fills a rectangle with color
fillRoundRect	Fills a round-cornered rectangle with color
fill3Drect	Fills a rectangle with color

14.8.2 Drawing of Rectangles

The following program shows two components on a frame: a drawing area with several rectangles of different sizes and a button with a listener.

Class *Drawfig* creates a frame with border layout manager for placing the two components. The first component is the drawing area with several rectangles. The drawing area is an object of class *Mydrawr* and placed in the center position of the frame. The button is placed in the south position.

```
import all java.awt
import all javax.swing
description
    This is the main class that presents an example
    of drawing simple objects.    */
class Drawfig is
  public
  description
      The main function.        */
  function main is
  constants
      define WIDTH = 300 of type integer
      define HEIGHT = 250 of type integer
  object references
      define dframe of class JFrame
      define cpane of class Container
      // object for drawing area
      define mdrawing of class Mydrawr
      // button
      define qbutton of class JButton
      define bhandler of class Bhandler
      define bordermanager of class BorderLayout
  begin
      create dframe of class JFrame using
            "Drawing Rectangles"
      set cpane = call getContentPane of dframe
      create mdrawing of class Mydrawr
      create qbutton of class JButton using "Exit"
      create bordermanager of class BorderLayout
      call setLayout of cpane using bordermanager
      create bhandler of class Bhandler
      call add of cpane using mdrawing,
            BorderLayout.CENTER
      call add of cpane using qbutton,
            BorderLayout.SOUTH

      // register the listener object with the
      // button object
      call addActionListener of qbutton
            using bhandler
      call setSize of dframe using WIDTH, HEIGHT
      call setVisible of dframe using true
  endfun main
```

```
endclass Drawfig
```

Several rectangles of different sizes and at different locations are drawn in class *Mydrawr*, which appears in the following lines of code.

```
import all java.awt
import all javax.swing
description
  This class draws several rectangles.  */
class Mydrawr inherits JComponent is
   public
   description
     Paint where the actual drawings are.  */
   function paint parameters gobj of
       class Graphics is
   constants
       define TIMES = 15 of type integer // number rectangles
   variables
       // position in drawing area
       define x of type integer
       define y of type integer
       // width and height
       define w of type integer
       define h of type integer
       define j of type integer // loop counter
   begin
       set x = 50
       set y = 20
       set w = 170
       set h = 170
       set j = 0
       for j = 0 to TIMES - 1 do
          // draw a circle
          call drawRect of gobj using x, y, w, h
          add 5 to x
          add 5 to y
          subtract 5 from w
          subtract 5 from h
       endfor
   endfun paint
endclass Mydrawr
```

Figure 14.6 shows the top part of the frame that contains the drawing area with several circles of different sizes and the bottom part of the frame that contains a single button for exiting the program when the user clicks it.

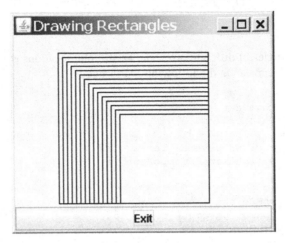

Fig. 14.6 A frame with rectangles

14.9 Summary

The Java packages AWT and Swing have a large number of predefined component and container classes for graphical user interfaces.

A graphical user interface provides the user a clear and attractive representation of relevant data, guide the user in the operation of the application, and facilitate his interaction with the program, and also provide some level of checking and verification of the input data.

A frame is the largest type of container. Graphical components and smaller containers are added to a frame in various manners, depending on the layout manager. Components and containers cannot be directly added to a frame; the content pane of the frame has to be used to add the graphical elements. Typical graphical elements are labels, buttons, text fields, and drawing areas. Types of containers are frames and panels.

Listener objects respond to the user in different ways. Buttons and text fields are components that generate events when the user clicks a button. These components can have object listeners attached. Listener objects handle the events that are generated by buttons and/or text fields. This is why the programs with graphical user interfaces (GUIs) are also called event-driven applications.

More detailed documentation of the various classes in the AWT and Swing packages for constructing graphical applications can be found on the Sun Microsystems Web pages.

14.10 Key Terms

frame	window	AWT
Swing	container	content pane
component	listener	pixel
layout manager	border	grid
flow	card	action event
image	label	text field
applet	panel	drawing
coordinate system	origin	picture

Exercises

14.1. Develop a program that carries out conversion from inches to centimeters and from centimeters to inches. The program must include a GUI for the user to select which conversion will be calculated, and then the user inputs data and gets the result on the frame.

14.2. Develop a program with two or more classes that draws a toy house and a few trees. Use lines, rectangles, ovals, and arcs.

14.3. Develop a program that converts temperature from degrees Fahrenheit to Celsius and vice versa. The program should present the appropriate GUI with the selection using two buttons, one for each type of conversion.

14.4. Investigate in the Web additional graphical elements. Design and implement a program that uses a GUI that includes a combo box to solve the temperature conversion problem.

14.5. After searching I the Web, design and implement a program that uses a GUI that includes a combo box to solve the problem for conversion from inches to centimeters and vice versa.

14.6. Develop a program that includes a GUI for inventory data. This consists of item code, description, cost, quantity in stock, and other data. Use labels, text fields, and buttons to calculate the total inventory value for each item.

14.7. Redesign the program in Exercise 14.6 and implement it using text areas. Search the Web for information on these graphical elements.

14.8. Research the Web for additional graphical elements. Design and implement a program that uses a GUI that includes a slider to solve the problem for conversion from inches to centimeters and vice versa.

14.9. Search the appropriate Web pages for additional graphical elements. Design and implement a program that uses a GUI that includes a slider to solve the temperature conversion problem.

14.10. Modify the salary problem implemented in class *Psalarygui*. The calculations of the salary increase and updating the salary should be done in the same class *Psalarygui*, instead of in class *Sal_listener*.

14.11. Redesign the GUI for the salary problem in Exercise 14.10. Use several panels and different layout managers and colors for the buttons than the ones included in the problem presented in this chapter.

Chapter 15
Exceptions

15.1 Introduction

Execution of a program can sometimes produce some kind of error. The most common type of runtime errors are division by zero, array indexing out of bounds, variable value out of range, illegal reference, and I/O errors. Well-designed programs should detect errors and take specified actions when errors occur.

An exception is an error or an unexpected condition that occurs while the program executes. The mechanism for detecting these errors or conditions and taking some action is known as exception handling.

15.2 Programming with Exceptions

The default exception handling capability of the language is to detect an error then abort the program and the runtime system displays the type of condition detected. For example: "Exception in thread main ArithmeticException: division by zero." The runtime system also prints a trace of the function calls.

When an error occurs, the run-time system of the language **throws** an exception at the point in the program where the error occurred. The exception can be handled at a different point in the program. Programming with exceptions involves dividing the code into two sections:

1. The purpose of the first section of code is to detect an exception. This includes an instruction sequence that might generate or throw an exception.
2. The purpose of the second section of code is to take some action to handle the exception.

J.M. Garrido, *Object Oriented Simulation: A Modeling and Programming Perspective*, 171
DOI: 10.1007/978-1-4419-0516-1_15,
© Springer Science + Business Media, LLC 2009

15.2.1 Checked and Unchecked Exceptions

There are several predefined exceptions in the Java class library. The exception hierarchy is divided into two categories of exceptions: *checked* and *unchecked* exception.

The first type, checked exception, can be controlled syntactically. The compiler checks that the exception is handled in the program. These exceptions are used for errors that are very likely to occur in the program.

Some of the methods in the Java library packages can generate or throw various types of checked exceptions. If it is possible for a checked exception to be generated in a function and if it does not handle the exception, then the header of the function must include the keyword **throws** followed by the exception type. The handling of the exception has to be carried out by another function that called the function that throws the exception. For example, the following function can throw an exception when invoked.

```
function rproc throws IOException is
. . .
endfun rproc
```

The second type of exceptions, *unchecked* exceptions, are very difficult to detect at compile time. These exceptions do not have to be handled in the program.

15.2.2 Handling of Exceptions

When an exception is thrown, the program will normally detect and handle the exception. There are two blocks of statements that are needed for detection and processing of exceptions. The first block is called a **try** block and it contains statements that might generate an exception. When an exception occurs on the **try** block, the second block, called the **catch** block, begins to execute immediately.

The **catch** block declares an object reference of type *Exception* as parameter. When an exception occurs, this parameter is passed and can be used in the block to get information about the exception. Method *getMessage*, defined in class *Exception*, can be used to get a description of the exception. The general syntactic forms of these two blocks of statements are:

```
try begin
    ⟨ statements ⟩
endtry
. . .
catch ⟨ parameters ⟩
begin
    ⟨ statements ⟩
```

endcatch

The **catch** block provides a name to the object reference of the exception object that is caught. With this object reference, the message of the exception object can be displayed and/or any other action can be implemented to handle the exception.

The following program, class *MyException*, implements an exception that occurs when the user types the value of the age that is zero or negative. The handling of the exception is carried by displaying information about the exception object, *lexcep_obj*, by invoking its method getMessage, and by executing the instructions that reread the value of age. All these statements appear in the **catch** block. If no exception occurs, the **catch** block does not execute, and the program proceeds normally.

```
description
   This program detects a possible exception in the
   value of age.
   If the age is zero or negative, an exception
      is thrown and caught. */
class MyException is
   public
   description
      This is the main function of the application.
       */
   function main is
   variables
      define age of type integer
      define increase of type float
      define salary of type float
      define cname of type string
      // message for exception
      define lmessage of type string
   object references
      define emp_obj of class Employeec
      define lexecep_obj of class Exception
   begin
      display "Enter name: "
      read cname
      display "Enter age: "
      read age
      //    Check for exception
      try begin
        if age <= 0
        then
           create lexecep_obj of class Exception
              using "Exception: age negative or zero"
           throw lexecep_obj
        endif
      endtry
      //
      catch parameters excobj of class Exception
      begin
```

```
            set lmessage = call getMessage of excobj
            display lmessage
            display "Retrying . . . "
            display "Enter age: "
            read age
         endcatch
         //
         display "Enter salary: "
         read salary
         create emp_obj of class Employeec using
             salary, age, cname
         set increase = call sal_increase of emp_obj
         set salary = get_salary() of emp_obj
         display "Employee name: ", cname
         display "increase: ", increase,
                       " new salary: ", salary
      endfun main
   endclass MyException
```

An exception is thrown when the user types a zero or negative value for the age,.
The exception is detected in the **try** block. To handle the exception, the statements
in the **catch** block are executed. These statements display the message that explains
and identifies the exception and allows the user to reenter the value for the *age*.

15.3 Summary

Errors can occur in a program and they indicate abnormal conditions during the
execution of the program. An exception is detected in a **try** block, which encloses
a sequence of statements that might throw an exception. The exception is handled
in a **catch** block, which encloses the sequence of statements that implement some
action in response to the exception. The simplest way to handle an exception is to
display information about the exception and terminate the program.

15.4 Key Terms

error	exception	detection
exception handling	checked exception	unchecked exception
`try` block	`catch` block	throw exception

Exercises

15.1. Explain the differences between throwing an exception and catching an exception. List and explain two or three examples.

15.2. Briefly explain the difference between detecting an exception and throwing an exception. Explain with examples. Why do most Java classes for input/output throw exceptions?

15.3. Explain the purpose of using exceptions in a program. Explain the options to deal with errors if a program is implemented without exceptions.

15.4. Explain the use of exceptions when dealing with program correctness. Hint: research Design by Contract.

Chapter 16
Input and Output

16.1 Introduction

Input/output is carried out with streams, except with GUIs. A stream is a sequence of bytes; the direction of the flow of data determines whether it is an input or an output stream—either incoming from a source or directed toward a destination.

Input and output files are associated with I/O streams. The various class packages allow the programmer to open, process, and close files.

16.2 Files

Files stored on a disk device are known as disk files. A disk file organizes data on a massive storage device such as a disk device. The main advantage of a disk file is that it provides permanent data storage; a second advantage is that it can support a large amount of data. A third advantage of a disk file is that the data can be interchangeable among several computers, depending on the type of storage device used. On the same computer, disk files can be used by one or more different programs.

A disk file can be associated with an input stream or with an output stream. It can be set up as the source of a data stream or as the destination of the data stream. Figure 16.1 illustrates the flow of data in an input and an output streams.

J.M. Garrido, *Object Oriented Simulation: A Modeling and Programming Perspective*,
DOI: 10.1007/978-1-4419-0516-1_16,
© Springer Science + Business Media, LLC 2009

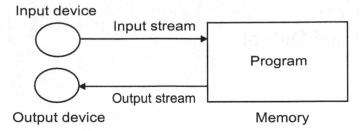

Fig. 16.1 Input and output data streams

16.2.1 Text and Binary Files

There are two general types of files: text files and binary files. Text files contain data that is coded as printable strings and are human-readable. A byte is coded as a single text character. An OOSimL source program is stored in a text file.

A binary file has data stored in the same way as represented in memory and is not human-readable. Especially for numeric data, the representation in memory is just ones and zeroes. A compiled program is stored in a binary file.

Binary files take less storage space and are more efficient to process. When reading or writing numeric data, there is no conversion from or to string format.

16.2.2 Input and Output Streams

The various streams available for I/O are defined in the `java.io` package. The streams are organized in a hierarchy of classes that are inherited by the classes that process files. Binary files are processed by classes that inherit classes *InputStream* and *OutputStream*. Text files are processed by classes that inherit classes *Reader* and *Writer*.

A *buffer*indexbuffer is a block of memory for temporarily storing data while being input or output. During data transfer, the buffer is used as an intermediate storage for data. Buffering is provided by several buffered streams, such as *BufferedInputStream*, *BufferedReader*, *BufferedOutputStream*, and *BufferedWriter*.

16.3 Using Text Files

A text file consists of a sequence of characters. Lines are separated by two characters, carriage return (CR) and line feed (LF); these are placed at the end of a line by pressing the Enter key[1]. A program that processes data on a file will normally perform the following sequence of steps:

1. *Open* the file for input or output. This step sets up the file for input or output; it attaches the file to a stream.
2. *Read* data from the file or *write* data to the file.
3. *Close* the file.

16.3.1 Reading Text Files

Two predefined classes are provided in the *io* package that are used to create objects for opening a text file for input: *BufferedReader* and *FileReader*.

Reading data from an input text file involves reading text lines from the input stream. The program that reads from the file has no information on the number of lines in the text file.

In the following lines of code, statements declare the two object references and create the corresponding objects for an input text file called "indata.dat."

```
define indatafile of class BufferedReader
define mreader of class FileReader
. . .
try begin
    create mreader of class FileReader
            using "indata.dat"
    create indatafile of class BufferedReader
            using mreader
endtry
//
catch parameters object lexc of
            class FileNotFoundException
begin
    display "Error opening file: ", "indata.dat"
    exit
endcatch
```

Because the opening of a text file for input can throw an exception if the file cannot be found, the statements that create the two objects must appear in a **try** block. To handle the exception, a **catch** block must immediately follow. If the input file cannot be opened, the statements shown in the **catch** block display an error message and terminate the program.

Once the input file has been opened, the program can start reading input streams from the file, line by line. To read a line of text data method *readLine* is invoked, which is defined in class *BufferedReader*. The data read is placed in a string variable.

---

[1] In Unix, only LF is placed at the end of the line.

The statement that reads a line of data must be placed in a **try** block because a reading error might occur. The exception is thrown by method *readLine*.

An additional statement is necessary to check whether the file still has data; otherwise, there would be an attempt to read data even if there is no more data in the input file. In this case, the value of the text read is *null*. The following statements define a **try** block with a while loop, which repeatedly reads lines of text from the text file.

```
try begin
    // Read data
    set inline = call readLine of indatafile
    while inline not equal null do
        // get name
        . . .
        // read next line
        set inline = call readLine of indatafile
    endwhile
endtry
```

Conversion is needed for numeric variables because the text file can only store string values. For example, *height* and *width* are variables of type **double**, so the string value read from the text file has to be converted to type **double**. The following statements read the text line (a string) from the file, and then convert the string value to a value of type **double** with method *Double.parseDouble*. For conversion to type **integer**, method *Integer.parseInt* is invoked.

```
// get value of height
set inline = call readLine of minfile
set height = call Double.parseDouble using inline
// get value of width
set inline = call readLine of minfile
set width = call Double.parseDouble
            using inline
```

16.3.2 Writing Text Files

To open a text file for output, two predefined classes are used to create the stream objects: *FileOutputStream* and *PrintWriter*. The following statements declare the two object references and create the corresponding objects to an output text file *outdata.dat*. The statements connect the disk file to an output stream, *moutstream*.

The opening of the file could generate an exception if the file cannot be created. For this reason, the statements must appear in a **try** block. To handle the exception, a **catch** block must immediately follow. If the output file cannot be created, an exception is thrown and statements in the **catch** block display an error message related to the exception and terminate the program.

```
define outdatafile of class FileOutputStream
define loutstream of class PrintWriter
. . .
try begin
   create outdatafile of class FileOutputStream
          using "outdata.dat"
   create loutstream of class PrintWriter
          using outdatafile
endtry
//
catch parameters object excep of class
                   FileNotFoundException
begin
    display "Error creating file outdata.dat"
    exit
endcatch
```

The output stream created is used for all output statements in the program with methods *print* and *println* of stream *moutstream.*

The numeric data must first be converted to a text string. For example, to convert an integer value to a string value, function *valueOf* of the class *String* is invoked. The following statements declare a variable of type **integer**, *itemnum*, declare a variable of type **string**, *numstr*, convert the value of the integer variable to a string, and assign the value to the string variable, *descrip.*

```
variables
   define itemnum of type integer
   define numstr of type string
. . .
set numstr = call String.valueOf using itemnum
```

16.3.3 Write File Application

In the following program, class *Outfilsal* writes employee data to a text file. Objects of class *Employee* calculate the salary increase and the updated salary.

```
import all java.io
description
  This program writes data to an
  output file.  */
class Outfilsal is
  public
  description
      This is the main function of the application.
      An object of class Employee calculates the
      salary increase and updates the salary.
```

```
      If the age is zero or negative, an exception
      is thrown and caught. This data is written to
      an output text file.        */
function main is
variables
      define age of type integer
      define more_data of type character
      define increase of type double
      define salary of type double
      define ename of type string
      define str_age of type string
      define str_inc of type string
      define str_sal of type string
      define file_name of type string
      define lmessage of type string // message for exception
object references
      define emp_obj of class Employee
      define myoutfile of class FileOutputStream
      define myoutstream of class PrintWriter
      // exception for negative age
      define lexecep_obj of class Exception
begin
      set myoutstream = null
      display "Enter name for output file: "
      read file_name
      // open ouput file
      try begin
         create myoutfile of class FileOutputStream
            using file_name
         create myoutstream of class PrintWriter
            using myoutfile
      endtry
      catch parameters e of
            class FileNotFoundException
      begin
         display "Error creating file mydata.txt"
         exit
      endcatch
      //
      set more_data = 'Y'
      while more_data equal 'Y' do
        display "Enter person name: "
        read ename
        display "Enter age: "
        read age
        //    Check for exception
        try begin
           if age <= 0
           then
              create lexecep_obj of class Exception
                 using "Exception: age negative or zero"
              throw lexecep_obj
           endif
        endtry
```

```
                catch parameters excobj of
                     class Exception
                 begin
                   set lmessage = call getMessage of excobj
                   display lmessage
                   display "Retrying . . . "
                   display "Enter age: "
                   read age
                endcatch
                // continue with processing
                display "Enter salary: "
                read salary
                create emp_obj of class Employee using
                     ename, salary, age
        //
   call increase_sal of emp_obj
                set increase =  call get_increase of emp_obj
                set salary = call get_salary of emp_obj
                display "Employee name: ", ename
                display "increase: ", increase,
                     " new salary: ", salary
                // write to output file
                call println of myoutstream using ename
                set str_age = call String.valueOf
                     using age
                call println of myoutstream
                     using str_age
                set str_inc =call String.valueOf
                     using increase
                call println of myoutstream using str_inc
                set str_sal = call String.valueOf
                     using salary
                call println of myoutstream using str_sal
                display "More data? (Yy/Nn): "
                read more_data
                if more_data equal 'y'
                then
                    set more_data = 'Y'
                endif
            endwhile
            call close of myoutstream
      endfun main
   endclass Outfilsal
```

16.3.4 Read File Application

The following application program consists of class *Readfilsal*, which reads data from the file created by the program presented in Section 16.3.3. This data file has the values of name, age, salary, and increase are each stored in a different line. The file stores these values for every person. The class computes and displays the total accumulated value of salary and the total accumulated value of increase for several persons.

```
import all java.io
description
     This class reads data from an input file
     and computes the total salary,
     total increase
     */
class Readfilsal is
  public
  description
     This is the main function of the application.
     */
  function main is
  variables
     define emp_name of type string
     define emp_age of type integer
     define emp_salary of type double

     define increase of type double
     define total_sal of type double
     define total_inc of type double

     define str_age of type string
     define file_name of type string
     define databuf of type string
     define lmessage of type string // message for exception
  object references
     define indatafile of class BufferedReader
     define lread of class FileReader
     define lexecep_obj of class Exception
  begin
     set indatafile = null
     set total_sal = 0.0
     set total_inc = 0.0
     display "Enter name for input file: "
     read file_name
     try begin
        // open input file
        create lread of class FileReader
           using file_name
        create indatafile of class BufferedReader
           using lread
     endtry
     //
     catch parameters e of class FileNotFoundException
     begin
         display "Error opening file: ", file_name
         exit
     endcatch
     //
```

```
        try begin
            // Read text line from input file
            set databuf = call readLine of indatafile
            while databuf not equal null do
                // get name
                set emp_name = databuf
                // get age
                set databuf = call readLine of indatafile
                set str_age = databuf
                // get salary
                set databuf = call readLine of indatafile
                set emp_salary = call Double.parseDouble
                        using databuf
                add emp_salary to total_sal
                // get increase
                set databuf = call readLine of indatafile
                set increase = call Double.parseDouble
                        using databuf
                add increase to total_inc
                //
                // Display and continue with processing
                display "Employee name: ", emp_name,
                        " age: ", str_age
                display " increase: ", increase,
                        " salary: ", emp_salary
                // read next line from file
                set databuf = call readLine of indatafile
            endwhile
        endtry
        catch parameters myexc of class Exception
        begin
            display "Error reading file: ", file_name
            exit
        endcatch
        display " "
        display "Total salary: ", total_sal
        display "Total salary increase: ", total_inc
        try begin
            call close of indatafile
        endtry
        catch parameters exc2 of class IOException
        begin
            display "Error closing file: ", file_name
            exit
        endcatch
    endfun main
endclass Readfilsal
```

A text file normally stores several fields per line, each separated by white spaces or blanks. For this, the program retrieves the individual string values, and convert these to the appropriate types (if needed), for every line of text read from the file.

Using the Java class *StringTokenizer* separates the individual substrings (tokens) from a text line. The following statements declare and create an object of class

StringTokenizer, read a line from the text file, and get two string variables, *var1* and *var2*, from the line.

```
// declare object ref for tokenizer
define tokenizer of class StringTokenizer
//

// read line from text file
set inbuf = call readLine of infile
//
// create tokenizer object
create tokenizer of class StringTokenizer using inbuf
//
// get a string variable from line
set var1 = call nextToken of tokenizer
//
// get another string variable from line
set var2 = call nextToken of tokenizer
```

The Java method *countTokens* can be invoked to get the number of substrings remaining on a line. This function returns a value of type **integer**. Another method, *hasMoreTokens*, returns true if there are substrings left on the line; otherwise, it returns false.

16.4 Summary

A data stream is a sequence of bytes. An I/O stream is a sequence of bytes in the input direction or in the output direction, which is treated as a source of data or a destination of data. I/O streams are normally connected with files.

The two important types of files are text and binary files. Only text files are explained in this chapter. Most of the statements for opening, reading, and writing files throw exceptions. Therefore, these statements must be placed in a `try` block. The input and output with text files are carried out to or from a text line, which is a string. If the data is numeric, then to or from the appropriate numeric type is necessary.

16.5 Key Terms

disk storage	storage device	type conversion
input stream	output stream	text file
binary file	open	close
read line	write line	

Exercises

16.1. Include exception handling for an empty name and age less than 18 in the program with class *Outfilsal*, discussed in section 16.3.3.

16.2. Develop a program that stores the inventory parts for a warehouse. Each inventory part has the following attributes: description, unit code, number of items in stock, and the unit cost. The program is to store the data in a text file and compute the total investment per item.

16.3. Develop a program that reads the inventory data from the text file written by the program in Exercise 16.2. The program must display the individual data on each inventory item, and print the total investment and revenue.

16.4. Include exception handling for a negative number of parts in stock, a zero or negative unit cost, and negative unit price, in the program in Exercise 16.3.

16.5. Include exception handling for a unit price equal to or less than the unit cost in the program of Exercise 16.3.

16.6. Develop a class with a GUI for inventory data in the inventory program in Exercise 16.2.

16.7. Develop a program that writes data to a text file with at least three fields per line.

16.8. Develop a program that reads data from a text file with several fields per line. The program must read the data file that was written in Exercise 16.7.

16.9. Develop an extension to the program developed in Exercise 16.1. The new program must declare and create an array of objects of class *Employee* and compute the lowest, highest, and average salary.

Chapter 17
Recursion

17.1 Introduction

Recursion is used to implement a repetitive task. It can sometimes be used to describe a solution in a simpler manner than with an iterative solution. Recursion is a design and programming technique by which a circular definition is employed, a structure is defined in terms of itself. Recursion can sometimes be simpler and clearer than an iterative solution to a problem. This allows the solution of a big problem by partitioning it into several smaller subproblems of the same kind and then we can combine the solutions to these subproblems. This way recursion can be used to describe complex algorithms.

The recursive approach to design and implement functions accomplishes the same goal as using the iterative approach for problems with repetitions. A function or method definition that contains a call to it is said to be recursive.

This chapter introduces the basic concepts that involve recursion and includes a problem-solving application of recursion using recursive function calls.

17.2 Defining Recursive Solutions

A recursive function calls itself from within its own body. A recursive operation achieves exactly what an operation with *iterations* achieves. In principle, any problem that can be solved recursively can also be solved iteratively. With iteration, a set of instructions is executed repeatedly until some *terminating condition* has been satisfied. Similarly with recursion, a set of instructions, most likely a part of a function, is invoked repeatedly unless some terminating condition has been satisfied.

A recursive function definition consists of two parts:

1. One or more *base cases* that define the terminating conditions. In this part, the value returned by the function is specified by one or more values of the arguments.

J.M. Garrido, *Object Oriented Simulation: A Modeling and Programming Perspective*,
DOI: 10.1007/978-1-4419-0516-1_17,
© Springer Science + Business Media, LLC 2009

2. One or more *recursive cases*. In this part, the value returned by the function depends on the value of the arguments and the previous value returned by the function. This is sometimes known as the winding phase.

The unwinding phase returns the values from the base case to each of the previous calls.

17.3 Examples of Recursive Functions

This section describes and explains three examples of functions that can be defined and implemented with recursion. The functions are: sum of squares, exponentiation, and list reversal.

17.3.1 Sum of Squares

The first example of a simple recursive function is *sum of squares*. The function must add all the squares of numbers from m to k, with $m \le k$. The informal description of the function $sq(m,k)$ is:

$$sq(m,k) = m^2 + (m+1)^2 + (m+2)^2 + \ldots + k^2.$$

The strategy of solution is to breakdown the problem into smaller subproblems, such that the smaller problems can be solved with the same technique as that used to solve the overall problem. The final solution is computed by combining the solutions to the subproblems.

A mathematical specification of this recursive function is as follows, assuming that $m \ge 0$ and $k \ge 0$:

$$ssq(m,k) = \begin{cases} m^2 + ssq(m+1,k), & \text{when } m < k \\ m^2, & \text{otherwise} \end{cases}$$

The recursive implementation of function *ssq* is defined in class *Sumsq*. This function is invoked in function *main* of class *Sumsq*.

```
use all java.util
description
   Tests sum of squares
   */
class Sumsq is
  public
  description
     This function is a test for sum of squares.
     It calls the recursive function, ssq
```

```
      */
      function main is
      variables
            define p of type integer
            define q of type integer
            define res of type integer
      begin           // body of function starts here
            set p = 3
            set q = 8
            set res = call ssq using p, q
            display "results: ", res
      endfun main
      //
      static function ssq return type integer
      parameters m of type integer, k of type integer
      is
      variables
            define res of type integer
      begin
            if m < k then
                  // recursive call
                  set res = call ssq using m+1, k
                  set res = m * m + res
                  return res
            else
                  set res = m * m
                  return res
            endif
      endfun ssq
      endclass Sumsq
```

17.3.2 Exponentiation

Another example of a recursive function is *exponentiation*, y^n. The informal description of exponentiation is:

$$y^n = y \times y \times y \times y \times \ldots \times y$$

For example,

$$y^3 = y \times y \times y$$

A mathematical specification of the recursive exponentiation function is as follows, assuming that $k \geq 0$:

$$y^k = \begin{cases} 1, & \text{when } k = 0 \\ y \times y^{k-1}, & \text{when } k > 0 \end{cases}$$

The base case in this recursive definition is the value of 1 for the function if the argument has value zero, that is $y^k = 1$ for $k = 0$. The recursive case is $y^k = y \times y^{k-1}$, if the value of the argument is greater than zero.

The following class includes a recursive implementation for the exponentiation function, *expn(y, k)*. The code defines a static function that is called by function *main* in class *Recexpn*.

```
use all java.util
description
   Tests sum of squares
 */
class Recexpn is
  public
  description
      This function is a test for exponentiation.
      It calls the recursive function, expn
      */
  function main is
   variables
       define p of type double
       define n of type integer
    define res of type double
    begin        // body of function starts here
       set p = 3.25
    set n = 8
    set res = expn(p, n)
    display "results: ", res
    endfun main
    //
    description
       This function computes the exponentiation of y
       Recursively. To the power of k,
       assuming that k > 0.
    */
    static function expn return type double
    parameters y  of type double, k of type integer is
    variables
        define res of type double
    begin
       display "expn ", y, " power ", k
       // base case
       if k == 0 then
          set res = 1.0
       elseif k < 0 then
          // exceptional case
          display "Negative value of k"
          set res = 1.0
       else
          // recursive case
          // k greater than 0
          // recursive call
          set res = y * expn(y, k-1)
          display "y = ", y, " k = ", k, " expn ", res
```

```
        endif
        return res
    endfun expn
endclass Recexpn
```

The computation of the recursive function *expn* involve successive calls to the function continue until it reaches the base case. After this simple calculation of the base case, the function starts calculating the exponentiation of *y* with power 1, 2, 3, and then 4.

17.3.3 Reversing a Linked List

An interesting set of recursive problems is the recursive processing of a linked list. Recursive reversal of a linked list is simpler and more elegant than performing the same operation iteratively.

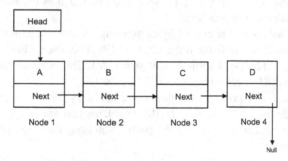

Fig. 17.1 Linked list of characters

Consider a simple list of characters, List = ('A', 'B', 'C', 'D'). Figure 17.1 shows a linked list with four nodes, each with a character. The overall task for this problem is to change the list so that the nodes will appear in reverse order.

To solve this problem recursively, a good strategy is to apply the divide and conquer approach. The first step is to split the list into a head and tail sublists. The head sublist contains only the first element of the list. The second sublist contains the rest of the list. The second step is to reverse (recursively) the tail sublist. The third step is to concatenate the reversed tail sublist and the head.

Figure 17.2 illustrates the general steps of reversing a linked list recursively. After partitioning the list, the head sublist contains only the first element of the list: *Hlist* = ('A'). The second sublist contains the rest of the list, *Tlist = ('B, 'C', 'D')*.

The recursive reverse operation continues to partition the tail sublist until a simple operation of reversing the sublist is found. Reversing a list containing a single

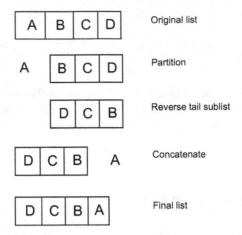

Fig. 17.2 Reversing a linked list of characters

element is easy, the reverse of the list is the same list. If the sublist is empty, the reverse of the list is an empty list. These will be included as the two base cases in the overall solution to the problem.

The overall solution is achieved by combining the concatenation or joining together the reversed tail sublist and the head sublist. The reversed tail sublist is Rlist = ('D', 'C', 'B'). The head sublist is Hlist = ('A'). The concatenation of the two sublists is *concat(Rlist, Hlist)* = *('D', 'C', 'B', 'A')*.

The solution to this problem requires three auxiliary functions: the first two are needed to divide the problem into smaller problems that are simpler to solve. The third function is needed to combine the partial solutions into the final overall solution to the problem.

The following class, *ChList*, implements the recursive reverse function and the auxiliary functions. Class *TestChList* implements function *main* that declares and creates an object of class *ChList* to build a linked list of characters and to reverse the list.

```
description
   This class represents a linked list. The methods are used to
   display, insert, and delete nodes.
   */
class ChList is
public
object references
      define head of class ChNode    // ref first node of list
      define last of class ChNode    // ref last node of list
public
description
   This is a constructor, it initializes the first and last
   node of the list. An empty list is created.
   */
function initializer is
```

```
begin
   set head = null
   set last = null
endfun initializer
//
description
   This function will return true if the list is empty
   */
function isEmpty return type boolean is
begin
 if head == null then
        return true   // List is empty
  else
return false  // list is not empty
 endif
endfun isEmpty
//
description
   This function will insert a node at the front of the list
   */
function insertFirst
           parameters pnode of class ChNode is
begin
   set pnode.next = head
   if head equal null then
      set last = pnode
   endif
   set head = pnode        // new first node
endfun insertFirst
//
function addnode parameters pnode of class ChNode is
begin
   // last node references current last node
   if last not equal null then
      set last.next = pnode
      set last = pnode
   else
      set head = pnode
      set last = pnode
   endif
endfun addnode
//
description
   This function will return a copy of the
   the node at the front of the list.
   It assumes that the list is not empty
   */
function getFirst return class ChNode
is
object references
 define temp of class ChNode
begin
 set temp = head
   return temp
```

```
endfun getFirst
//
description
   This function will remove node at the front of the list.
   It assumes that the list is not empty
   */
function deleteFirst is
object references
 define temp of class ChNode
begin
 set temp = head
 set head = head.next  // reference to the next node in list
 set temp = null        // destroy the deleted node
endfun deleteFirst
//
description
   This function traverses the list starting from node pnode
   and displays on the console
   the data of the nodes of the list.
   */
function display_data parameters pnode of class ChNode is
object references
   define current of class ChNode
begin
   display "List fist-->last : "
   set current = pnode
   while current != null do      // traverse list to last node
      call current.display_data  // display data in node
      set current = current.next // next node
   endwhile
   display ""
endfun display_data
//
// This function returns the ref of node at head of list
function get_hsub return class ChNode
parameters plist of class ChNode is
object references
   define thead of class ChNode
begin
   set thead = plist
   set thead.next = null
   return thead
endfun get_hsub
//
// partition the list
// returns ref to tail sublist
function get_tsub return class ChNode
parameters plist of class ChNode is
object references
   define Tlist of class ChNode // tail sublist
begin
   set Tlist = plist.next
   return Tlist
endfun get_tsub
```

```
//
// concatenate two sublists
function conclist return class ChNode
parameters L1 of class ChNode, L2 of class ChNode
is
object references
    define tnode of class ChNode
begin
    set tnode = L1
    while tnode.next not equal null do
       set tnode = tnode.next
    endwhile
    set tnode.next = L2
    set tnode = L1
    return tnode
endfun conclist
//
function reverse return class ChNode
parameters plist of class ChNode is
object references
    define tailt of class ChNode
    define headt of class ChNode
    define rnode of class ChNode
    define result of class ChNode
begin
    if plist equal null then
       return null
    elseif plist.next equal null then
       return plist
    else
       // partition list into tail and head sublists
       set tailt = call get_tsub using plist
       set headt = call get_hsub using plist
       //
       // reverse tail sublist
       set rnode = call reverse using tailt
       //
       // concatenate reversed tail sublist and head
       set result = call conclist using rnode, headt
       return result
    endif
endfun reverse
endclass ChList
```

17.4 Recursive Executions

The executions of the iterative and the recursive solutions to a problem are quite different. For the recursive solution, we must understand its implementation well to be able to develop and use it. We must understand the *runtime stack*.

Recall from previous chapters that a stack is a data structure (a storage structure for data retention and retrieval) based on a last in first out (LIFO) discipline. For example, if a stack is constructed with integer values, the last value that was inserted is at the top of the stack and must be removed before any other can be removed.

When a value is inserted on the top of a stack, the operation is known as *push*, and the stack grows up. When a value is removed from the stack, the operation is known as *pop*, and the stack shrinks. In other words, a stack grows or shrinks depending upon the insertion or removal of items from the stack.

Execution of a computer program involves two broad steps: allocating storage to hold data and then attaching a set of instructions to perform computations on the data held by the allocated storage.

Generally, storage is provided for objects, constants, and functions that have local variables, constants, and parameter variables. Because recursion involves only a function, focus here is only on the associated storage of a function: local variables, constants, and parameter variables. Operating systems create a process for each program to be executed and allocate a portion of primary memory to each process. This block of memory serves as a medium for the runtime stack, which grows when a function is invoked and shrinks when the execution of a function is completed.

During the execution of a process, there may be several functions involved in processing; the first function is always the main function, which invokes other functions if specified by the instructions. Whenever a function is invoked, the runtime system dynamically allocates storage for its local variables, constants, and parameter variables declared within the function from the allocated chunk of memory. In fact, this data is placed in a data structure known as a *frame* or *activation record* and inserted on the stack with a *push* operation. After the execution of the invoked function is completed, the frame created for that function is removed from the top of the stack with *pop* operation.

Obviously, the first frame is always for function *main*, as processing starts with this function. A frame is created to provide storage for each function. The *runtime stack* refers to a stack-type data structure (LIFO) associated with each process provided and maintained by the system. The runtime stack holds data of all the functions that have been invoked but not yet completed processing. A runtime stack grows and shrinks depending on the number of functions involved in processing and the interaction between them.

If function *main* is the only function involved in processing, there is only one frame in the stack with storage for all the variables, locals and constants. If function *main* invokes another function, A, then the stack grows only by one frame. After the function A completes execution, the memory block allocated to its frame is released and returned to the system.

17.5 Summary

A recursive function definition contains one or more calls to the function being defined. In many cases, the recursive function is very powerful and compact in defining the solution to complex problems. The main disadvantages are that it demands a relatively large amount of memory and time to build stack.

As there is a choice between using iterative and recursive algorithms, so programmers must evaluate the individual situation and make a good decision for their use.

17.6 Key Terms

base cases	recursive case	recursive call
terminating condition	recursive solution	iterative solution
winding phase	unwinding phase	stack
recursive functions	list functions	auxiliary functions
LIFO	push operation	pop operation
Activation frame	activation record	runtime stack

Exercises

17.1. Develop a program with a recursive function that computes and displays the factorial of n.

17.2. Develop a program with a recursive function that finds and displays n natural numbers that are even.

17.3. Develop a program with a recursive function that displays the letters in a string in reverse order.

17.4. Develop a program with a recursive function that reverses the letters in a string.

17.5. Develop a program with a recursive function that checks whether a given string is a palindrome. A palindrome is a string that does not change when it is reversed. For example: "madam,", "radar,", and so on.

17.6. Develop a program with a recursive function that performs a linear search in an array of integer values.

17.7. Develop a program with a recursive function that performs a binary search in an array of integer values.

Chapter 18
Threads

18.1 Introduction

Problems that include multiple tasks are normally implemented with programs that consist multiple *threads*, one thread for each task.

Multi-threading is a programming technique that allows the execution of multiple threads that are executed concurrently. On of the most common applications for threads are programs that use GUIs and animations. This chapter presents the basic concepts of threading and an example of programming with multiple threads.

18.2 Programming with Multiple Threads

In programs with multiple threads, each task is implemented as a *thread*. A thread object reference must be declared and the thread object created. Thread objects have a different behavior than other objects in a program. After creating a thread object, it must be started and then it takes a life of its own, by executing its main body until completion.

After creating a thread, it can then be started. This executes the main body of the thread. It can then be paused and resumed, until it becomes null.

The Java *Thread* class is a library class used to define threads. Class *Thread* includes the following methods: *start()*, *run()*, *sleep()*, *join()*, *yield()*, and others.

The main body of the thread is defined in method *run()*. The *start()* method starts the thread executing by calling method *run()* of the thread. When this method completes, the thread terminates.

J.M. Garrido, *Object Oriented Simulation: A Modeling and Programming Perspective*,
DOI: 10.1007/978-1-4419-0516-1_18,
© Springer Science + Business Media, LLC 2009

18.3 Defining Thread Classes

The definition of a thread class involves simply defining a class that inherits class *Thread*, which is a library class. Another way to define a thread class involves defining a class that implements the *Runnable* interface.

With the first technique, a subclass of class *Thread* overrides method *run()*. This is shown in the following portion of code:

```
description
   This class defines a thread. */
class Mthread inherits Thread is
public
description
  This is the main body of the thread
  */
function run is
       //
endfun run
endclass Mthread
```

With the thread class defined, a thread object reference is declared, then the thread object is created and started. This is shown in the following portion of code:

```
object references
   define mtref of class Mthread
   ...
begin
   ...
   create mtref of class Mthread
   start thread mtref    // start running the thread
   ...
```

The second technique involves three steps. The first step is defining a class that implements the *Runnable* interface and overrides method *run()*. This is shown with the following portion of code:

```
description
  This class defines a thread class by
  Implementing Runnable.
  */
class Mthread implements Runnable is
  public
  description
     This is the main body of the thread
     */
  function run is
       //
  endfun run
endclass Mthread
```

The second step is declaring an object reference and creating an object of the thread class previously defined.

The third step is declaring the object reference and creating a thread object of class *Thread*. The object reference from the previous step is used as an argument. The thread object can now be started. This is shown in the following portion of code:

```
object references
   define work of class Mthread
   define mthr of class Thread
   ...
begin
   ...
   create work of class Mthread
   create mthr of class Thread using work
   start thread mthr
```

18.4 More on Thread Behaviors

A thread can be suspended for a specified time interval by calling method *sleep()*. The execution of statement `sleep(150)` will pause the thread for 150 milliseconds. Method *yield()* will allow another thread to execute. It is similar to the *sleep()* method, but without any specific time.

A call to method *join()* waits until another thread completes its current execution phase. This method allows several threads coordinate their activities. For example, Thread *T1* calls this method in Thread *T2* that causes Thread *T1* to block until Thread *T2* has completed, and then Thread *T1* can continue. When the reference to the thread is assigned a null value, it stops at the current instruction and terminates.

18.4.1 Suspending A Thread

A thread can be suspended for a specified time interval then reactivated. Method *sleep* is used by a thread to suspend itself; the method is a static method that requires an argument of type **long**. The following line of code calls method *sleep* with an argument of value 200 to suspend a thread for 200 milliseconds:

```
call Thread.sleep using 200
```

While the thread is suspended, it can be interrupted by another thread; this call must be placed in a *try* block so it can check for an exception. The code is as follows:

```
try begin
   call Thread.sleep using 200
endtry
```

```
catch parameters e of class InterruptedException
begin
    // ignore exception
endcatch
```

18.4.2 Interrupting a Thread Object

One thread can interrupt the execution of another thread. The first thread invokes method *interrupt* of the second thread. In the following example, a thread interrupts the thread that has been created and started previously; the main method includes a call to the interrupt method of the second thread.

```
...
// interrupt mythread
call mythread.interrupt
...
```

The interrupted thread will have a special interrupt flag set to indicate that it has been interrupted. If the thread being interrupted is sleeping, an exception is thrown (as shown above). The block of instructions to execute when this event occurs (interrupt) is placed in a *catch* block.

```
try begin
    call Thread.sleep using 200
endtry
catch parameters e of class InterruptedException
begin
    // just a message to screen
    display "Thread interrupted ...."
endcatch
```

The interrupted flag of a thread is to indicate that the thread was interrupted. The call to method *sleep* clears the interrupted flag when it throws the exception. Usually, when a thread is executing a method and it is interrupted, it should be able to raise an exception of class *InterruptedException*.

The *isInterrupted* method is called to check the interrupted status of a thread. This method returns **true** if the thread has been interrupted; it returns **false** if the thread has not been interrupted. This method does not change the interrupted status of the thread. For example, the following code checks for the interrupted flag and executes appropriate instructions in a thread:

```
...
set intstatus = call Thread.isInterrupted
if intstatus equal true then
    ...             // appropriate instructions
    display "Thread was interrupted"
else
    ...             // other instructions
    display "Thread was not interrupted, ..."
```

```
endif
...
```

To check and clear the interrupted flag in a thread, the *interrupted* method is invoked; it is a static method of class *Thread*. The following code invokes this method and displays the interrupted status of the thread:

```
set intstatus = call Thread.interrupted
display "Status for thread: ", intstatus
```

18.4.3 Thread Priorities

Scheduling is the selection of which thread to execute next. The priority is an integer value. The threads (including the main thread) have a default priority of 5. Threads are normally scheduled with their default priorities. The system threads, such as the thread of the garbage collector, the AWT windows thread, and others, have a higher priority (in the range of 6 to 10).

To change the priority of threads, Java provides several constants and methods used for priority assignments. Any priority changes must be done with care, and JVM may not actually use the new priorities in the expected manner.

Method *getPriority* is invoked to get the current priority of a thread. To set the priority of a thread to a different value, method *setPriority* is invoked. A thread can be rescheduled to execute any time after a pause by relinquishing the processor to another thread. The static method *yield* indicates the scheduler to execute the next pending thread. The following code gets the priority of a thread, and if it is 5 or less, it is set to the maximum priority possible, otherwise the current thread yields the processor to another scheduled thread.

```
define my_prior\ of type integer
...
set my_prior = call mythread.getPriority
if  my_prior <= 5 then
    call mythread.setPriority using Thread.MAX_PRIORITY
else
    call Thread.yield    // yield execution of this thread
...
```

18.4.4 Thread Coordination

To obtain mutual exclusion in the thread behavior, a thread can obtain a *lock* on an object by invoking a *synchronized* instance method of that object. Only one thread can invoke the method, all other threads are excluded from invoking the method and have to wait. The threads that are waiting are suspended (or blocked) until one is enabled to invoke the method.

To declare a synchronized method, the non-static method must include the **synchronized** modifier in the method header. This will ensure that only one thread be allowed to execute the method at a time. The following code defines a class that includes a synchronized method as one of its members. The main method instantiates this class and two threads that invoke the synchronized method of the object created.

```
class Mexcoord inherits Object is
    public
    // other public definitions
    //
    // a synchronized method that can only be invoked
    // by one thread at a time
    synchronized function exclus is
        // ...
    endfun exclus
endclass Mexcoord // end of class definition

    function main is
      define mobj of class Mexcoord
      define mthread1 of class ThClass
      define mthread2 of class ThClass
      // ...
      create mobj of class My_exclusive
      //
      // create two threads and passing object
      // as argument to constructor

      create mthread1 of class Thclass using my_obj
      create mthread2 of class Thclass using my_obj

      //  ...
      // the two threads will invoke method
      // exclus of the object
      start thread mthread1
      start thread mthread2
      // ...
    endfun main
```

18.4.5 The Wait/Notify Mechanism

A set of threads may need to be coordinated and accomplish some level of communication. The wait/notify mechanism is used. A thread will *suspend* itself waiting for a condition until it is notified that there has been a change. This condition will typically be a check on the value of a variable. A second thread changes the condition and notifies the first thread. At this instant, the first thread can continue, if possible.

A thread first acquires a lock on a member object then it invokes method *wait* on the object. The thread releases the lock on the object and is suspended until notified or interrupted.

If the second thread cannot get the lock on the object, the thread waits until it can get exclusive access to the lock on the same object. Once the thread gets access to the lock on the object, the thread invokes method *notify*. In the following code, first thread gets suspended.

```
try begin
   call mobj.wait
endtry
catch parameters e of class InterruptedException
begin
    display "Thread interrupted on wait "
endcatch
```

18.5 Summary

This chapter is a short introduction to threads and basic principles of thread pro-gramming. The thread supports multi-tasking inside one program. It is a necessary mechanism for event-driven programming and network programming. The JVM schedules threads but using several methods of class *Thread* can change the order of execution of a set of threads. Thread synchronization is achieved by using several methods of class *Thread*.

18.6 Key Terms

threads	multithreading	processes
tasks	control sequence	preempt
animation	lightweight process	concurrent execution
thread priorities	mutual exclusion	thread coordination
thread suspension	wait/notify	

18.7 Exercises

Exercises

18.1. Explain and give three examples of multi-tasking.

18.2. Explain why threads are important.

18.3. Write a description of a typical application that uses multiple threads.

18.4. Investigate and explain the use of threads needed in event-driven programming.

18.5. Develop a program that displays and updates the time on a digital clock. One thread keeps time in a loop. Another thread updates the screen on every second.

Chapter 19
Linked lists

19.1 Introduction

A linked list is a data structure that stores a collection of data items of the same or similar types. This data structure is dynamic in the sense that the number of data items can change. A linked list can grow and shrink during the execution of the program that is manipulating it. Recall that an array is also a data structure that stores a collection of data items, but the array is static; once it is created, more elements cannot be added to it.

Linked lists and arrays are considered low-level data structures that are used to implement higher-level data structures, such as stacks and queues that are manipulated by an appropriate algorithm.

This chapter explains in some detail the basic forms of simple linked lists, double-ended linked lists, and multiple linked lists. The operations possible on linked lists and some applications that manipulate linked lists are also discussed.

19.2 General Form of a Linked List

In its most general form, a linked list is a chain of node objects. Each node has two basic components:

- A data item of some specified type or a reference to a data object of some specified class
- A reference to the next node object in the list

The last node on a linked list has a reference with value *null*. Figure 19.1 illustrates the general form of a simple linked list. When comparing linked lists with arrays, the main differences observed are:

- Linked lists are dynamic in size; arrays are static in size

J.M. Garrido, *Object Oriented Simulation: A Modeling and Programming Perspective*,
DOI: 10.1007/978-1-4419-0516-1_19,
© Springer Science + Business Media, LLC 2009

- In linked lists, items are linked by references and based on many node objects; whereas, an array is a large block of memory with the elements located contiguously.
- The nodes in a linked list are referenced by relationship not by position; to find a data item, always start from the first item (no direct access). Access to the elements in an array is carried out using an index.

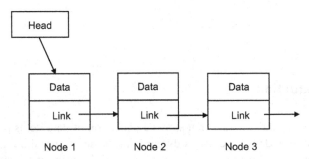

Fig. 19.1 A simple linked list

19.3 Node Objects

As mentioned previously, every node in a simple linked list has a data component and a link to the next node. These nodes can be located anywhere in memory and do not have to be contiguous in memory. The following listing is the implementation of class *PNode*, which includes a reference, *data*, to an object of class *Person* as its first attribute. The second attribute, *next*, is a reference to an object of class *PNode*. This component will actually be a reference to the next node in the linked list.

```
description
   This class represents a node as a building block for
   constructing a linked list. The attributes are
     the data object and a link to the next node.
   */
class PNode is
   public
   object references
       define data of class Person // data item
       define next of class Node   // link to the next node
   description
       This is the constructor, it initializes a Node object,
       a reference to a Person object is passed
       */
   function initializer parameters idata of class Person
```

```
   is
   begin
      set data = idata      // reference to an Person object
      set next = null
   endfun initializer
   //
   description
      This funtion displays the data object on the console.
      */
   function display_data is
   begin
      // invoke display of the Person object
      call display_data of data
   endfun display_data
   //
endclass PNode
```

19.4 Linked Lists

A linked list is a chain of nodes, it is an object that contains a reference to the first node. The nodes are also objects, which may themselves contain references to data objects. Some of the basic operations defined on a simple linked list are:

- Create an empty list
- Inserting an item at the front of the list
- Get a copy of the data item at the front of the list
- Deleting the item at the front of a list
- Traversing the list to display all the data items in the list
- Check whether the list is empty
- Find a node that contains a specified data item

The following listing contains the definition of class *LList*. The methods in the class implement the operations listed previously for linked lists.

```
description
    This class represents a linklist. The methods are used to
    display, insert, and delete nodes.
    */
class LList is
 public
 object references
    define head of class PNode // reference to first node
 public
 description
    This is a constructor, it initializes the reference to
    the first node of the list. An empty list is created.
    */
```

```
function initializer is
begin
     set head = null
endfun initializer
//
description
    This function will return true if the list is empty
    */
function isEmpty return type boolean is
begin
        if head == null then
            return true    // List is empty
        else
            return false   // list is not empty
endif
endfun isEmpty
//
description
   This function will insert a node at the front of the list
   */
function insertFirst
             parameters idata of class Person is
object references
    define newLink of class PNode
begin
    create newLink of class PNode using idata
    // new node references current head node
    set newLink.next = head
    set head = newLink        // new first node
endfun insertFirst
//
description
    This function will return a copy of the reference to
    the data of the node at the front of the list.
    It assumes that the list is not empty
    */
function getFirst return class Person
is
object references
    define temp of class PNode
    define tperson of class Person
begin
    set temp = head
    set tperson = temp.data
    return tperson
endfun getFirst
//
description
    This function will remove node at the front of
    the list. It assumes that the list is not empty
    */
function deleteFirst is
object references
    define temp of class PNode
```

```
begin
     set temp = head
     set head = head.next   // reference to next node
     set temp = null        // destroy deleted node
endfun deleteFirst
//
description
     This function traverses the list until a Person object
     is found with the specified person number. The function
     returns a reference to the Person object.
     */
function find_data return class Person
parameters pernum of type long
is
variables
     pnum of type long
object references
     define cperson of class Person
     define current of class PNode
begin
     set current = head
     while current != null do      // traverse list
        set cperson = current.data
        set pnum = cperson.get_num()
        if pnum == pernum
        then
             return cperson
        endif
        set current = current.next // next node
     endwhile
     return null
endfun find_data
//
description
     This function traverses the list and displays on
     the console the data objects of the nodes of the list.
     */
function display_data is
object references
     define current of class PNode
begin
     display "List fist-->last : "
     set current = head
     while current != null do       // traverse list
        call current.display_data  // display data
        set current = current.next // next node
     endwhile
     display ""
endfun display_data
endclass LList
```

The constructor basically creates an empty linked list. Method *isEmpty* checks whether the list is empty by examining the value of attribute *head*, which is a reference to the first node in the list. The value of this reference has a value *null* when the list is empty.

Although there are two possible places to add or insert nodes to the linked list, the front or the back, for simple linked list, insertion at the front of the list is simpler. Method *insertFirst* creates a new node and inserts the new node to the front of the list. This method is a pure mutator method. Figure 19.2 shows the insertion of a new node to the front of the list.

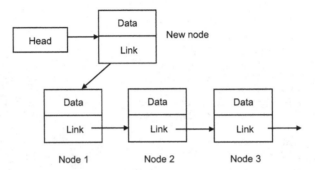

Fig. 19.2 Inserting a new node to front of a linked list

Method *deleteFirst* removes and destroys the node at the front of the linked list. This is a pure mutator method.

Method *getFirst* gets a copy of the data attribute, which is a reference to an object of class *Person*. This method does not change the state of the list object; it is a pure accessor method. Method *display_data* displays the data on each and every node of the linked list. It traverses the list starting with the first node. This method does not change the state of the linked list object.

A useful operation is the removal of a node that contains a specific data. This operation has to traverse the list starting from the node at the front of the list, examining each node until it finds the one with the data. Method *remove* in class *LList* removes the node when the data is found. The function does not return a value; it is a pure mutator function. The following listing has the implementation of method *remove*.

```
description
     This function traverses the list until a person object
     is found with the specified person number. The function
     removes the node from the list.
     */
function remove
parameters pernum of type long
is
variables
    define pnum of type long
```

```
object references
   define cperson of class Person
   define current of class PNode
   define prev of class PNode
begin
   set current = head
   set prev = head
   while current != null do        // traverse list to last node
      set cperson = current.data
set pnum = cperson.get_pnum()
      if pnum == pernum
      then
         if prev == head
         then
            set head = current.next
         else
            set prev.next = current.next
         endif
         set current = null   // destroy node
         return
      endif
      set prev = current
      set current = current.next // next node
   endwhile
   return
endfun remove
```

19.5 Linked List with Two Ends

The previous section described linked list with only one end, which references the first node. This reference is also known as the head of the list. Adding a reference to the last node provides the linked list with more flexibility. With two ends, a linked list has two references: a reference to the first node, the *head* of the list, and a reference to the last node, the *tail* of the list. Figure 19.3 illustrates this type of linked list.

With the reference to the last node (the *tail*), in addition to the reference to the first node (the *head*), the linked list now provides the ability to directly add a new node to the back of the list without traversing it from the front.

The following listing is a partial implementation of class *FTLList*, which includes the two attributes *head* and *tail*. This class also includes an additional function, *addTail*, that directly inserts a node at the tail of the list.

```
description
   This class implements a linked list with two ends.
   */
class FTLList is
```

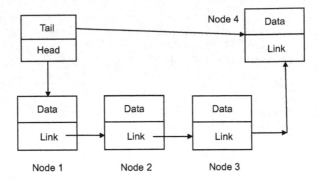

Node 3

Fig. 19.3 A linked list with two ends

```
public
object references
   define head of class PNode // reference to first node
   define tail of class PNode // reference to last node
   . . .
description
   This function will insert a node at the tail
   of the list    */
function insertTail
            parameters idata of class Person is
object references
   define newNode of class PNode
begin
   create newNode of class PNode using idata
   if head == null    // is list empty?
   then
      set head = newNode
   endif
   // current tail to reference new node
   set tail.next = newNode
   set tail = newNode      // new last node
endfun insertTail
   . . .
endclass FTLList
```

19.6 Nodes with Two Links

Linked lists that manipulate nodes with only one link, a reference to the next node, can only traverse the linked list in one direction, starting at the front and towards the tail of the list. To further enhance the flexibility of a linked list, a second link is included in the definition of the nodes. This second link is a reference to the previous link. These linked lists are also known as *doubly linked lists*. Figure 19.4 illustrates the general form of a linked list with nodes that have two links: a reference to the next node and a reference to the previous node.

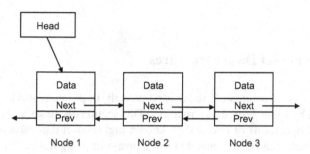

Fig. 19.4 A linked list with two links per node

The following listing is the source code for the implementation of class *DPNode*, which represents a node with two links.

```
description
  This class represents a node as a building block for
  constructing a doubly linked list. The attributes are
  the data object, a link to the next node, and a
  link to the previous node.
  */
class DPNode is
  public
  object references
      define data of class Person // data item
      define next of class DPNode   // link to next node
      define prev of class DPNode   // link to previous node
  description
    This is the constructor, it initializes a Node object
    on creation, a reference to a Person object is passed
    */
  function initializer parameters idata of class Person
  is
  begin
    set data = idata     // reference to an Person object
    set next = null
    set prev = null
```

```
   endfun initializer
   //
   description
     This funtion displays the data object on the console.
     */
   function display_data is
   begin
       // invoke display of the Person object
       call display_data of data
   endfun display_data
   //
 endclass DPNode
```

19.7 Higher-level Data Structures

Higher-level data structures are those used directly in problem solving and can be implemented by lower-level data structures. This section discusses and describes the structure and operations of two widely-known higher-level data structures: queues and stacks. These can be implemented using arrays or using linked lists.

19.7.1 Queues

A queue is a dynamic data structure that stores a collection of data items and that has two ends: the *head* and the *tail*. The main characteristics of a queue are:

- Data items can only be inserted at the tail of the queue
- Data items can only be removed from the head of the queue
- Data items must be removed in the same order of that in which they are inserted into the queue. The data structure is also known as a first in and first out (FIFO) data structure.

The data items in a queue may be variables of a simple type, or references to data objects. Figure 19.5 illustrate the form of a queue. It shows the insertion point at the tail and the removal point at the head of the queue. The operations that manipulate a queue are:

- *isEmpty*, returns true if the queue is empty; otherwise returns false.
- *isFull*, returns true if the queue is full; otherwise returns false.
- *copyHead*, returns a copy of the data object at the head of the queue without removing the object from the queue.
- *removeHead*, removes the head item from the queue
- *insertTail*, inserts a new data item into tail of the queue.
- *queueSize*, returns the number of data items in the queue.

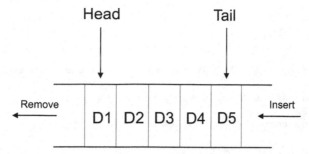

Fig. 19.5 A queue as a dynamic data structure

The following listing is the source code for class *LQueue*, which implements a queue structure based on the linked list with two ends developed previously. The class defines an integer variable, *count*, which represents the current number of data items or objects in the queue. Class *LQueue* implements the operations mentioned above.

```
description
    This class defines a queue implemented with a simple
    linked list.
    Class FTList is used as the underlying implementation
    of a linked list with two ends.
    */
class LQueue is
 private
 constants
    define N = 100 of type integer   // capacity of queue
 variables
    define count of type integer     // current number items
 object references
    define mList of class FTLList
 public
 description
  This is a constructor, it creates an empty queue.
    */
 function initializer is
 begin
    set count = 0
    create mList of class FTLList
 endfun initializer
 //
 description
   This function will return true if the queue is empty
    */
 function isEmpty return type boolean is
 variables
    define temp of type boolean
 begin
    set temp = call mList.isEmpty   // FTList object empty?
```

```
      return temp
   endfun isEmpty
   //
   description
     This function will return true if the queue is full
      */
   function isFull return type boolean is
   variables
      define temp of type boolean
   begin
      // is FTList object full?
      if count == N
      then
         set temp = true
      else
         set temp = false
      endif
      return temp
   endfun isFull
   //
   description
     This function will insert node at the tail of the
     queue. It assumes the queue is not full.
      */
   function inserTail
           parameters idata of class Person is
   begin
      call mList.insertTail using idata
      set count = count + 1
   endfun inserTail
   //
   description
      This function will return a copy of the data in
      the node at the head of the queue.
      */
   function copyHead return class Person is
   object references
    define tperson of class Person
   begin
    set tperson = call mList.getFirst
      return tperson       // return ref Person object
   endfun copyHead
   //
   description
      This function will remove the node at the head
      of the queue. It assumes the queue is not empty.
      */
   function removeHead is
   begin
      call mList.deleteFirst
      set count = count - 1
   endfun removeHead
   //
   description
```

```
      This function will return the number of
      data objects in the queue.
      */
  function queueSize return type integer is
  begin
      return count      // return number of data items
  endfun queueSize
  //
  endclass LQueue
```

19.7.2 Stacks

A stack is another dynamic data structure that stores a collection of data items. The main difference with a queue is that a stack has only one end: the *top* of the stack. The main characteristics of a stack are:

- Data items can only be inserted at the top of the stack
- Data items can only be removed from the top of the stack
- Data items are removed in reverse order of that in which they are inserted into the stack. The data structure is also known as a last in and first out (LIFO) data structure.

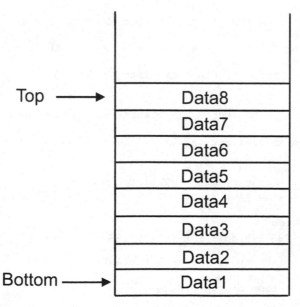

Fig. 19.6 A stack as a dynamic data structure

In a similar manner to a queue, the data items in a stack may be variables of a simple type, or references to data objects. Figure 19.6 illustrate the form of a queue. It shows the top of the stack as the insertion point and the removal point. The operations that manipulate a stack are:

- *isEmpty*, returns true if the stack is empty; otherwise returns false.
- *isFull*, returns true if the stack is full; otherwise returns false.
- *copyTop*, returns a copy of the data object at the top of the stack without removing the object from the queue.
- *pop*, removes the data item from the top of the stack.
- *push*, inserts a new data item to the top of the stack.
- *stackSize*, returns the number of data items in the stack.

The following listing is the source code for class *LStack*, which implements a stack structure based on the linked list with two ends developed previously. The class defines an integer variable, *count*, which represents the current number of data items or objects in the stack. Class *LStack* implements the operations mentioned above.

```
description
   This class defines a stack implemented with a simple
   linked list. Class FTList is used as the underlying
   implementation of a linked list with two ends.
   */
class LStack is
 private
 constants
    define N = 100 of type integer   // capacity of stack
 variables
    define count of type integer     // number of items
 object references
    define mList of class FTLList
 public
 description
  This is a constructor, it creates an empty stack.
  */
 function initializer is
 begin
    set count = 0
    create mList of class FTLList
 endfun initializer
 //
 description
   This function will return true if the stack is empty
   */
 function isEmpty return type boolean is
 variables
    define temp of type boolean
 begin
    set temp = call mList.isEmpty   // FTList object empty?
    return temp
```

```
endfun isEmpty
//
description
   This function will return true if the stack is full
   */
function isFull return type boolean is
variables
   define temp of type boolean
begin
   // is FTList object full?
   if count == N
   then
      set temp = true
   else
      set temp = false
   endif
   return temp
endfun isFull
//
description
   This function will insert node to the top of the stack.
   It assumes the stack is not full.
   */
function push parameters idata of class Person is
begin
   call mList.insertFirst using idata
   set count = count + 1
endfun push
//
description
   This function will return a copy of the data in
   the node at the top of the stack.
   */
function copyTop return class Person is
object references
 define tperson of class Person
begin
 set tperson = call mList.getFirst
   return tperson       // return ref to Person object
endfun copyTop
//
description
   This function will remove the node at the top of
   the stack. It assumes the stack is not empty.   */
function pop is
begin
   call mList.deleteFirst
   set count = count - 1
endfun pop
//
description
   This function will return the number of
   data objects in the stack.
   */
```

```
function stackSize return type integer is
begin
   return count      // return number of data items
endfun stackSize
//
endclass LStack
```

19.8 Generic Classes

To enhance flexibility and the reuse of classes, generics parameters are used to specify a type or class. A generic parameter is usually denoted by one or two characters, such as *G*, *G1*, *G2*, and so on.

The following example shows the syntax to define a class for a generic node, *GNode*, that will store data items of a generic class *G*.

```
description
   This class represents a generic node as a building
   block for constructing a linked list. The attributes
   are the data object and a link to the next node.
   */
class GNode of G is
   public
   object references
      define data of class G // data item
      define next of class GNode  // link to the next node
   description
      This is the constructor, it initializes a Node object
      on creation, a reference to an object of a generic
      class G is passed
      */
   function initializer parameters idata of class G
   is
   begin
      set data = idata     // ref to object of gen class G
      set next = null
   endfun initializer
   //
endclass GNode
```

To declare an object reference with the generic class *GNode*, an actual class must be specified, also known as a parameterized type. The following statements declare an object reference, *lnode*, of the generic class *GNode* and using class *Person* as the actual class.

```
define lnode of class GNode of Person
```

The following code defines a generic class, *GList* using the generic class *GNode* and parameter type *G*.

```
description
    This class represents a generic linked list. The methods
    are used to display, insert, and delete nodes.
    */
class GList of G
is
 public
 object references
    define head of class GNode of G // ref to the first node
 public
 description
    This is a constructor, it initializes the first node
    of the list. An empty list is created.
    */
 function initializer is
 begin
    set head = null
 endfun initializer
 //
 description
    This function will return true if the list is empty
    */
 function isEmpty return type boolean is
 begin
     if head == null then
         return true    // List is empty
       else
         return false  // list is not empty
 endif
 endfun isEmpty
 //
 description
    This function will insert a node at the front of the list
    */
 function insertFirst
             parameters idata of class G is
 object references
    define newLink of class GNode of G
 begin
    create newLink of class GNode of G using idata
    // new node references current first node
    set newLink.next = head
    set head = newLink        // new first node
 endfun insertFirst
 //
 description
    This function will return a copy of the reference
    to the data of the node at the front of the list.
    It assumes that the list is not empty
    */
```

```
function getFirst return class G
is
object references
 define temp of class GNode of G
 define tdata of class G
begin
    set temp = head
    set tdata = temp.data
    return tdata
endfun getFirst
//
description
    This function will remove node at the front of the
    list. It assumes that the list is not empty
    */
function deleteFirst is
object references
 define temp of class GNode of G
begin
 set temp = head
 set head = head.next   // ref to the next node
 set temp = null        // destroy the deleted node
endfun deleteFirst
//
description
    This function traverses the list until a data object
    is found equal to the specified object. The function
    returns a reference to the the data object.
    */
function find_data return class G
parameters pdata of class G
is
object references
    define cdata of class G
    define current of class GNode of G
begin
    set current = head
    while current != null do      // traverse to last node
       set cdata = current.data
       if cdata.equals(pdata)
       then
          return cdata
       endif
       set current = current.next // next node
    endwhile
    return null  // not found
endfun find_data
//
description
    This function traverses the list until a data object
    is found equal the specified data object. The function
    removes the node from the list.
    */
function removeNode
```

```
    parameters pdata of class G
    is
    object references
       define cdata of class G
       define current of class GNode of G
       define prev of class GNode of G
    begin
       set current = head
       set prev = head
       while current != null do        // traverse to last node
          set cdata = current.data
          if cdata.equals(pdata)
          then
             if prev == head
             then
                set head = current.next
             else
                set prev.next = current.next
             endif
             set current = null    // destroy node
             return
          endif
          set prev = current
          set current = current.next // next node
       endwhile
       return
    endfun removeNode
 endclass GList
```

19.9 Using Java Collections Framework

A collection – also known as a container – is an object that groups and stores multiple elements into a single unit. Several operations are defined to store, retrieve, and manipulate data.

A collections framework is a unified architecture for representing and manipulating collections. The collections include:

- Interfaces: These are abstract data types that represent collections. Interfaces allow collections to be manipulated independently of the details of their representation. In object-oriented languages, interfaces generally form a hierarchy.
- Implementations: These are the concrete implementations of the collection interfaces. In essence, they are reusable data structures.
- Algorithms: These are the methods that perform useful computations, such as searching and sorting, on objects that implement collection interfaces. The algorithms are said to be polymorphic: that is, the same method can be used on many different implementations of the appropriate collection interface. In essence, algorithms are reusable functionality.

When you declare a Collection instance you can and should specify the type of object contained in the collection. The core collection interfaces are:

- Collection – the root of the collection hierarchy. A collection represents a group of objects known as its elements.
- Set – a collection of elements with duplicate elements. This interface is used to represent sets.
- List – an ordered collection that can contain duplicate elements. The client of a List can decide where in the list each element is inserted and can access elements by their integer index.
- Queue – a collection used to hold multiple elements. A Queue provides additional insertion, extraction, and inspection operations. Queues can order elements in a FIFO (first-in, first-out) manner. Priority queues order elements according to a supplied comparator or the elements' natural ordering. Every Queue implementation must specify its ordering properties.
- Map – an object that maps keys to values. A Map cannot contain duplicate keys; each key can map to at most one value.

19.9.1 Declaring and Creating Collection Object References

The Collections classes use *generic* definitions, which allow the use of parameterized types. In declaring a reference to a collection, a specific type or class is used to specify the class of the data objects in the collection.

There are two general-purpose *List* implementations: *ArrayList* and *LinkedList*. For example, the following statements declare and create a *LinkedList* collection of objects of class *Person*.

```
object references
      define mylist of class LinkedList of Person
 . . .
      create mylist of class LinkedList of Person
```

19.9.2 Operations on List Collections

Lists may contain duplicate elements. In addition to the operations inherited from Collection, the List interface includes operations for the following: Positional access – manipulates elements based on their numerical position in the list Search – searches for a specified object in the list and returns its numerical position Iteration – extends Iterator semantics to take advantage of the list's sequential nature Rangeview – performs arbitrary range operations on the list. The following specifications are of some of the most common operations of class *LinkedList*.

- *add*, appends the specified element to the end of this list. Inserts the specified element at the specified position in this list.

- *addFirst*, inserts the specified element at the beginning of this list.
- *addLast*, appends the specified element to the end of this list.
- *clear*, removes all of the elements from this list.
- *contains*, returns true if this list contains the specified element.
- *element*, retrieves, but does not remove, the head (first element) of this list.
- *get*, returns the element at the specified position in this list.
- *getFirst*, returns the first element in this list.
- *getLast*, returns the last element in this list.
- *indexOf*, returns the index of the first occurrence of the specified element in this list, or -1 if this list does not contain the element.
- *remove*, retrieves and removes the head (first element) of this list.
- *remove*, removes the element at the specified position in this list.
- *remove*, removes the first occurrence of the specified element from this list, if it is present.
- *removeFirst*, removes and returns the first element from this list.
- *removeLast*, removes and returns the last element from this list.
- *size*, returns the number of elements in this list.

The following statements apply several operations to the linked list, *mylist* created previously.

```
variables
     define j of type integer
object references
     define mylist of class LinkedList of Person
     define personobj of class Person
. . .
     // add an object of class Person to the end of
     // the linked list
     call mylist.add using personobj
     call mylist.addLast using personobj
     call mylist.addFirst using personobj
     //
     // get a copy of an object of the linked list
     set personobj = call mylist.element
     set personobj = call mylist.getFirst
     set personobj = call mylist.getLast
     set personobj = call mylist.get using j
     //
     // remove an object from the linked list
     set personobj = call mylist.removeFirst
     set personobj = call mylist.removeLast
     //
     // set elemant j of the list to personobj
     call mylist.set using j, personobj
```

19.10 Summary

Linked lists are dynamic data structures for storing data items of the same or related class. Each of these values is known as an element. After the list has been declared and created, it can grow or shrink by adding or removing data items, also known as nodes. Lists can have one or two ends. Each node may have one or more links. A link is a reference to another node of the linked list.

Queues and stacks are examples of higher level data structures and can be implemented with arrays or by linked lists.

Generic classes from the Java Collections Framework can also be used to implement linked lists and stacks.

19.11 Key Terms

linked lists	nodes	links
dynamic structure	low-level structures	high-level structures
next	previous	queues
stacks	Collection Framework	generics

Exercises

19.1. Class *LList* implements a linked list with only one end. Define a function that adds a new data item of class Person to the end of the list.

19.2. Class *LList* implements a linked list with only one end. Define a function that removes the data item of class Person from the end of the list.

19.3. Class *LList* implements a linked list with only one end. Define a function that adds a new data item of class Person after a given node of the list. The indicated node is specified by its relative position in the list.

19.4. Class *LList* implements a linked list with only one end. Define a function that removes a specified data item of class Person from the list. The indicated node is specified by its relative position.

19.5. Class *LList* implements a linked list with only one end. Define a function that adds a new data item of class Person after a given node of the list. The indicated node is specified by the person number in the node.

19.6. Class *FTLList* implements a linked list with two ends. Define a function that removes the data item of class Person from the end of the list.

19.7. Class *FTLList* implements a linked list with two ends. Define a function that adds a new data item of class Person after a given node of the list. The indicated node is specified by its relative position in the list.

19.8. Class *FTLList* implements a linked list with two ends. Define a function that removes a specified data item of class Person from the list. The indicated node is specified by its relative position.

19.9. Implement a class, *DLList* similar to *FTLList* but with double-link nodes. These nodes were defined in class DPNode.

19.10. Class *DLList* implements a linked list with only one end and nodes with two links. Define a function that adds a new data item of class Person to the end of the list.

19.11. Class *DLList* implements a linked list with only one end and nodes with two links. Define a function that removes the data item of class Person from the end of the list.

19.12. Class *DLList* implements a linked list with only one end and nodes with two links. Define a function that adds a new data item of class Person after a given node of the list. The indicated node is specified by its relative position in the list.

19.13. Class *DLList* implements a linked list with only one end and nodes with two links. Define a function that removes a specified data item of class Person from the list. The indicated node is specified by its relative position.

19.14. Class *DLList* implements a linked list with only one end and nodes with two links. Define a function that adds a new data item of class Person after a given node of the list. The indicated node is specified by the person number in the node.

19.15. Class *LQueue* implements a queue data structure. How does it help to use instead double-link nodes? Explain.

19.16. Class *LQueue* implements a queue data structure. Modify this class and implement it with nodes of class *DPNodes*.

19.17. Class *LQueue* implements a queue data structure. Modify this class and implement it with a linked of class *LList*.

19.18. Class *LStack* implements a stack data structure. How does it help to use instead double-link nodes? Explain.

19.19. Class *LStack* implements a stack data structure. Modify the class definition and use instead double-link nodes.

19.20. Class *LStack* implements a stack data structure. How does it help to use instead a linked list with a single end? Explain.

19.21. Class *LStack* implements a stack data structure. Modify the class definition and use instead a linked list with a single end.

19.22. Class *GList* implements a generic linked list data structure. Modify the class definition and implement instead a linked list with two ends.

19.23. Class *GList* implements a generic linked list data structure. Modify the class definition and implement instead a linked list with a single end and generic nodes with two links.

19.24. Class *GList* implements a generic linked list data structure. Modify the class definition and implement instead a linked list with two ends and generic nodes with two links.

19.25. Class *LQueue* implements a queue data structure. Modify this class and implement it with class *LinkedList* from the Java Collections Framework.

19.26. Class *LStack* implements a stack data structure. Modify this class and implement it with class *LinkedList* from the Java Collections Framework.

19.27. Class *LQueue* implements a queue data structure. Modify this class and implement it as a generic class using class *LinkedList* from the Java Collections Framework.

19.28. Class *LStack* implements a stack data structure. Modify this class and implement it as a generic class using class *LinkedList* from the Java Collections Framework.

Chapter 20
Using Assertions with Programming

20.1 Introduction

One of the most important factors in software quality is reliability, which depends on correctness and robustness. A program is correct if it performs according to its specification, it is robust if it handles abnormal situations that were not covered in the specification in a graceful manner.

Reliability, although desirable in software construction regardless of the approach, is particularly important in the object-oriented approach because of the special role given to reusability. It is very important for reusable software components to be correct.

Constructing reliable object-oriented software depends on certain language characteristics. One of these is strong typing, which helps in catching inconsistencies before they have had time to become bugs. Another factor is garbage collection, which removes the specter of devious memory management errors. Another factor is the reuse of verified component libraries.

Finally, for the construction of reliable object-oriented software, a systematic approach is needed for specifying and implementing object-oriented software components and their interactions in a software system.

20.2 Using Assertions in Programming

Assertions are *Boolean* expressions that define correct program states at arbitrary locations in the code. Assertions used in programming are: *preconditions* that have to be satisfied on method invocation, *post-conditions* that are checked after method execution, and *class invariants* that express conditions for the consistency of data.

Bertrand Meyer developed an approach of software engineering called Design by Contract. This design approach specifies a contract between a supplier class and its client classes. The point of this approach is to state very clearly and precisely the

J.M. Garrido, *Object Oriented Simulation: A Modeling and Programming Perspective*, 233
DOI: 10.1007/978-1-4419-0516-1_20,
© Springer Science + Business Media, LLC 2009

respective responsibilities between the supplier class and the client classes. The key elements of the method are *assertions*.

Using Design by Contract improved software quality can by achieved by:

- Specifying the communication between components as accurately as possible.
- Defining the mutual obligations and expected results of the communication process.

These mutual obligations are called contracts, and assertions are used to check whether an application complies with a contract. An assertion is a boolean expression, inserted at a specific point in a program's execution, which must be true. Failure of an assertion is typically a symptom of a bug in the software, so it must be reported to the user. The Design by Contract approach identifies three basic types of assertions:

- Preconditions: Obligations that the client must fulfill in order to call the external component correctly.
- Postconditions: Expected results after the execution of the external component.
- Class invariants: Conditions that must remain unchanged after the execution of the external component.

These assertions in a class specify a contract between its instances and their clients. According to the contract a server promises to return results satisfying the post-conditions if a client requests available services and provides input data satisfying the preconditions. Class invariants must be satisfied before and after each service. Neither party to the contract (these are the clients and servers) shall be allowed to rely on something else than stated explicitly in the contract.

The objects of the client class must guarantee certain conditions before calling a method on the objects of the supplier class, these conditions are the preconditions. Objects of the supplier class guarantee certain conditions are met after the method call, these conditions are the postconditions. Some important goals of Design by Contract are:

- Reduced test effort by separating contract checks from regular application logic.
- Saved debugging effort due to improved monitoring where failures occur close to the faults, as well as improved up-to-date and unambiguous documentation of interfaces.

If the preconditions and postconditions are included in a form that the compiler can check, then any violation of the contract between objects of the client class and objects of the supplier class can be detected immediately.

The notion of Design by Contract is focus in the systematic approach to object-oriented software construction, first implemented in the Eiffel programming language.

20.2.1 Preconditions

Preconditions specify conditions that must hold before a method can execute. As such, they are evaluated just before a method executes. Preconditions involve the system state and the arguments passed into the method.

Preconditions specify obligations that a client of a software component must meet before it may invoke a particular method of the component. If a precondition fails, a bug is in a software component's client.

20.2.2 Postconditions

In contrast, postconditions specify conditions that must hold after a method completes. Consequently, postconditions are executed after a method completes. Postconditions involve the old system state, the new system state, the method arguments, and the method's return value.

Postconditions specify guarantees that a software component makes to its clients. If a postcondition is violated, the software component has a bug.

20.2.3 Class Invariants

A class invariant specifies a condition that must hold anytime a client could invoke an object's method. Invariants are defined as part of a class definition. In practice, invariants are evaluated anytime before and after a method on any class instance executes. A violation of an invariant may indicate a bug in either the client or the software component.

20.3 Advantages of Using Assertions

Some of the advantages of using assertions in Design by Contract include the following. Design by Contract provides:

- It provides an approach that helps improve the construction of error-free object-oriented software systems.
- A method for dealing with abnormal cases using exception handling.
- An effective framework for debugging, testing and, more generally, improved software quality.
- A method for documenting software components.
- An improved understanding of the object-oriented method and, more generally, of software construction.

Including assertions in classes provide a powerful tool for finding errors. Assertion monitoring is a way to check what the software does against what its developer described it should do. This results in a good approach to debugging, testing, in which the search for errors is based on consistency conditions provided by the developers themselves.

This approach reduces significantly the number of bugs, and improves software reliability.

20.4 Specification of Classes

To improve software reliability, the external description of a software component must be stated as precisely as possible.

The presence of a component's specification, significantly helps to guarantee the module's correctness, and is a good basis for systematic testing and debugging.

With the Design by Contract approach, these specifications (or contracts) govern the interaction of software component with the other components.

Using more formal specifications is stated with a formal specification language such as Z and VDM. These specification languages are typically non-executable.

20.4.1 The Notion of a Contract

Contracts are agreements between two parties when one of them (the supplier) performs some task for the other (the client). Each party expects some benefits from the contract, and accepts some obligations in return. Usually, what one of the parties sees as an obligation is a benefit for the other party. The aim of the contract document is to state and describe as precise as possible these benefits and obligations.

Using assertions the notation is precise and may be used to capture the semantics of various operations, but avoids any implementation commitment. Table 20.1 shows the general relationship between a supplier and a client, viewed as a contract.

	Obligations	Benefits
Client	*Must ensure method precondition*	*Will benefit from postcondition*
Supplier	*Must ensure method postcondition*	*Assume precondition*

Table 20.1 Obligations in a contract between Client and Supplier.

20.4.2 Class Invariants

Preconditions and post-conditions apply to individual operations, implemented as functions or methods. An assertion that describes a property which holds of all instances of a class is called a class invariant.

Class invariants are constraints that characterize the semantics of a class. This notion is important for configuration management and regression testing, since it describes the deeper properties of a class: not just the characteristics it has at a certain moment of its evolution, but the constraints which must also apply to subsequent changes.

Viewed from the contract theory, an invariant is a general clause which applies to the entire set of contracts defining a class.

20.4.3 Improved Documentation

An important advantage of contracts is that they provide a standard way to document software modules, as classes. To provide client programmers with a more appropriate description of the interface properties of a class, that is, the external view of a class. These forms of class description do not include any implementation detail but only the essential usage information, the contract.

The external description of classes serves as the basic tool for documenting libraries and other software elements. It also serves as a central communication between software developers. It also facilitates software design and project management, as it encourages developers and managers to discuss the key issues (interface, specification, inter-module protocols) rather than internal (implementation) details.

The external description of a class retains headers and assertions of the class features, as well as invariants. This form of a class without implementation can be written as a formal class specification.

20.5 Using Assertions with OOSimL

The following example introduces the use of the two assertions, precondition and postcondition, in a simple function using the OOSimL language:

```
description
   This function inserts an element x to a list, the element
   must be retrievable through key.  */
function put
parameters x of class Element,
           key of type string
is
precondtion
    count <= capacity and key.length() > 0
```

```
begin
    ... instructions of insertion algorithm ...
postcondition
    find(key) == x and
    count == old_count + 1
endfun put
```

The **precondition** clause introduces an input condition, or precondition; the **postcondition** clause introduces an output condition, or postcondition. Both of these conditions are examples of assertions, or logical conditions (contract clauses) associated with software elements.

In the precondition, *count* is the current number of elements and capacity is the maximum number. In the post-condition, the boolean query which tells whether a certain element is present invoking function *find*, which returns the element associated with a certain key. The variable *old_count* refers to the value of *count* on entry to the routine, e.g., in the previous state of the object.

In OOSimL, class invariants are written using the keyword **invariant** followed by a boolean expression. Class invariants are written after all attribute declarations. The following example how a simple invariant of a class is written:

```
invariant
        count >= 0 and
        count <= capacity
```

The following example in the OOSimL illustrates the use of assertions and the Design by Contract principle in a class specification.

```
import all oosimlib
description
   This class represents employee data. The attributes are
      salary, age, employment date, and name.
   */
class Employee is
  private
  variables
        define salary of type double
        define age of type integer
        define name of type string
        define sal_increase of type double
  object references
        define employ_date of class EmpDate
  invariant
        get_salary() >= 0.0 and
        get_increase() >= 0.0 and
        get_age() >= 18
  //
  public
  //
  description
     This is the constructor, it initializes an Employee
       object on creation.
      */
```

```
function initializer
parameters iname of type string,
           isalary of type double,
           iage of type integer
is
precondition
   isalary >= 1000.00
postcondition
   get_increase() == 0.0
endfun initializer
//
description
  This funtion sets the employment date of the
  employee object.
  */
function set_employdate
parameters day of type integer,
           month of type integer,
           year of type integer
is
precondition
    year >= 1990
postcondition
    employ_date != null
endfun set_employdate
//
description
  This funtion gets the salary of the employee object.
  */
function get_salary return type double is
endfun get_salary
//
description
  This function returns the age of the employee object.
  */
function get_age return type integer is
endfun get_age
//
description
  This function returns the name of the employee object.
  */
function get_name return type string is
endfun get_name
//
description
    This function computes the salary increase and
    updates the salary of an employee.
    */
function increase_sal is
postcondition
    get_increase() > 0.0
endfun increase_sal
//
description
```

```
      This function returns the salary increase for
      the Employee object.
      */
   function get_increase return type double
   is
   endfun get_increase
   //
   description
      This function displays the attributes of the
      Employee object
      */
   function display_emp is
   endfun display_emp
endclass Employee
```

The complete class definition, which includes the implementation of the class follows.

```
import all oosimlib
description
   This class represents employee data. The attributes are
      salary, age, employment date, and name.
   */
class Employee is
   private
   variables
       define salary of type double
       define age of type integer
       define name of type string
       define sal_increase of type double
   object references
       define employ_date of class EmpDate
   invariant
       get_salary() >= 0.0 and
       get_increase() >= 0.0 and
       get_age() >= 18
   //
   public
   //
   description
     This is the constructor, it initializes an Employee
     object on creation.
     */
   function initializer
   parameters iname of type string,
              isalary of type double,
              iage of type integer
   is
   precondition
     isalary >= 1000.00
   begin
     //
     set salary = isalary
     set age = iage
```

```
   set name = iname
   set sal_increase = 0.0
   set employ_date = null
postcondition
   get_increase() == 0.0
endfun initializer
//
description
   This funtion sets the employment date of the
   employee object.
   */
function set_employdate parameters day of type integer,
                                    month of type integer,
                                    year of type integer
 is
object references
   define temp_date of class EmpDate
precondition
   year >= 1990
begin
   create temp_date of class EmpDate
              using day, month, year
   set employ_date = temp_date
postcondition
   employ_date != null
endfun set_employdate
//
description
  This funtion gets the salary of the employee object.
  */
function get_salary return type double is
begin
   return salary
endfun get_salary
//
description
  This function returns the age of the employee object.
  */
function get_age return type integer is
begin
   return age
endfun get_age
//
description
  This function returns the name of the employee object.
  */
function get_name return type string is
begin
   return name
endfun get_name
//
description
   This function computes the salary increase and
   updates the salary of an employee.
```

```
      */
   function increase_sal is
     constants    // constant data declarations
        define percent1 = 0.045 of type double
        define percent2 = 0.05 of type double
     begin              // body of function starts here
        if salary > 45000.0
        then
           set sal_increase = salary * percent1
        else
           set sal_increase = salary * percent2
        endif
        add sal_increase to salary    // update salary
   postcondition
        get_increase() > 0.0
   endfun increase_sal
   //
   description
      This function returns the salary increase for the object.
      */
   function get_increase return type double
   is
    begin
       return sal_increase
   endfun get_increase
   //
   description
      This function displays the attributes of the
      Employee object
      */
   function display_emp is
      begin
         display name, " ", age, " ", salary
      endfun display_emp
   endclass Employee
```

20.6 Loop Invariants and Loop Variants

Loop invariants and variants are used to help verify the *correctness* of loops. A loop invariant is a boolean expression that evaluates to *true* on every iteration of the loop. This boolean expression normally includes variables used in the loop.

20.6.1 Loop Invariants

The loop invariant has to be true before each iteration of the loop body, and also after each iteration of the loop body. If the invariant is true before entering the loop, it must also be true after exiting the loop.

The initial value of the loop invariant helps determine the proper initial values of variables used in the loop condition and body. In the loop body, some statements make the invariant false, and other statements must then re-establish the invariant so that it is true before the loop condition is evaluated again. In OOSimL, a loop invariant is written using the keyword **loopinv** followed by a boolean expression.

Invariants can serve as both aids in recalling the details of an implementation of a particular algorithm and in the construction of an algorithm to meet a specification.

20.6.2 Loop Variants

The loop variant is an integer expression that always evaluates to a non-negative integer value and decreases on every iteration. The loop variant helps to guarantee that the loop terminates (in a finite number of iterations). In OOSimL, a loop variant is written using the keyword **loopvariant** followed by an integer expression.

20.6.3 Examples in OOSimL

The following function definition finds the maximum value in an integer array. To invoke the function, two arguments are used: the integer array and the current number of elements in the array.

```
function max_array return type integer
   parameters
       a array[] of type integer,
       num_elements of type integer
   is
   variables                               // local variables
       define i of type integer            // use as array index
       define max_elem of type integer     // maximum so far
   precondition
       num_elements > 0 and a != null
   begin
       set i = 1
       set max_elem = a[0]
       while i < num_elements
       loopinv                             // loop invariant
           max_elem >= a[i-1]
       loopvariant                         // loop variant
           num_elements - i
       do
           if a[i] > max_elem
           then
               set max_elem = a[i]
           endif
           increment i
       endwhile
```

```
        return max_elem
    endfun max_array
```

In the loop code above, the **loopinv** keyword followed by a boolean expression defines the loop invariant. This boolean expression is true after loop initialization and maintained on every iteration. This is the general property of a loop invariant.

```
    loopinv                          // loop invariant
        max_elem >= a[i]
```

The loop variant is an integer expression that decreases in value on every iteration of the loop. In OOsimL it is written after the keyword **loopvariant**. For this example, the loop variant is defined as follows:

```
    loopvariant                      // loop invariant
        num_elements - i
```

As another example, the following portion of code defines a function to compute the greatest common divisor.

```
function gcd return type integer
    parameters a of type integer, b of type integer is
    set x = a
    set y = b
    precondition
        a > 0 and b > 0
    begin
    while x != y do
        if x > y
        then
            set x = x  y
        else
            set y = y  x
        endif
    endwhile
endfun gcd
```

In the loop code above, the following boolean expression is true after loop initialization and maintained on every iteration. This is the general property of a loop invariant. Using OOSimL syntax:

```
loopinv
        x > 0 and y > 0
```

The *gcd* function, included above, the variant is: *max(x,y)*. In OOsimL, the syntax for this construct appears as:

```
loopvariant
        max (x, y)
```

20.7 Summary

An important property of software is correctness. The notion of client and supplier contracts specifies all operations in terms of responsibilities and obligations. Contracts in software systems are expressed in programming with assertions. With the OOSimL language, preconditions, postconditions, and class invariants enables specification of the classes. These assertions together with loop invariants and variants can help improve program correctness. Contract violations are signaled as exceptions during program execution.

20.8 Key Terms

correctness	robustness	reliability
class specification	contracts	assertions
precondition	postcondition	class invariant
loop invariant	loop variant	exception
obligations	benefits	client
supplier		

Exercises

20.1. Discuss whether a class invariant should be checked at the start of an initializer function (constructor). What is the solution to this?

20.2. Add assertions to class *LList*, which represents a linked list and discussed in Chapter 19. Test the modified class with class *TestList* or a similar class.

20.3. Add assertions to class *FTList*, which represents a linked list with two ends and discussed in Chapter 19. Test the modified class with class *TestList* or a similar class.

20.4. Discuss whether a higher-level class, such as one that represents a stack, or the low-level implementation class representing a linked list, should be specified with assertions. Explain. Which class is more appropriate to specify with assertions?

20.5. Add assertions to class *LStack*, which represents a stack and discussed in Chapter 19. Test the modified class with class *TestList* or a similar class.

20.6. Add assertions to class *LQueue*, which represents a queue and discussed in Chapter 19. Test the modified class with class *TestList* or a similar class.

Part III
Discrete-Event Simulation

This part presents an introduction to object-oriented discrete-event simulation. The OOSimL simulation language is used for all implementation of simulation models.

Chapter 21
Models of Single-Server Systems

21.1 Introduction

This chapter presents an introduction to the general structure of an object-oriented simulation model with OOSimL. The basic form of simple single-server models is discussed. Modeling with *UML* diagrams, modeling with simulation activity diagrams, and object-oriented programming are explained and are used for developing a single-server model.

21.2 Object-Oriented Simulation with OOSimL

A process is an active object that carries out a sequence of logically related activities ordered in time. The process-interaction approach to simulation benefits from the advantages of object-oriented modeling since a process is modeled as an active object.

During a simulation run, all the active objects of the software model *interact* with each other in some way or another. The process interaction approach to discrete event simulation is based on object-oriented modeling and programming.

In an object-oriented programming language such as OOSimL, an entity type is defined as a class, and an object is an instance of that class.

For example, in a simple traffic light control system, an automobile is modeled as a process and defined in a thread class. The model may include several automobiles as processes of the same type; these are represented as instances, or objects, of the automobile class. The attributes of a process are represented as attributes of the class. The behavior of a process is modeled by the operations that can be performed by the process; these are implemented as methods in the thread class.

In addition to processes, a simulation model often includes other entities that do not behave as processes. These entities are modeled as *passive* objects; that is, they

J.M. Garrido, *Object Oriented Simulation: A Modeling and Programming Perspective*,   249
DOI: 10.1007/978-1-4419-0516-1_21,
© Springer Science + Business Media, LLC 2009

do not have a life of their own. A simulation model normally consists of several active objects and several passive objects.

The simulation software library provides classes to help develop the simulation models. When the model runs, it creates instances of some of these library classes and inherits other library classes. All classes in the simulation model that represent processes are defined by inheriting class *Process* from the class library.

Other classes in the library provide various functionalities (e.g., the generation of random numbers, the definition and use of priority queues, and so on).

The simulation approach applied to all the simulation models presented in this book is the process interaction approach to discrete-event simulation. This approach is the most powerful one since it is adequate for large and complex systems. The other advantage of this approach is that it is inherently object-oriented.

21.3 Implementing A Simulation Model

A model consists of an assembly of classes, which define the structure and behavior of all objects in the model. Some of these objects are *active objects*, the other objects are *passive*. The active objects are also called processes and have a predefined general behavior. The passive objects correspond to queues or other resources; the active objects use these passive objects as resources.

A simulation model is implemented with either a general-purpose programming language, or a simulation language. Simulation is the activity of carrying out experiments with the simulation model to study the behavior and obtain performance estimates of the system represented by the model.

The general behavior of a process is defined in class *Process*, which is included in the OOSimL simulation library. A process is an active object and is an instance of a class that inherits class *Process*.

21.3.1 General Form of a Model

A simulation models must include definitions of the classes for active objects and the classes for passive objects. Some passive objects are created directly from a library class (e.g., *Squeue* library class).

The general steps in implementing a simulation model are as follows:

1. Define all classes for the active objects (processes), these classes inherit from the library class *Process*.
2. Define the main class, which is also a class for an active object of the model.

All class definitions for active objects must include a method called *Main_body*. This method is the main sequence of execution for the active object (process). The main class must include method *main*.

21.3.2 The Main Class

The main class implements the general logic that starts and shuts down the simulation. This class must implement method *main*. All important variables and object references are declared in it. The structure of the main class is:

1. Declare variable(s) for the queue size
2. Declare variables for the workload parameters and system parameters
3. Declare variables for the total calculations
4. Declare a reference to an object of class *Simulation*
5. Declare references for the active objects of the simulation model
6. Declare references to the queues and other passive objects
7. Declare references for the output files
8. Define the *initializer* method
9. Define method *main*
10. Define the main body of the class

21.3.3 Method main

Method *main* include the following general steps:

1. Create an object of the library class *Simulation* using a title for the model.
2. Create all the objects used in the model.
3. Start the simulation by invoking the *start_sim* function of the simulation object.
4. Setup the output files.
5. Create the queues and other passive objects.
6. Create and start an object of this class, the main object of the model.

21.3.4 Method main_body

Method *Main_body* implements the logic on every active object in the model. The implementation of this method in the main class should include the following general steps:

1. Create and start the active objects declared in this class.
2. Start the simulation run using the declared simulation period.
3. Calculate total results.

Execution of the simulation program is carried out under control of the simulation executive.

Several simulation models discussed run as console applications, others include a graphical interface. Additional details on the use and distributions of OOSimL and sample models are included in the Psim Web page:

http://science.kennesaw.edu/~jgarrido/psim.html

21.4 General Structure of Single-Server Models

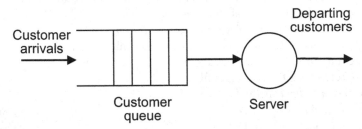

Fig. 21.1 Model of a single-server system

In a model of a single-server system, there is only one server process that provides service to the customer processes. An example of a graphical description of a single-server model is shown in Figure 21.1. The single-server model includes the following components:

- The arrival of customers, indicated with an arrow pointing to the tail of the queue
- The customers that arrive requesting service
- The customer queue, which is the waiting line for customers
- The server, which takes the next customer from the head of the queue and services it

A queue is a data structure that represents a waiting line and has two ends, the *head* and the *tail*. A queue is defined as a passive entity. An arriving customer process enters the queue at its tail. A customer can only leave the queue if it is at the head. The order of arrival of customers is retained in a simple queue, which follows first-in-first-out (FIFO) ordering. The server removes the customer at the head of the queue then provides service to this customer. Figure 21.2 illustrates these general properties of a queue.

21.5 A Model for The Car-Wash System

The Carwash system consists of a single Carwash machine, the server process. Arriving cars join a line to wait for service. The car at the head of the line is the one that is next serviced by the Carwash machine. After the car wash is completed, the

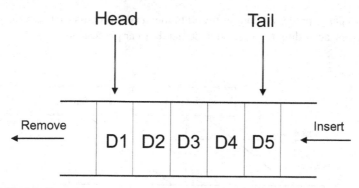

Fig. 21.2 Model of a queue

car leaves the system. Cars are considered the customers of the system, as they are the processes requesting service from the server.

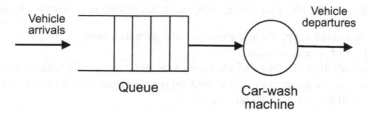

Fig. 21.3 Model of the Carwash system

21.5.1 The Conceptual Model

The model of this system is a typical single-server queuing model. There is a single process representing the Carwash machine. This process is the server of the model. There are several processes, the car processes. These are the customers of the model. Finally, there is a single process representing the arrivals of cars, and which represents the environment of the system. The model of the simple Carwash system consists of the following processes:

- The *Car* processes, which represent the customers to be serviced by the Carwash machine. There are many instances of this process that are created and actually executed (each one is an object of class *Car*).
- The *Arrivals* process, which creates car arrivals according to the inter-arrival period. This process represents the environment.

- The *Machine* process, which represents the server process that services the car processes, according to the service demand of car processes.

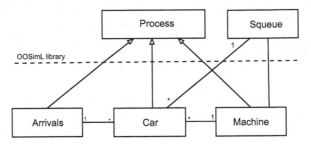

Fig. 21.4 The UML class diagram for the Carwash system

During execution of the simulation model, all active objects or processes interact among themselves and/or carry out their individual behaviors for the duration of the simulation period. There are several relevant types of events in this simple model:

1. The arrivals of car processes, which have to join the queue.
2. The start of service of a car
3. The completion of service of the current car process. At this same instance, the server process attempts to get the next car process from the queue, and if there is none, will transition to the idle state.

Figure 21.4 shows the UML class diagram for the simple Carwash system. Figure 21.5 shows the UML communication diagram with the interactions among the processes mentioned above. Figure 21.6 shows the UML state diagram for a Car process in the Carwash system.

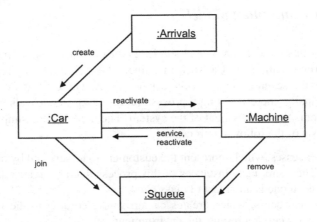

Fig. 21.5 The UML communication diagram for the Carwash system

Two models of the Carwash system are discussed: a deterministic model and a stochastic model. In both models, the time is measured in generic simulation time units.

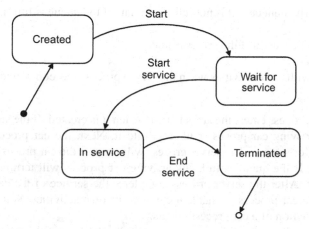

Fig. 21.6 A state diagram for a Car process

21.5.2 The Car-Wash Deterministic Model

A deterministic version of the model for the Carwash system has predetermined arrivals and service periods. This model has the following workload description:

1. Customer proceeses arrive at instants 0, 2, 5, 8, 12, 13, 17, 22, and 23;
2. A Carwash service takes 4 time units.

21.5.2.1 The Arrivals Process

The arrivals process represents the environment that generates new customers. There is a single arrivals process in this model. The following sequence of activities describes the arrivals process:

1. Wait until the clock advances to the next arrival event, i.e., by a time interval equal to the inter-arrival period.
2. Create a customer (car) object with service period equal to 4.0 time units.
3. Repeat from step 1 for all arriving car processes.

The arrivals process creates a set of customer processes in sequence; each one created at a specified instant.

21.5.2.2 The Car Process

A car process includes the service period as one of its relevant attributes and the following sequence of activities describe their behavior:

1. Join the arrival queue if it is not full. Terminate if the queue is full (i.e., the car is rejected).
2. Reactivate the server if the server is idle.
3. Suspend self.
4. Continue with own activities when the server process has completed the service.
5. Terminate.

Every car process enters the arrival queue when it is created. If the server process is idle, the arriving car process will reactivate it. Next, the car process suspends itself to wait for service. The server process will remove the car process at the head of the queue. If the queue is full, any arriving car process will terminate and will cease to exist. After the server process completes the service of the car process, it reactivates the car process to enable it continue its own activities. Some time after, normal termination of a car process occurs.

Part of the behavior of the car process includes the process interaction with the arrivals process. The other process interaction occurs with the server process, i.e., when the car process reactivates the server process from its idle state. Other interactions are:

• The server process removes or dequeues the car process to start its service, and
• After completing service, the server process reactivates the car process.

21.5.2.3 The Server Process

The description of the Carwash machine (server) process in this model, assumes that the arrival queue follows the FIFO order. There is only one object of the class *Server* in this model. The behavior of the server process can be described by the following sequence of activities:

1. While the arrival queue is not empty, execute the following activities:

   a. Remove the car process at the head of the queue.
   b. Carry out the service on the car process.
   c. Reactivate the car process.

2. Wait (in the idle state) until the next car process arrives, then start from step 1.

In the description above, the service activity on the car takes some finite period, called the *service period*. Every activity takes some given finite amount of time to be carried out. The simulation clock is advanced by a period that corresponds to the duration of the service. When executing step 2, the server process suspends itself if there are no car processes in the queue and changes to the idle state. The server process will be reactivated only when an arrival event occurs, the queue becomes non-empty with the new car process.

21.5.2.4 Results of Running the Deterministic Model

It is possible to manually simulate a small deterministic model like the Carwash model. This is a single server system because there is only one server process servicing several car processes and is simple enough for hand-calculation.

The relevant events that occur during simulation run of the model at specific instants (discrete points in time) are shown in Table 21.1. At time 0, the processes start their activities. The simulation starts when an arrival of a car process occurs and the process enters the queue. The server process starts servicing the car process immediately. The next event for the server process occurs at time 4, when the process' service interval completes. At simulation time of value 2, the second car process (number 2) arrives. It enters the queue waiting for the server process to remove it from the queue and start its service. At time 4, the server process completes service of car number 1. The server process then removes car process number 2 from the queue and starts its service. This goes on until the simulation time is 24 and the server process goes into the idle state because there are no more car processes.

Table 21.1 Events in the Car-Wash Model

Time	Process	Event	Next Event
0	arrivals	starts	
0	server	starts	
0	car 1	arrives	
0	server	begins service	4
2	car 2	arrives	
4	server	completes service	4
4	server	begins service	8
5	car 3	arrives	
8	car 4	arrives	
8	server	completes service	8
8	server	begins service	12
12	car 5	arrives	
12	server	completes service	12
12	server	begins service	16
13	car 6	arrives	
16	server	completes service	16
16	server	begins service	20
20	server	completes service	20
20	server	begins service	24
24	server	completes service	24
24	server	starts waiting	

The number of car processes in the queue at the relevant points in time is shown in Table 21.2. An important performance measure is the *wait time* of the car processes. Table 21.3 includes for every car process the arrival time, the start time for the service, and the car wait times.

Table 21.2 Queue Size in the Car-Wash Model

Time	Q Size
0	0
2	1
4	0
5	1
8	1
12	1
13	2
16	1
20	0

Table 21.3 Processes Waiting Time

Process	Arrival	Start Service	Wait Time
car 1	0	0	0
car 2	2	4	2
car 3	5	8	3
car 4	8	12	4
car 5	12	16	4
car 6	13	20	7

21.5.3 The Car-Wash Stochastic Model

Most practical systems have entities with one or more attributes that change values in a non-deterministic manner, i.e., to model the uncertainty in the behavior of the real system. Systems are usually modeled and simulated with stochastic models. The main differences between the stochastic model and the deterministic model are:

- The arrival events are random events, i.e., it is not known exactly when a car arrival event will occur.
- The service periods are also random, i.e., it is not known exactly how much time it will take the machine to wash a particular car.

A stochastic model includes random variables to implement the uncertainty attributes. In the Carwash model, the random variables for this model are:

- the inter-arrival period for each car process, and
- the service period for each car process.

The actual values for these attributes depend on some probabilistic distribution.

21.5.3.1 The Server Process

As in the deterministic model, a description of the server process assumes that the arrival queue for car processes follows the FIFO order. The following sequence of activities defines the behavior of the server process:

1. While the arrival queue is not empty, execute the following activities:

    a. Remove the car process at the head of the queue.
    b. Carry out the service of the car process.
    c. Reactivate the car process so it will continue its own activities.

2. Wait (in the idle state) until the next car process arrives, then start from step 1.

The servicing of a car process takes some finite period, called the *service period*. The simulation clock is advanced by a period that corresponds to the duration of the activity.

When executing step 2, the server process suspends itself and changes to the idle state if there are no car processes in the queue. The server process will be reactivated by a new car when an arrival event occurs; and the queue becomes non-empty.

21.5.3.2 The Arrivals Process

As mentioned before, in this model there is only one arrivals process. The behavior of the arrivals process can be described by following sequence of activities:

1. Generate a random inter-arrival period.
2. Wait until the clock advances by an amount equal to the inter-arrival period.
3. Generate a random service period.
4. Create a car process with its random service period.
5. Repeat from step 1.

It is not known exactly when a car process will arrive. In addition, the required service period is not known. Thus, the arrivals entity description includes the generation of two random numbers:

- The generation of an inter-arrival period for an arrival event;
- The generation of a service period.

These two random numbers are drawn from two different probability distributions. The decision of which probability distribution to use results from statistical analysis based on observations carried out previously on the real system or a similar system.

The arrivals process creates a sequence of car processes; one car process is created at every inter-arrival period. Every car process has a different service period.

21.5.3.3 The Car Process

There are several car processes created by the arrivals process. Each car process includes its service period as one of its relevant attributes. The following sequence of activities describes the behavior of a car process:

1. Join the car queue if it is not full.
2. Reactivate the server process if the server is in its idle state.
3. Suspend (itself), go into the idle state to wait for service.
4. Service completed, continue with own activities.
5. Terminate (itself) if the queue is full (i.e., the car process is rejected), or after the server process has completed the service, resume activities and terminate.

After a car process is created, it enters the car queue. If the server is idle, the new car process will reactivate it. The next activity of the car process is suspend itself to wait for service. If the queue is full, the arriving car process will terminate and will cease to exist. After the server process completes servicing the car process, this process continues with its own activities and then terminates.

The server process removes the car process at the head of the queue to start its service. During the servicing of a car, there is a joint participation of the two processes: the server process and a car process. This type of synchronization is called *process-to-process cooperation*. During the period of cooperation, one of the processes takes a leading role, the server process, and the other process takes a passive role, the car process.

21.6 Activity Diagrams

Activity diagrams are used to specify process-based discrete- event models. The main focus is on the dynamic behavior of the model. These diagrams help describe the operations of the processes involved and the synchronization that is present when processes interact with each other.

Processes can enter waiting lines or queues and be suspended; from this state they can be reactivated by other processes. For example, in the Carwash model, the car processes enter a queue and transition to the idle state. The machine process removes a car process from the queue to service it. All queues are passive objects and are different from the processes.

21.6.1 Activity Symbols

The flow of control in the diagram is composed of a sequence of symbols that denote different type of activities and synchronization actions, all joined by lines and arrows.

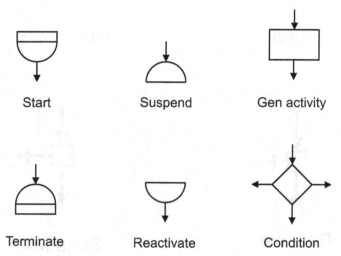

Fig. 21.7 Activity symbols

Figure 21.7 shows the basic symbols used in the activity diagrams. The lower semicircle with a bar below a process name, indicates the start of a process life cycle. The inverted form of this symbol indicates the termination of the process. The upper semicircle indicates that the object enters its idle state; a possible arrow in a non vertical inclination denotes the synchronization with another process.

The lower semicircle symbol indicates reactivation of the activity sequence; this symbol can also have an arrow in a non-vertical inclination that shows synchronization with another process. A vertical rhombus indicates the evaluation of some condition; there are two possible outcomes, Y or N.

A general activity is represented by a rectangular box; the label in the box is the name of the activity. This activity symbol is usually called a *delay* because a finite interval elapses while the activity is carried out and before the process can proceed to the next activity. The arrows show the direction of the flow activity sequence.

Figure 21.8 shows the symbols used to describe process interactions and indicate signals and direct synchronization among processes. The *synchronization send* denotes when a signal is sent to a condition queue; this symbol can also denote an interrupt to another process. This symbol can also be used to send an item to a queue. The *synchronization receive* indicates an item being received from a queue.

The symbols for *cooperate* describe the effect of the cooperation among processes. The symbol for *schedule* describe a process that schedules itself or another

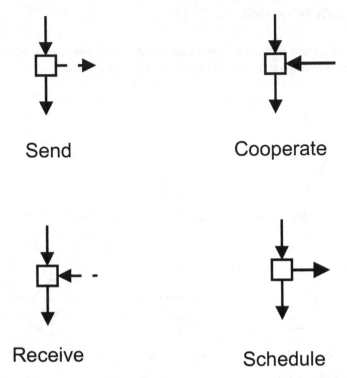

Send   Cooperate

Receive   Schedule

Fig. 21.8 Process interaction symbols

process after some time interval; it can also denote the reactivation of another process.

21.6.2 Process Interaction

The activity diagram of the Carwash model describes the interactions between the arrivals process and a car process that it creates. The other process interaction occurs between a car process and the server process, since the car process reactivates the server process from its idle state. The server process dequeues the car process, and after service is complete, the server reactivates the car process.

Figure 21.9 shows the activity diagram for the Car-Wash model, which describes the activities and interactions of the processes in the model.

Processes usually interact with other processes during a simulation run. For example, in the model for the Carwash system, the arrivals process creates one or more car (customer) process; the machine process (server) services the car processes. The newly created car processes must re-activate the machine process if this has become

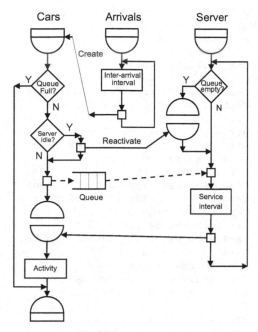

Fig. 21.9 Activity diagram of the Carwash model

idle. The machine process must wait (in the idle state) for car processes if the arrival queue is empty.

21.6.2.1 Results from a Simulation Run

The results of a simulation run of the stochastic Carwash model is produced on the two output files generated by the simulation run. One file includes a listing of the sequence of events and the other file includes the summary statistics and performance metrics computed.

The trace of a simulation run of the multi-server model is shown in Listing 21.1 and appears in file carwtrace.txt.

Listing 21.1 Trace of a simulation run of the single-server Carwash model.

```
OOSimL model: Simple Model of Car-Wash System
Simulation date: 9/19/2008 time: 13:47
---------------------- TRACE ----------------------------
Time: 0 Arrivals  holds for 9.839
Time: 0 Wash_machine deactivated
Time: 9.839 Arrivals  holds for 10.372
Time: 9.839 Car1 enqueued into Customer Queue
Time: 9.839 Wash_machine to reactivate
Time: 9.839 Car1 deactivated
```

```
Time: 9.839 Car1 dequeued from Customer Queue
Time: 9.839 Wash_machine holds for 13.354
Time: 20.212 Arrivals  holds for 3.211
Time: 20.212 Car2 enqueued into Customer Queue
Time: 20.212 Car2 deactivated
Time: 23.193 Car1 to reactivate
Time: 23.193 Car2 dequeued from Customer Queue
Time: 23.193 Wash_machine holds for 10.743
Time: 23.193 Car1 terminating
Time: 23.423 Arrivals  holds for 17.068
Time: 23.423 Car3 enqueued into Customer Queue
Time: 23.423 Car3 deactivated
Time: 33.936 Car2 to reactivate
Time: 33.936 Car3 dequeued from Customer Queue
Time: 33.936 Wash_machine holds for 11.203
Time: 33.936 Car2 terminating
Time: 40.491 Arrivals  holds for 9.237
Time: 40.491 Car4 enqueued into Customer Queue
Time: 40.491 Car4 deactivated
Time: 45.139 Car3 to reactivate
Time: 45.139 Car4 dequeued from Customer Queue
Time: 45.139 Wash_machine holds for 11.273
Time: 45.139 Car3 terminating
Time: 49.728 Arrivals  holds for 3.253
Time: 49.728 Car5 enqueued into Customer Queue
   . . .
Time: 403.316 Car35 terminating
Time: 413.782 Car36 to reactivate
Time: 413.782 Car37 dequeued from Customer Queue
Time: 413.782 Wash_machine holds for 10.743
Time: 413.782 Car36 terminating
Time: 424.524 Car37 to reactivate
Time: 424.524 Car38 dequeued from Customer Queue
Time: 424.524 Wash_machine holds for 10.957
Time: 424.524 Car37 terminating
Time: 435.481 Car38 to reactivate
Time: 435.481 Car39 dequeued from Customer Queue
Time: 435.481 Wash_machine holds for 10.967
Time: 435.481 Car38 terminating
Time: 446.448 Car39 to reactivate
Time: 446.448 Car40 dequeued from Customer Queue
Time: 446.448 Wash_machine holds for 9.666
Time: 446.448 Car39 terminating
Time: 456.115 Car40 to reactivate
Time: 456.115 Car41 dequeued from Customer Queue
Time: 456.115 Wash_machine holds for 11.403
Time: 456.115 Car40 terminating
Time: 467.518 Car41 to reactivate
Time: 467.518 Car42 dequeued from Customer Queue
Time: 467.518 Wash_machine holds for 9.868
Time: 467.518 Car41 terminating
Time: 477.386 Car42 to reactivate
Time: 477.386 Wash_machine deactivated
Time: 477.386 Car42 terminating
```

```
------------------------------------------------------------

End Simulation of Simple Model of Car-Wash System
  date: 9/19/2008 time: 13:47
```

The summary statistics of a simulation run of the single-server model for the Carwash system is shown in Listing 21.2 and appears in file `carwstatf.txt`. This shows the summary statistics and various results calculated at the end of the simulation run.

Listing 22.2 Summary statistics of a simulation run of the model.

```
OOSimL model: Simple Model of Car-Wash System
Simulation date: date: 9/19/2008 time: 13:47
--------------------STATISTICS REPORT--------------------
------------------------------------------------------------
Squeue: Customer Queue
Capacity of queue: 40
Number of observations: 84
Max number of objects in queue: 15
Average number of objects in queue: 2
Average time in queue: 5.583055910617741
Queue utilization: 0.3632765518093226
Queue usage: 0.19106458005225158
------------------------------------------------------------
Random generator: Inter-arrival
Distribution: Negative exponential
Number of obs: 42
Seed: 7
Mean: 7.5
------------------------------------------------------------
Random generator: Service Period
Distribution: Normal
Number of obs: 42
Seed: 13
Mean: 11.25
Standard deviation: 1.25
------------------------------------------------------------

End Simulation of Simple Model of Car-Wash System
  date: 9/19/2008 time: 13:47

Total number of cars serviced: 42
Car average wait period: 81.885
Average period car spends in the shop: 93.017
Machine utilization: 0.992
```

21.7 Implementing The Simulation Model

The implementation of the Carwash model consists of four classes: *Server*, *Car*, and *Arrivals*, in addition to the main class, *Carwash*. There is one passive object, of class *Squeue* for the simple queue, *car_queue*, defined as the queue for waiting car processes.

The Java implementation of the Carwash model is stored in various files; these are: `Carwash.osl`, `Arrivals.osl`, `Car.osl`, and `Server.osl` . All the files of this model are archived in the file `carwash.jar`.

Listing 21.3 shows the source code for the implementation of class *Carwash*. The implementation of the Carwash model presents only one way to structure the classes. This implementation uses several global variables, i.e., public static variables declared in the main class, *Carwash*. An improved model implementation would use a smaller number of such variables and would also emphasize a better application of the principle of information hiding. Exercise 12 below delays with this issue.

Listing 5.3 Implementation of class *Carwash* of the model.

```
use all java.io
use java.text.DecimalFormat
use all psimjava

description
A single-server model of a Carwash system
arriving cars (customers) join a queue to wait for service
The server is a Carwash machine that services one car at
a time. Service consists of a complete external wash of
a car.

OOSimL model J. Garrido, Jan 10, 2008
Main class: Carwash

This class sets up simulation parameters and creates the
relevant objects.
There are four types of active objects of classes: Carwash,
    Server, Arrivals, and Car.
There is one passive object, the car_queue of class Squeue.
The arrivals object creates the various car objects that
arrive at random intervals.
Random variables: inter-arrival period of a negative
exponential distribution and service period of a Normal
distribution.

File: Carwash.osl
*/
public class Carwash as process is
    private
    object references
        //
        // files for reporting
```

```
      define   static statf of class PrintWriter   // stats
      define   static tracef of class PrintWriter  // trace
   public
   variables
      // input car queue size
      define static totalQSize = 40 of type integer
      //
      // simulation period
      define static simPeriod = 1200.0 of type double
      //
      // time to close arrival of cars
      define static close_arrival = 300.5 of type double
      //
      // mean car inter-arrival interval
      define static MeanInterarrival = 7.5 of type double
      //
      // mean car service interval
      define static MeanServiceDur = 11.25 of type double
      //
      // standard deviation of service interval
      define StdServiceDur = 1.25 of type double
      //
      // Accumulative variables
      //
      // accumulated customer service time
      define static custServiceTime = 0.0 of type double
      // accumulated customer sojourn time
      define static custSojournTime = 0.0 of type double
      // accumulated car waiting time
      define static custWaitTime = 0.0 of type double
      // accum server idle time
      define static accum_idle = 0.0 of type double
      // current number of customers serviced
      define static num_serviced = 0 of type integer
      // current number of cars that arrived
      define static num_arrived = 0 of type integer
      // current number of cars rejected
      define static num_rejected = 0 of type integer
      //
   object references
      //
      // Simulation model essential objects
      define static sim of class Simulation
      //
      // Queues for the model
      // queue for arrived waiting cars
      define static car_queue of class Squeue
      //
      // Classes for the active objects of the model
      define static wash_machine of class Server
      //
      define static genCust of class Arrivals
      define static shop of class Carwash
      define model of class SimModel
```

```
      //
      // constructor
      function initializer parameters ss of class String is
      begin
            call super using ss
      endfun initializer
      //
      function main is
      begin
          // set-up simulation with an object of class
          // simulation
          simulation title "Simple Car-Wash System"
          //
          // setup files for reporting
          trace file "carwtrace.txt"
          statistics file "carwstatf.txt"
          //
          // create queues (passive objects)
          create car_queue of class Squeue using
                "Customer Queue", totalQSize
          //
          // Create and start the main active objects of
          //  the model
          create shop of class Carwash using "Car Wash Shop"
          start object shop
      endfun main
      //
      // This function is called by the class object with
      //    interactive I/O
      function pbegin parameters sm of class SimModel is
        variables
          define jin of type integer
          define din of type double
        begin
          set model = sm
          call println of model using
                "Simple Model of a Car-Wash System"
          // call model.println using
          //    "Input workload parameters for Car Wash Model"
          // Input parameters
          call model.readInt using "Type queue size (40): "
                return to jin
          if jin > 0 then
            set totalQSize = jin
          endif
          //
          set din = model.readDouble
                ("Type simulation period (1200.0): ")
          if din > 0.0 then
            set simPeriod = din
          endif
          //
          call model.readDouble using
                "Type close time (300.5): "
```

```
        return value to din
            if din > 0.0 then
                set close_arrival = din
            endif
            //
            set din = model.readDouble
                    ("Type mean inter-arrival period (7.5): ")
            if din > 0.0 then
                set MeanInterarrival = din
            endif
            //
            call model.readDouble using
                "Type mean service period (11.25): "
    return to din
            if din > 0.0 then
                set MeanServiceDur = din
            endif
            //
            call model.readDouble using
                "Type service time standard dev (1.25): "
    return value to din
            if din > 0.0 then
                set StdServiceDur = din
            endif
            //
            // set-up simulation
            simulation title "Simple Model of Car-Wash System"
            //
            // Set up report files
            trace file "carwtrace.txt"
            statistics file "carwstatf.txt"
            //
            // Create  passive objects: queues
            create car_queue of class Squeue using
                "Customer Queue", totalQSize  // passive obj
            //
            // start main active object in model

            start self
    endfun pbegin
    //
    //
    method Main_body is
    variables
        define pname of type string
        define machutil of type double
        //
        // formatting strings
        define fmtout1 of type string
        define fmtout2 of type string
        define fmtout3 of type string
        define dispouta of type string
        define dispoutb of type string
        //
```

```
object references
    define dfmt of class DecimalFormat
begin
    access statistics file
    //
    // create the other active objects of the model
    create wash_machine of class Server
          using "Wash_machine"
    create genCust of class Arrivals
          using "Arrivals ", MeanInterarrival,
             MeanServiceDur, StdServiceDur
    start thread genCust
    start thread wash_machine
    //
    // display "Workload - car mean inter-arrival: ",
    //       MeanInterarrival, " mean service: ",
    //          MeanServiceDur
    //
    // starting simulation
    start simulation with simPeriod
    //
    // set formatting to round output to 3 dec places
    create dfmt of class DecimalFormat using "0.###"
    //
    display "Total number of cars serviced: ",
       num_serviced
    statwrite "Total number of cars serviced: ",
          num_serviced
    if num_serviced > 0
    then
      set fmtout1 = call dfmt.format using
          custWaitTime/num_serviced
      display "Car average wait period: ", fmtout1
      statwrite "Car average wait period: ", fmtout1
      //
      set fmtout2 = call dfmt.format using
          custSojournTime/num_serviced
      display "Average period car spends in the shop: ",
          fmtout2
      statwrite
          "Average period car spends in the shop: ",
          fmtout2
    endif
    //
    // machine utilization
    set machutil = (simPeriod - accum_idle)/simPeriod
    set fmtout3 = call dfmt.format using machutil
    //
    statwrite "Machine utilization: ", fmtout3
    display "Machine utilization: ", fmtout3
    //
    set dispouta = "Cars serviced: " concat
                num_serviced concat "\n" concat
                "Avg wait: " concat
```

```
                    dfmt.format(custWaitTime /
                        num_serviced) concat "\n"
        set disputb = disputa concat
                    "Mach util: " concat

                    dfmt.format((simPeriod-accum_idle)/
                        simPeriod) concat
                    "\n" concat
                    "Avg per in shop: " concat
                    dfmt.format(custSojournTime/num_serviced)
            call model.println using disputb
            exit
        endmethod Main_body
    endclass Carwash
```

The simulation period is declared as a variable of type `double`; the name of the variable is *simperiod*. A similar variable is declared for the closing arrivals of car processes.

Object reference *sim* of class *Simulation*, is a reference to an object that sets up the simulation. It is declared in class *Carwash*, and used in method *main* with the statement **simulation title**. This object assigns a name to the simulation. In method *Main_body*, using statement **start simulation using**, it is used to start the simulation for the period defined in variable *simPeriod*.

The object of class *Carwash* is the main object of the application. This object starts the simulation; at the end, it prints the results and terminates the simulation.

Every class needs access to the *oosimlib.jar* library package of the OOSimL language. The **use** statement in the first line of code gives access to the *psimjava* directory of this library.

Every class that defines active objects needs to include the clause **as active** in the header of the class definition. A few attributes of class *Carwash* are declared as global variables or global constants.

The queue for car processes is declared with name *car_queue*. A variable of type integer, *totalQSize*, defines the capacity of the car queue, with a default value of 40.

Listing 21.4 shows the source code that implements class Arrivals of the model.

Listing 21.4 Implementation of class *Arrivals* of the Carwash model.

```
use all psimjava
description
  The model of the Carwash system
  OOSimL version J Garrido, Jan 2008

  This class defines the behavior of the environment
  that generates car arrivals randomly.
  The object of this class creates and starts the car objects
  at specific instants called arrival events.
  An negative exponential distribution is used to generate
  random numbers that correspond to the inter-arrival period.
  The service periods for car objects are random
```

```
      variables from a Normal distribution.
      */
   class Arrivals as process is

      private
      object references
          // car inter-arrival random period
          define  arrivalPeriod of class NegExp
          //
          // car service period random number
          define  servicePeriod of class Normal
      public
      function initializer parameters name of type string,
          Mean_arr of type double, Mean_serv of type double,
          stdserv of type double is
      begin
        call super using name
        //
        // create random number generator using mean
        //   inter-arrival period
        // exponential distribution
        create arrivalPeriod of class NegExp using
           "Inter-arrival", Mean_arr
        //
        // create random number generator using mean
        //   service period
        // Normal distribution
        create servicePeriod of class Normal using
           "Service Period", Mean_serv, stdserv
        display name, " created"
      endfun initializer
      //
      function Main_body is
        variables
            // inter-arrival period for car object
            define inter_arr of type double
            // service period
            define serv_per of type double
            define simclock of type double
            define carname of type string
        object references
            define carobj of class Car
      begin
        assign simulation clock to simclock
        display "Arrivals starting main body at: ", simclock
        //
        // repeat until time to close arrivals
        while simclock < Carwash.close_arrival do
           // generate inter-arr
           assign random value from arrivalPeriod to inter_arr
           hold self for inter_arr        // wait for inter-arr
           increment Carwash.num_arrived
           //
           // generate service interval
```

```
            assign random value from servicePeriod to serv_per
            set simclock = get_clock()
            display "Arrivals creating Car at: ", simclock
            set carname = "Car" concat Carwash.num_arrived
            //
            create carobj of class Car using carname, serv_per
            start object carobj
        endwhile
        display "Arrivals terminates"
        terminate self
    endfun Main_body
endclass Arrivals
```

Listing 21.5 shows the source code that implements class *Arrivals* of the model.

Listing 21.5 Implementation of class *Server* of the Carwash model.

```
use all psimjava
description
    OOSimL model of the Carwash system

    J Garrido, Feb. 2008

    This class defines the server object, which
     is the Carwash machine. It takes the car at the head of
    the queue and services the car. When the machine completes
    service of the car, it gets another car from the queue
    If the queue is empty, it goes into its idle state
*/
class Server as process is
  private
  object references
      define currentCustomer of class Car   // current customer

    function serviceCustomer is
    variables
        define startTime of type double        // start of service
        define service_per of type double      // service period
        define objname of type string
        define ccustname of type string
        define ccustservt of type double       // service time
        define simclock of type double
    begin
        if Carwash.car_queue is not empty
        then
            // get customer from head of waiting queue
            remove currentCustomer of class Car from
                Carwash.car_queue
            //
            set objname = get_name()
            set ccustname = currentCustomer.get_name()
```

```
    // get cust service time
    set ccustservt = currentCustomer.get_serv_dur()
    assign simulation clock to startTime  // service start
    display objname, " begins service of: ", ccustname,
        " at: ", startTime, " for ", ccustservt
    tracewrite objname, " begins service of: ", ccustname

    //
    // accumulate waiting time for this customer (car)
    set Carwash.custWaitTime = Carwash.custWaitTime +
        (startTime - currentCustomer.get_arrivalT())
    //
    set service_per = currentCustomer.get_serv_dur()
    hold self for service_per
    //
    assign simulation clock to simclock
    add (simclock - startTime) to Carwash.custServiceTime
    display objname, " completes service of: ", ccustname,
        " at: ", simclock
    tracewrite objname, " completes service: ", ccustname

    reactivate currentCustomer now   // let car continue
  else
    return
  endif
endfun serviceCustomer
//
public
function initializer parameters name of type string is
begin
  call super using name
  // display name, " created at: ", simclock
endfun initializer
//
function Main_body is
variables
  define startIdle of type double
  define idle_period of type double     // idle period
  define simclock of type double        // simulation time
  define cname of type string           // name attribute
begin
  set cname = get_name()
  assign simulation clock to simclock
  display cname, " starting main body at ", simclock
  //
  while simclock < Carwash.simPeriod do
    if Carwash.car_queue is empty
    then
        // queue is empty
        set startIdle = get_clock()  // start idle time
        display cname, " goes idle at ", simclock
        suspend self         // suspend server
        //
        // reactivated by a car object
```

```
                // queue must now be nonempty
                display cname, " reactived"
                set simclock = get_clock()
                set idle_period = simclock- startIdle
                add idle_period to Carwash.accum_idle
                display cname, " reactivated at " + simclock
            endif
            call serviceCustomer    // service the car
        endwhile
        terminate self
    endfun Main_body
    //
endclass Server
```

Listing 21.6 shows the source code that implements class *Car* of the model.

Listing 21.6 Implementation of class *Car* of the Carwash model.

```
use all psimjava
description
   The model of the Carwash system
   OOSIM1 version,  J Garrido, Feb. 2008

   This class defines behavior of car objects
   After a car object is created it joins the queue to wait
   for service. It it finds the server object idle,
   it reactivates the server object.
*/
class Car as process
 is
  private
  variables
     define customerNum of type integer   // customer number
     define arrivalTime of type double     // cust arrival time
     define service_dur of type double     // service interval
  public
  //
  function initializer parameters name of type string,
                                  dur of type double is
  begin
     call super using name
     set customerNum = Carwash.num_arrived
     assign simulation clock to arrivalTime
     set service_dur = dur
     display name, " arrives at time ", arrivalTime
  endfun initializer
  //
  function get_arrivalT return type double is
  begin
     return arrivalTime
```

```
    endfun get_arrivalT
    //
    function get_serv_dur return type double is
    begin

        return service_dur
    endfun get_serv_dur
    //
    function Main_body is
    variables
        define simclock of type double
        define pname of type string
        define a of type double      // bogus
    begin
        assign clock to simclock
        set pname = call get_name
        display pname, " requests service at time ", simclock
        // check if there is still space available in queue
        if Carwash.car_queue is not full  then
            // queue not full
            display pname, " joins queue at time ", simclock
            insert self into Carwash.car_queue  // enqueue car
            if Carwash.wash_machine is idle
            then
                display "Activating server at time ", simclock
                reactivate Carwash.wash_machine now
                // call Thread.yield
            endif
            //
            suspend self                    // to wait for service
            // service completed, do final computation
            increment Carwash.num_serviced  // customers serviced
            // total time in the system: custSojournTime
            assign simulation clock to simclock
            set Carwash.custSojournTime =
                Carwash.custSojournTime +
                (simclock - arrivalTime)
            display pname, " terminates at ", simclock
            terminate self                  // terminates itself
        else
            // queue full, abandon hope
            increment Carwash.num_rejected
            display pname, " rejected, queue full "
            terminate self          // terminate this object
        endif
    endfun Main_body
endclass Car
```

21.8 Graphical User Interfaces

Programmers can access standard graphical packages available mainly with the Java class libraries. These include the ACM package for GUI and the standard Java packages *AWT* (Abstract Windows Toolkit) and *Swing*. Using the classes in these packages, a programmer can design and implement very good graphical interfaces (GUI) for the software model of the Carwash system.

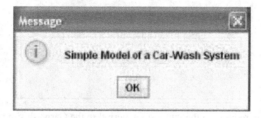

Fig. 21.10 First dialog box in the Carwash simulation

Simple Input/output with graphical interface can be implemented with very little effort using the ACM library. Figure 21.10 shows the first dialog box that appears when the simulation run is started.

Figure 21.11 shows the dialog box that appears requesting the user to enter the value for the queue size and also showing the default value. Figure 21.12 shows the dialog box that appears requesting the used to enter the value for the simulation period and also showing the default value.

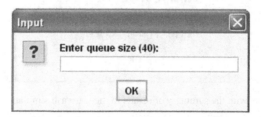

Fig. 21.11 Dialog box requesting the queue size in the Carwash simulation

The main advantage of this graphical interface is that the user of the model of the Carwash system can provide any set of values for the model's workload, and simulation parameters. Otherwise, the model uses the default values.

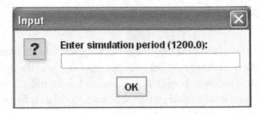

Fig. 21.12 Dialog box requesting the simulation period in the Carwash simulation

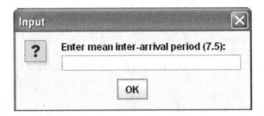

Fig. 21.13 Dialog box requesting the inter-arrival period in the Carwash simulation

The rest of the dialog boxes for the other input parameters for the simulation run appear in a similar manner. The last dialog box in the simulation run displays a short summary of the results. Figure 21.14 shows the last dialog box in the simulation run.

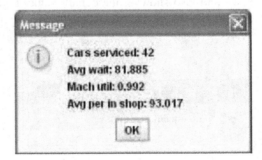

Fig. 21.14 Dialog box with the summary of results in the Carwash simulation

Different graphical interfaces can be implemented using the OOSimL and Java integration. Graphical animation is a slightly more complex design of graphical interfaces. This graphical interface can show the arrival of the processes into the system, the simulation clock advancing through the various events, the plot with the variations of the size of the queue, and a different format for the input parameters.

21.9 Summary

This chapter explains the basic concepts of the process interaction approach to simulation. The UML and the activity diagrams are used to help describe the conceptual model of the Carwash system. A simulation model can be implemented in an appropriate object-oriented simulation language or in a suitable object-oriented programming language. The Carwash model is implemented and explained in some detail.

This chapter introduces some of the details of modeling processes and the interactions that occur among these processes. The process interaction approach to discrete-event simulation is more suitable for complex and large-scale models than other approaches to simulation.

A simple graphical user interface is shown for the model of the Carwash system. More complete and complex graphics can be designed for simulation models.

21.10 Key Terms

single servers	UML diagrams	activity diagrams
OOSimL library	deterministic model	stochastic model
inter-aarival interval	service interval	wait time
server idle interval	queue size	event sequence
random events	FIFO order	process interaction
GUI	graphical animation	

Exercises

21.1. Write a list of systems that would have a similar model as the one for the Carwash system.

21.2. Change the time that the car wash closes arrivals but before the simulation ends. How would the model deal with this condition or operational mode? How useful is this?

21.3. In the model of the Carwash system, include the computations for the server utilization and the proportion of rejected car processes.

21.4. Compute the server utilization, the proportion of useful time (servicing cars), with respect to the total simulation time. Use the deterministic and the stochastic models for the (single server) Carwash system.

21.5. Describe a model of the Carwash system with two or three servers. How would this change or improve the simulation?

21.6. Design the Carwash model for two or more servers. Write the complete description of the process definitions involved.

21.7. Hand simulate the deterministic Carwash model with the same arrivals and fixed service time used in the example explained for a two-server model.

21.8. Completely develop a Carwash model with two servers.

21.9. Carry out a manual simulation using the same values for random arrivals and random service times of the stochastic model of the Carwash system for a two-server model.

21.10. Compute the server utilization, the proportion of useful time (servicing cars), with respect to the total simulation time. Use the deterministic and the stochastic models for the two-server Carwash system.

21.11. Compute the average car waiting time for the same cases applied to Exercise 21.9.

21.12. Discuss the limitations of the graphical user interface developed for the model of the Carwash system. Design a more complete graphical interface and explain its advantages. Discuss ways to implement this graphical interface.

21.13. Modify the implementation of the Carwash model using a smaller number of global variables, i.e., public static variables. How does this improve information hiding? Discuss.

Chapter 22
Models of Multi-Server Systems

22.1 Introduction

Multi-server systems include more that one server, and these provide service to the customers arriving into the customer queue(s). The models of multi-server systems can be designed with several similar servers or with different types of servers.

A large set of practical problems involves the study of systems with multiple servers. Many real-world problems can be modeled with this scheme. The simplest multi-server models include a single customer queue. Other models include multiple queues, of which the simplest are those with a separate queue for every server.

22.2 Queuing Models

A queuing model is one that includes at least one queue. The simplest type of queuing models is the single-server model. The server gets the next customer to serve from head of the customer queue.

The three categories of queuing models that can be analyzed with simulation are:

1. single-server models
2. multi-server models
3. queuing networks

The workload parameters for these models usually include the following:

- The mean inter-arrival interval for customers;
- The mean service interval required by customers.

The customer inter-arrival intervals usually follow an exponential probability distribution and the customer service intervals usually follow an exponential or normal probability distribution. The queue size is an important system parameter in the simulation model.

Some of the performance measures to be computed for queuing models are:

J.M. Garrido, *Object Oriented Simulation: A Modeling and Programming Perspective*,
DOI: 10.1007/978-1-4419-0516-1_22,
© Springer Science + Business Media, LLC 2009

- The average number of customers waiting (i.e., the number of customers in the queue)
- The average time that a customer spends in the system, the average sojourn time
- The total number of customers serviced in a given interval, the system throughput
- The percentage of the total time that the server is actually carrying out the servicing of the customers, the server utilization
- The percentage of customers rejected because of the limited queue size. (These customers arrive when the queue is full.)

Examples of queuing systems in the real world are:

- Computer systems
- Communication systems and networks
- Teller facilities in a bank
- Production systems
- Transport and material handling
- Repair and maintenance systems

22.3 Multi-Server Queuing Models

In a multi-server model, any of the servers can provide the service demanded by a customers waiting in the customer queue. Figure 22.1 illustrates the general structure of a multi-server model for the Carwash system.

The servers that are not busy, are usually stored in server queue. An arriving customer will remove the server at the head of the server queue and reactivate the server. The system has several servers providing service to customers. All servers are alike, e.g., there is only one type of server. In a similar manner, all customers are alike, there is only one type of customer.

If the demand for service is high enough, it may be necessary to add more servers. If the customer wait time is too high and/or the throughput (the number of serviced customers) is too low, more servers are included to improve the performance of the model.

If the arrival rate of a system is not high enough, it may not be convenient to increase the number of servers because the server utilization will be lower. If the demand for service is much greater than the service capacity of the system, then adding more servers can be justified.

22.4 The Carwash System

The model of the Carwash system has K wash-machines — the server objects, and the customers are car objects that receive service from any server object. A customer

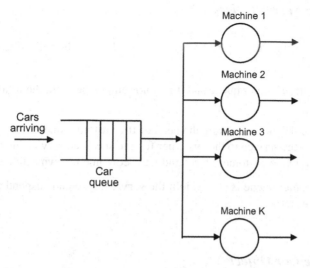

Fig. 22.1 A multi-server model

waits in the queue until a server becomes available. The server then removes the customer from the customer queue and starts servicing to it.

The multi-server model has an array of K server objects. This array is needed first, so that customer can reference any server, second every server will compute its own to idle time. The model also has a server queue that server objects join when they become idle. The size of this queue is relatively short, the capacity of the queue is K.

The general behavior of the model can be described by the following sequence of operations:

1. A new car object (customer) arrives and checks if there is any server available in the server queue. If so, the car removes the server at the head of the server queue and reactivates it.
2. The car joins the car queue to wait for service.
3. When a server becomes available, it removes the car from the car queue.
4. The server provides the service for service interval of the car object.
5. When the service has completed, the car object continues its own activities and the server becomes available.
6. If the server finds that the car queue is empty, the server object becomes available, is made idle, and joins the server queue.

The model has two queues, one for cars waiting for service and one for servers waiting for cars. As in the single-server model, the queues in this model are simple, i.e., they follow a first-in-first-out (FIFO) order.

22.4.1 The Server Object

The behavior of the server process can be described by the following sequence of activities:

1. Examine the customer queue and if it is not empty, perform the following activities:

   a. Remove the customer from the head of the customer queue
   b. Perform the service to the customer for the specified service interval
   c. Reactivate the customer object and let it continue its own activities

2. If the customer queue is empty, join the server queue and suspend itself to wait (in the idle state).

22.4.2 The Car Object

The behavior of a car process is started by the *Arrivals* process. The service interval is the only relevant attribute of a car object. The behavior of a car object can be described by the following sequence of activities:

1. Examine the car queue and if it is not full, join the queue.

   a. Check whether there is an available server object by examining the server queue and if not empty, remove the server object from the head of the server queue.
   b. Reactivate the server object.
   c. Suspend itself and go into the idle state.
   d. Reactivated by the server object after completed the service, continue with own individual behavior before terminating.

2. If the car queue is full, terminate immediately , the car has been rejected.

22.4.3 The Arrivals Object

The purpose of the *Arrivals* process is to generate customer arrivals. The behavior of this object can be described by the following sequence of activities:
   Repeat while the clock time is less than the close-arrival period.

1. Generate a random inter-arrival time interval.
2. Wait until the simulation clock advances by a time interval equal to the inter-arrival interval.
3. Generate a random customer service interval.
4. Create a customer object.

The generation of the random time intervals is needed because it is not known exactly when a customer object will arrive, and its required service period cannot be known either. Thus, the Arrivals process includes the generation of two random numbers: the generation of an inter-arrival interval and the generation of a service interval. These two random numbers are drawn from the appropriate probability distributions.

The Arrivals object creates a sequence of customer objects, one for every inter-arrival interval that elapses. Each customer object has its own service interval.

22.4.4 Simulation Outputs

As mentioned before, there are two types of simulation outputs for every simulation run, the summary statistics and the trace. The summary statistics of a simulation run of the multi-server model for the Carwash system is shown in Listing 22.1 and appears in file mcarwstatf.txt. This shows the summary statistics and various results calculated at the end of the simulation run.

Listing 22.1 Summary statistics of a simulation run of the model.

```
OOSimL model: Multi-server Model of Carwash System
Simulation date: date: 9/12/2008 time: 10:20
------------------STATISTICS REPORT------------------
Squeue: Server Queue
Capacity of queue: 5000
Number of observations: 55
Max number of objects in queue: 5
Average number of objects in queue: 0
Average time in queue: 1.8143043935034617
Queue utilization: 0.05896471131942732
Queue usage: 0.02207403678762545
------------------------------------------------------
Squeue: Car Queue
Capacity of queue: 60
Number of observations: 518
Max number of objects in queue: 12
Average number of objects in queue: 2
Average time in queue: 1.2372902832578605
Queue utilization: 0.47352449896848325
Queue usage: 0.19306883795002866
------------------------------------------------------
Random generator: Inter-arrival
Distribution: Negative exponential
Number of obs: 259
Seed: 7
Mean: 2.5
------------------------------------------------------
Random generator: Service Interval
Distribution: Uniform
```

```
Number of obs: 259
Seed: 0
Lower bound: 10.25
Upper bound: 14.5
------------------------------------------------------------

End Simulation of Multi-server Model of Carwash System
    date: 9/12/2008 time: 10:20

Total number of cars serviced: 259
Car average wait period: 10.734
Average period car spends in the shop: 23.227
Machine 0 utilization: 0.984
Machine 1 utilization: 0.98
Machine 2 utilization: 0.984
Machine 3 utilization: 0.984
Machine 4 utilization: 0.976
```

The other output of a simulation run is the trace, which is the sequence of events that occur at various simulation time instants. The trace of a simulation run of the multi-server model is shown in Listing 22.2 and appears in file mcarwtrace.txt.

Listing 22.2 Trace of a simulation run of the multi-server Carwash model.

```
OOSimL model: Multi-server Model of Carwash System
Simulation date: 9/12/2008 time: 10:20
----------------------- TRACE ----------------------------
Time: 0 Wash_machine 0 to idle state
Time: 0 Wash_machine 0 enqueued into Server Queue
Time: 0 Wash_machine 0 deactivated
Time: 0 Wash_machine 1 to idle state
Time: 0 Wash_machine 1 enqueued into Server Queue
Time: 0 Wash_machine 1 deactivated
Time: 0 Wash_machine 2 to idle state
Time: 0 Wash_machine 2 enqueued into Server Queue
Time: 0 Wash_machine 2 deactivated
Time: 0 Wash_machine 3 to idle state
Time: 0 Wash_machine 3 enqueued into Server Queue
Time: 0 Wash_machine 3 deactivated
Time: 0 Wash_machine 4 to idle state
Time: 0 Wash_machine 4 enqueued into Server Queue
Time: 0 Wash_machine 4 deactivated
Time: 0 Arrivals  holds for 3.28
Time: 3.28 Arrivals  holds for 3.457
Time: 3.28 Car1 enqueued into Car Queue
Time: 3.28 Wash_machine 0 dequeued from Server Queue
Time: 3.28 Car1 activating Wash_machine 0
Time: 3.28 Wash_machine 0 to reactivate
Time: 3.28 Car1 deactivated
Time: 3.28 Car1 dequeued from Car Queue
Time: 3.28 Wash_machine 0 stats service of Car1
Time: 3.28 Wash_machine 0 holds for 13.352
Time: 6.737 Arrivals  holds for 1.07
Time: 6.737 Car2 enqueued into Car Queue
```

```
Time:  6.737 Wash_machine 1 dequeued from Server Queue
Time:  6.737 Car2 activating Wash_machine 1
Time:  6.737 Wash_machine 1 to reactivate
Time:  6.737 Car2 deactivated
Time:  6.737 Car2 dequeued from Car Queue
Time:  6.737 Wash_machine 1 stats service of Car2
Time:  6.737 Wash_machine 1 holds for 12.14
Time:  7.808 Arrivals  holds for 5.689
Time:  7.808 Car3 enqueued into Car Queue
Time:  7.808 Wash_machine 2 dequeued from Server Queue
Time:  7.808 Car3 activating Wash_machine 2
Time:  7.808 Wash_machine 2 to reactivate
Time:  7.808 Car3 deactivated
Time:  7.808 Car3 dequeued from Car Queue
Time:  7.808 Wash_machine 2 stats service of Car3
Time:  7.808 Wash_machine 2 holds for 10.468
. . .
Time:  667.097 Wash_machine 1 completes service of Car256
Time:  667.097 Car256 to reactivate
Time:  667.097 Wash_machine 1 to idle state
Time:  667.097 Wash_machine 1 enqueued into Server Queue
Time:  667.097 Wash_machine 1 deactivated
Time:  667.097 Car256 terminating
Time:  673.19 Wash_machine 3 completes service of Car258
Time:  673.19 Car258 to reactivate
Time:  673.19 Wash_machine 3 to idle state
Time:  673.19 Wash_machine 3 enqueued into Server Queue
Time:  673.19 Wash_machine 3 deactivated
Time:  673.19 Car258 terminating
Time:  673.596 Wash_machine 4 completes service of Car259
Time:  673.596 Car259 to reactivate
Time:  673.596 Wash_machine 4 to idle state
Time:  673.596 Wash_machine 4 enqueued into Server Queue
Time:  673.596 Wash_machine 4 deactivated
Time:  673.596 Car259 terminating
-----------------------------------------------------------------
End Simulation of Multi-server Model of Carwash System
    date: 9/12/2008 time: 10:20
```

22.5 OOSimL Implementation of the Model

The OOSimL implementation of the multi-server Carwash model is stored in file mcarwash.jar. The source files included are: MCarwash.osl, Car.osl, Server.osl, and Arrivals.osl. The additional source file SimModel.osl is necessary to carry out the GUI I/O with the ACM classes.

The OOSimL implementation of class *Car* is shown in Listing 22.3 and appears in file Car.osl.

Listing 22.3 OOSimL Implementation of class Car.

```
use all psimjava
description
  The model of the multi-server Carwash system
  OOSimL version,  J Garrido, August 2008

  This class defines behavior of car objects
  After a car object is created it joins the queue to wait for
  service. It first lokks in the server queue. If it finds
  a server object idle, it reactivates the server object.
*/
class Car as process
 is
  private
  variables
      define customerNum of type integer    // customer number
      define arrivalTime of type double      // arrival time
      define service_dur of type double      // service interval
  public
  //
  function initializer parameters cname of type string,
                                  dur of type double is
  begin
    call super using cname
    set customerNum = MCarwash.num_arrived
    assign simulation clock to arrivalTime
    set service_dur = dur
    // display cname, " arrives at time ", arrivalTime
  endfun initializer
  //
  function get_arrivalT return type double is
  begin
     return arrivalTime
  endfun get_arrivalT
  //
  function get_serv_dur return type double is
  begin
     return service_dur
  endfun get_serv_dur
  //
  function Main_body is
  variables
      define simclock of type double
      define cname of type string
      define servname of type string
  object references
      define wmach of class Server
  begin
     assign clock to simclock
     set cname = call get_name
     // display cname, " requests service at time ", simclock
     // check if there is space available in the Carwash shop
     if MCarwash.car_queue is not full  then
```

```
        // queue not full
        display cname, " joins queue at time ", simclock
        insert self into MCarwash.car_queue  // enqueue car
   //
        // now check for available (idle) servers
        if MCarwash.servQueue is not empty
        then
            // get next available server
            remove object wmach of class Server from
                MCarwash.servQueue
            set servname = wmach.get_name()
            display cname, " activating server ", servname,
                " at ", simclock
            tracewrite cname, " activating ", servname
            reactivate wmach now
            // call Thread.yield
        endif
        //
        suspend self                    // to wait for service
        // service completed, do final computation
        increment MCarwash.num_serviced    // cust serviced
        // total time in the system: custSojournTime
        assign simulation clock to simclock
        set MCarwash.custSojournTime =
            MCarwash.custSojournTime +
            simclock - arrivalTime)
        // display cname, " terminates at ", simclock
        terminate self                  // terminates itself
    else
        // queue full, abandon hope
        increment MCarwash.num_rejected
        // display cname, " rejected, queue full "
        tracewrite cname, " rejected, queue full"
        terminate self                  // terminate this object
    endif
  endfun Main_body
endclass Car
```

A second queue in the multi-server model of the Carwash system is declared with reference name *server_queue* and is used to place the idle server objects (when there are no customer objects waiting). The size of the queue depends on the number of server objects in this model, which is represented by a constant *N*.

The OOSimL implementation of class *Server* is shown in Listing 22.4 and appears in file `Server.osl`.

Listing 22.4 OOSimL Implementation of class Server.

```
use all psimjava
description
   OOSimL model of the multi-server Carwash system
   J Garrido, August 2008
```

```
    This class defines the server objects, which represent
    is the Carwash machines.
    A server object takes the car at the head of
    the queue and services the car. When the machine completes
    service of the car, it gets another car from the car queue
    If the car queue is empty, it joins the server queue and
    goes into its idle state (suspends itself)
*/
class Server as process is
  private
  variables
      define snum of type integer            // server number
  object references
      define currentCustomer of class Car    // current customer
  function serviceCustomer is
  variables
      define startTime of type double        // start of service
      define service_per of type double      // service interval
      define objname of type string
      define ccustname of type string
      define ccustservt of type double       // service interval
      define simclock of type double
  begin
      if MCarwash.car_queue is not empty
      then
          // get customer from head of waiting queue
          remove currentCustomer of class Car
                from MCarwash.car_queue
          //
          set objname = get_name()
          set ccustname = currentCustomer.get_name()
          // get cust service time
          set ccustservt = currentCustomer.get_serv_dur()
          assign simulation clock to startTime  // service start
          // display objname, " begins service of: ", ccustname,
          //   " at: ", startTime, " for ", ccustservt
          //
          tracewrite objname, " stats service of ",
                ccustname
          //
          // accumulate waiting time for this customer (car)
          set MCarwash.custWaitTime = MCarwash.custWaitTime +
                (startTime - currentCustomer.get_arrivalT())
          //
          set service_per = currentCustomer.get_serv_dur()
          hold self for service_per
          //
          assign simulation clock to simclock
          add (simclock - startTime) to MCarwash.custServiceTime
          //display objname, " completes service of: ",
          //   ccustname, " at: ", simclock
          tracewrite objname, " completes service of ",
                ccustname
          reactivate currentCustomer now    // let car continue
```

```
      else
         return
      endif
   endfun serviceCustomer
   //
   public
   function initializer
   parameters name of type string,
             servnum of type integer is
   begin
      call super using name
      set snum = servnum
      display name, " created"
   endfun initializer
   //
   function Main_body is
   variables
     define startIdle of type double
     define idle_period of type double      // idle period
     define simclock of type double         // simulation time
     define sname of type string            // server name
   begin
     set sname = get_name()
     assign simulation clock to simclock
     display sname, " starting main body at ", simclock
     //
     while simclock < MCarwash.simPeriod do
       if MCarwash.car_queue is empty
       then
           // car queue is empty
           set startIdle = get_clock()  // start idle period
           // display sname, " goes idle at ", simclock
           tracewrite sname, " to idle state"
           // join available server queue
           insert self into MCarwash.servQueue
           suspend self          // suspend server
           //
           // reactivated by a car object
           // queue must now be nonempty
           set simclock = get_clock()
           set idle_period = simclock- startIdle
           add idle_period to MCarwash.accum_idle[snum]
           display sname, " reactivated at " + simclock
       endif
       call serviceCustomer   // service the car
     endwhile
     terminate self
   endfun Main_body
   //
 endclass Server
```

22.6 Models With Multiple Queues

Multi-server models can include more than one customer queue and the simplest models in this group are those that include a separate queue for every server. Each server object owns a queue and a customer object will receive service from only one server object. The queues are simple queues — FIFO queues.

These models are considered to have several service stations in parallel, each station with a single server and a queue. Figure 22.2 shows a multi-server system with multiple queues.

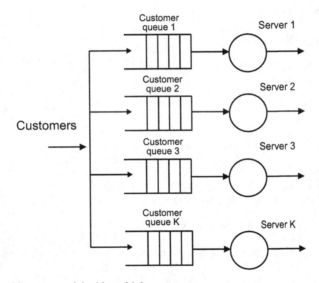

Fig. 22.2 A multi-server model with multiple queues

Arriving customers normally select the station with the shortest queue. If all the queues have the same size, then an arriving customer joins the first queue. If a queue is full, the customer will ignore it. If all the queues are full, the customer is rejected and terminates.

22.6.1 The Customer Object

The behavior of a customer object can be described by the following sequence of activities:

1. Join the shortest customer queue that is not full.

    a. Reactivate the server object of the queue if the server is idle.

b. Suspend itself and go to the idle state.

c. After the service has been completed, continue own activities.

d. Terminate.

2. If all the customer queues are full, terminate (e.g., the customer object is rejected).

Every customer object enters the shortest arrival queue when created. If the server of the selected queue is idle, the customer object reactivates the server object. The next activity of the customer object is to suspend itself, since the server object will remove it from its customer queue. If all the customer queues are full, the arriving customer object terminates immediately. After a customer object has received service, it continues its own activities, then it terminates.

22.6.2 The Server Object

The behavior of the server object can be described by the following sequence of activities. Continuously repeat the following steps:

1. Repeat while the customer queue for this server is not empty

a. Remove the customer object from the head of the corresponding customer queue

b. Perform the service to the customer object

c. Reactivate the customer object.

2. If the customer queue is empty, suspend itself and wait in the idle state until the next customer object arrives.

3. When reactivated by a customer object, start from step 1.

In this multi-queue model each server object examines and removes customer objects from its own customer queue only. For this reason, there is no need for a server queue as each server object will wait in its idle state if the corresponding customer queue is empty. The behavior of the arrivals object is the same as in the previous models.

22.7 Queuing Networks

A queuing network is a more general model than the ones considered previously, it consists of a number of interconnected stations. The stations are interconnected in such a way that the outputs of one station are used as inputs to one or more other stations. Each station has its own server and queue, it can consist of one or more servers and a queue.

Each service station in a queuing network provides a different type of service. In a queuing network, a customer object will usually request service from several service stations.

Customer objects enter the system at one or more entry stations, are routed through the network demanding service from various stations, and exit the network from one or more stations. Figure 22.3 shows a general queuing network with six stations.

In queuing systems, customers request service from several service stations. For example, in a data communication network the data packets are the customers and they travel from service station to service station until each packet reaches its final destination.

The analysis of the general behavior of these queuing networks considers stochastic processes for inputs, service periods, and for outputs. Customer arrivals occur randomly from the external environment to one or more stations in the network and are assumed to follow a Poisson distribution.

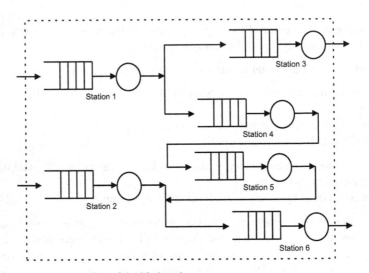

Fig. 22.3 A queuing network model with 6 stations

22.8 Summary

The general behavior of basic multi-server queuing models is discussed in this chapter. The general approach is to consider that performance metrics can be improved by increasing the number of servers, but this depends on the overall goals of the system or model. The three major parameters considered are the average customer waiting time, the total number of customers that received service over a given period, and the average number of customer in the queues.

The multi-server single queue model system and the multi-server multi-queue model are analyzed, both are variations of the simple the Carwash system. These models are implemented in OOSimL. Many practical problems can be solved with this simple queuing mechanism. The supermarket and the bank teller machines are only two common examples.

22.9 Key Terms

multiple servers	multi-queue
performance improvement	server queue

Exercises

22.1. Modify the OOSimL implementation of the Carwash system and include additional performance measures. The server utilization is a good candidate measure.

22.2. Compare the multi-server model to the single server model. Use the server utilization and the proportion of rejected customers. Carry out at least four simulation runs.

22.3. Modify the OOSimL implementation the multi-server model of the Carwash system to implement multiple queues.

22.4. Repeat exercise 22.3 and compare the two multi-server models.

22.5. List the conflicting performance measures. Under what circumstance will one have more weight than the other? Apply this to exercises 1 through 4. Is the behavior of these models fair (to all arriving customers)? What are the alternatives? Give two examples of applications where the unfairness of these models can become important.

22.6. Change the mean service time for customers and carry out more simulation runs. Redo the problem in Exercise 22.4.

22.7. Rewrite the simulation model implementation of the multi-server Carwash system and use a smaller number of global variables, i.e., public static variables in the main class.

Chapter 23
Models with Priorities

23.1 Introduction

Models with multiple types of customers are also known as models of multi-class systems. The queuing models described in previous chapters had only one customer type, so all customers were treated alike. In models with multiple types of customers, each customer type has its own mean arrival rate, mean service period, and other workload parameters. Usually, each customer type is given a priority.

A priority is used by the server object to select a customer for service. The server normally selects the customer with the highest priority. The priority affects the order of removal from the queue — the queue discipline. In previous models, there was only one type of customer and the simple discipline first-in-first-out (FIFO) was always implied.

There are many applications for queuing models with priorities. Some examples are:

- Computer communication networks, in which data may be routed in different ways, according to the message priorities
- Medical attention in a hospital, in which patients are attended according to the degree of the emergency
- Operating systems, in which processes are serviced according to the process' priority

All simulation models with priorities include at least one priority queue for arriving customers. A priority queue is a queue that stores customers in order of priority and uses FIFO ordering for customers with the same priority. Customers with the highest priority are always at the head of the queue.

J.M. Garrido, *Object Oriented Simulation: A Modeling and Programming Perspective*,
DOI: 10.1007/978-1-4419-0516-1_23,
© Springer Science + Business Media, LLC 2009

23.2 Priorities With Single-Server Models

Customer objects of different types arrive and join a priority queue. The priority is assigned by the arrivals object. Since customer objects of the various types have different mean inter-arrival periods and different mean service periods, for each type of customers a different arrivals object is created. Each arrivals object creates customer objects of the same type. Figure 23.1 shows the general structure of a model of a single-server system with priorities.

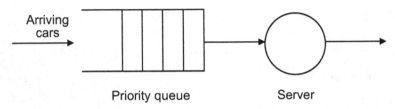

Fig. 23.1 Model of a simple system with priorities

23.2.1 Process Priorities

The priority of a process is an integer value and represents its relative importance in relation to other processes. In OOSimL, the highest priority value is 0. To access the priority of a process, the statement **assign priority** is used. The general structure of the statement follows.

assign priority [**of** ⟨ ref_variable ⟩] **to** ⟨ prio_var ⟩

For example, the following lines of code gets the priority of process referenced by *machine*, assigns it to variable *mach_prio*, and gets the priority of the current process and assigns it to variable *myprio*.

```
define mach_prio of type integer    // priority of machine
define myprio of type integer       // priority of self
define machine of class Server      // reference to object
...
assign priority of machine to mach_prio
assign priority to myprio           // get priority of self
```

To set the priority of a process, the statement **fix priority** is used. The general structure of the statement follows.

fix priority ⟨ prio_var ⟩ [**to** ⟨ ref_variable ⟩]

For example, the following lines of code set the priority 5 to the current process, then it sets priority 1 to another process referenced by *machine*.

```
fix priority 5
fix priority 1 to machine
```

The following lines of code increase the priority of a process referenced by *machine* by 1. The code defines an integer variable *m_priority* to store the priority of the process.

```
define m_priority of type integer
...
assign priority of machine to m_priority
increment m_priority              // increment current priority
fix priority m_priority to machine  // set new priority
```

23.2.2 Priority Queues

Priority queues allow the simulation model to retrieve or remove objects from the queue, based on the priority of the objects or processes. As such, priority queues do not behave as FIFO queues. A priority queue is an object of class *Pqueue*. The OOSimL statements in this section are used to define and manipulate priority queues.

23.2.2.1 Create Objects of Class Pqueue

The constructor for creating a priority queue requires the name of the queue, the optional number of different priorities, and the queue size for all priorities, which is also optional. If the second argument is not included, the number of priorities is assigned to 300 (default). If the third argument is not included, the assigned default queue size is 1,000 for every priority.

The following lines of code declare and create the priority queue with reference name *cust_queue*, with queue name "Customer Queue", using 8 different priorities, and size (capacity) of 25 customers for every priority.

```
define cust_queue of class Pqueue      // declare priority queue
...
// create priority queue
create cust_queue of class Pqueue using "Customer Queue", 8, 25
```

23.2.2.2 Priority Queue Length

This **assign** statement gets the current size (total number of processes) in the specified priority queue. An integer value that corresponds to the current length of the queue is assigned to the specified integer variable. The general structure of the statement follows.

assign length of ⟨ `queue_ref` ⟩ **to** ⟨ `variable` ⟩

For example, the following lines of code get the current length of priority queue *cust_queue* (defined above) and assign this value to variable *mqlength*.

```
define mqlength of type integer
...
assign length of cust_queue to mqlength    // get queue length
```

23.2.2.3 Check Priority Queue Empty

In a similar manner as for simple queues, the **if** statement with the **empty** condition checks if a queue is empty.

For example, the following lines of code check if queue object *cust_queue* (defined above) is empty. The current process suspends itself if the queue is empty, otherwise, it proceeds to remove an object from the queue.

```
if cust_queue is empty then
    // if queue is empty, suspend here
    suspend self
    ...
else
    // dequeue object
    ...
endif
```

23.2.2.4 Queue Length with Priority

This **assign** statement gets the number of processes of a specified priority in a priority queue, and assigns it to a specified (integer) variable.

assign length of ⟨ `queue_ref` ⟩ **with priority** ⟨ `prio_var` ⟩
to ⟨ `variable` ⟩

For example, the following line of code gets the current number of processes in the priority queue *cust_queue*, with priority *l_prio*, and assigns this number to variable *num_proc*.

```
assign length of cust_queue with priority l_prio to num_proc
```

23.2.2.5 Insert Object Into Priority Queue

The **insert** statement inserts the specified object into the priority queue. The size of the queue is increased by one. The priority of the process is automatically taken from the object to insert. The general structure of the statement follows.

> **insert** ⟨ ref_variable ⟩ **into** ⟨ queue_ref ⟩
> **insert self into** ⟨ queue_ref ⟩
> **enqueue** ⟨ ref_variable ⟩ **into** ⟨ queue_ref ⟩
> **enqueue self into**⟨ queue_ref ⟩

The following lines of code insert (enqueue) object *cust_obj* into priority queue *pcust_queue*.

```
define cust_prio = 3 of type integer
define cust_obj of class Customer   // reference customer
...
// enqueue customer process
insert cust_obj into pcust_queue
```

23.2.2.6 Remove Object with Specified Priority

This statement removes (dequeues) an object or process of a specified priority, from a priority queue. After removal, the size of the queue is reduced by one, as a result of this operation. The general structure of the statement is as follows:

> **remove** [**object**] ⟨ ref_var ⟩ **of class** ⟨ cl_name ⟩
>   **from** [**queue**] ⟨ queue_ref ⟩ **with priority** ⟨ prio_variable ⟩
> **dequeue** [**object**] ⟨ ref_var ⟩ **of class** ⟨ cl_name ⟩
>   **from** [**queue**] ⟨ queue_ref ⟩ **with priority** ⟨ prio_variable ⟩

For example, the following lines of code remove (dequeue) a customer process from queue *cust_queue* and assigns a reference *cust_obj* to it, given priority *cust_prio*.

```
define cust_prio of type integer
...
remove object cust_obj of class Customer from queue cust_queue
    with priority cust_prio
```

The reference to class Customer is necessary to specify the type of object or process) dequeued. If no priority is specified, the statement removes the highest priority process from the priority queue.

23.3 Car Wash Model with Priorities

The following process descriptions are related to the model of the Carwash system with priorities. The system has vehicles (cars) of various types: small cars, luxury cars, sport utilities, etc. Each type of vehicle usually has a different mean arrival rate and a different mean service period.

23.3.1 Description of the Server Object

A description of the server assumes that the arrival queue for car objects uses priority ordering. The server always takes the car with the highest priority from the car queue. The following sequence of activities defines the behavior of the server object:

1. While the car queue is not empty, execute the following activities:

   a. Remove the car object at the head of the queue.
   b. Perform the service of the car object.
   c. Reactivate the car object so it will continue its own activities.

2. Wait (in the idle state) until the next car object arrives, then start from step 1.

   As with previous models, the servicing of a car object takes some finite time interval known as the *service interval* of the car object. The simulation clock is advanced by an interval that is the duration of the service activity.

   When the car queue is empty, the server object suspends itself and changes to the idle state. The server object will be reactivated by a new car object on arrival; and the queue becomes non-empty.

23.3.2 The Arrivals Objects

In this model there are several types of customers, each one with a different priority. There are several Arrivals objects created, one for each car priority. Each Arrivals object generates the customers of that priority. The following sequence of activities defines the behavior of an Arrivals object.

1. Repeat until close arrivals or until simulation period expires:

   a. Generate a random inter-arrival period.
   b. Wait until the clock advances by an amount equal to the inter-arrival period.
   c. Generate a random service period.
   d. Create a car object with its random service period, and its priority.

2. Terminate

   Every Arrivals object generates two random numbers:

- The generation of an inter-arrival interval for an arrival event
- The generation of a service interval

These two random numbers are drawn from two different probability distributions. The decision of which probability distribution to use results from statistical analysis based on observations carried out previously on the real system or a similar system.

The Arrivals object creates a sequence of car objects of a specified priority. One car object is created after every inter-arrival time interval. Every car object has a different service interval.

23.3.3 The Car Objects

As mentioned previously, the car objects are grouped into categories (or types), and a different priority is assigned to each group by the corresponding arrivals object. There are several car objects created by each arrivals object.

Each car object includes its priority (type) in addition to its service period, as part of its relevant attributes. A car object joins the car queue according to its priority. The following sequence of activities describes the behavior of each car object:

1. Join the car queue if it is not full
2. Reactivate the server object if the server is idle
3. Suspend (itself), go into the idle state to wait for service
4. After the service is completed, continue with own activities
5. Terminate
6. If the queue is full, terminate (i.e., the car object is rejected)

After a car object is created, it enters the car queue by priority. If the server is idle, the car object will reactivate the server. The car object then suspends itself and waits for service. If the queue is full, the arriving car object will terminate immediately.

The server object removes the car object from the head of the queue and starts its service.

23.3.4 Outputs of a Simulation Run

The summary statistics output of a simulation run of the model of Carwash system with priorities, appears in Listing 23.1. This output also shows the values of the following performance measures for every priority:

- Throughput, i.e., the numbers of cars serviced;
- Average wait period for the cars.

Listing 23.1 Summary statistics of a simulation run.

```
OOSimL model: Model of Carwash System with Priorities
Simulation date: date: 9/17/2008 time: 8:21
-------------------STATISTICS REPORT-----------------------
----------------------------------------------------------
Priority queue: Cust Queue
Capacity of queue: 200
Number of observations: 586
Max number of objects in queue: 146
Average number of objects in queue: 69
Average time in queue: 1.7935666936304733
Queue utilization: 0.8617723660473778
Queue usage: 0.4789908220792021
----------------------------------------------------------
Random generator: Inter-arrival type 4
Distribution: Negative exponential
Number of obs: 29
Seed: 55
Mean: 25.2
----------------------------------------------------------
Random generator: Inter-arrival type 3
Distribution: Negative exponential
Number of obs: 122
Seed: 43
Mean: 5.2
----------------------------------------------------------
Random generator: Inter-arrival type 2
Distribution: Negative exponential
Number of obs: 35
Seed: 31
Mean: 14.2
----------------------------------------------------------
Random generator: Inter-arrival type 1
Distribution: Negative exponential
Number of obs: 75
Seed: 19
Mean: 8.5
----------------------------------------------------------
Random generator: Inter-arrival type 0
Distribution: Negative exponential
Number of obs: 120
Seed: 7
Mean: 5.2
----------------------------------------------------------
Random generator: Service Period type 4
Distribution: Normal
Number of obs: 29
Seed: 61
Mean: 2.2
Standard deviation: 0.0
----------------------------------------------------------
Random generator: Service Period type 3
```

```
Distribution: Normal
Number of obs: 122
Seed: 49
Mean: 3.5
Standard deviation: 0.85
-----------------------------------------------------------------
Random generator: Service Period type 2
Distribution: Normal
Number of obs: 35
Seed: 37
Mean: 3.0
Standard deviation: 0.85
-----------------------------------------------------------------
Random generator: Service Period type 1
Distribution: Normal
Number of obs: 75
Seed: 25
Mean: 2.6
Standard deviation: 0.85
-----------------------------------------------------------------
Random generator: Service Period type 0
Distribution: Normal
Number of obs: 120
Seed: 13
Mean: 4.6
Standard deviation: 0.85
-----------------------------------------------------------------

End Simulation of Model of Carwash System with Priorities
   date: 9/17/2008 time: 8:21

Total cars of type 0 serviced : 120
Car type 0 average wait period: 10.587397344561573
Total cars of type 1 serviced : 68
Car type 1 average wait period: 235.79209727808004
Total cars of type 2 serviced : 35
Car type 2 average wait period: 442.1166150740475
Total cars of type 3 serviced : 41
Car type 3 average wait period: 750.9129750062083
Total cars of type 4 serviced : 29
Car type 4 average wait period: 701.8389044542504

Total number of cars serviced: 293
Car average wait period: 286.414
Average period car spends in the shop: 289.953
Machine utilization: 0.994
```

The trace of the simulation run shows the sequence of events that occurred during the simulation run and appears in Listing 23.2.

Listing 23.2 Trace of a simulation run of the model with priorities.

```
OOSimL model: Model of Carwash System with Priorities
```

```
Simulation date: 9/17/2008 time: 8:21
------------------------ TRACE ------------------------------
Time: 0 Car Wash System with priorities holds for 1200
Time: 0 Arrivals0 holds for 6.822
Time: 0 Arrivals1 holds for 11.208
Time: 0 Arrivals2 holds for 18.667
Time: 0 Arrivals3 holds for 6.76
Time: 0 Arrivals4 holds for 32.927
Time: 0 Wash_machine deactivated
Time: 6.76 Arrivals3 holds for 9.962
Time: 6.76 Car1 priority 3 arrives
Time: 6.76 Car1 enqueued into Cust Queue
Time: 6.76 Wash_machine to reactivate
Time: 6.76 Car1 deactivated
Time: 6.76 Entity: Car1 dequeued from Cust Queue
Time: 6.76 Wash_machine begins service of Car1 type 3
Time: 6.76 Wash_machine holds for 3.812
Time: 6.822 Arrivals0 holds for 7.191
Time: 6.822 Car2 priority 0 arrives
Time: 6.822 Car2 enqueued into Cust Queue
Time: 6.822 Car2 deactivated
Time: 10.572 Wash_machine completed service of Car1
Time: 10.572 Car1 to reactivate
Time: 10.572 Entity: Car2 dequeued from Cust Queue
Time: 10.572 Wash_machine begins service of Car2 type 0
Time: 10.572 Wash_machine holds for 6.03
Time: 10.572 Car1 terminating
Time: 11.208 Arrivals1 holds for 3.771
Time: 11.208 Car3 priority 1 arrives
Time: 11.208 Car3 enqueued into Cust Queue
Time: 11.208 Car3 deactivated
Time: 14.014 Arrivals0 holds for 2.227
Time: 14.014 Car4 priority 0 arrives
Time: 14.014 Car4 enqueued into Cust Queue
   . . .
Time: 1037.185 Entity: Car366 dequeued from Cust Queue
Time: 1037.185 Wash_machine begins service of Car366 type 4
Time: 1037.185 Wash_machine holds for 2.2
Time: 1037.185 Car348 terminating
Time: 1039.385 Wash_machine completed service of Car366
Time: 1039.385 Car366 to reactivate
Time: 1039.385 Entity: Car374 dequeued from Cust Queue
Time: 1039.385 Wash_machine begins service of Car374 type 4
Time: 1039.385 Wash_machine holds for 2.2
Time: 1039.385 Car366 terminating
Time: 1041.585 Wash_machine completed service of Car374
Time: 1041.585 Car374 to reactivate
Time: 1041.585 Entity: Car380 dequeued from Cust Queue
Time: 1041.585 Wash_machine begins service of Car380 type 4
Time: 1041.585 Wash_machine holds for 2.2
Time: 1041.585 Car374 terminating
Time: 1043.785 Wash_machine completed service of Car380
Time: 1043.785 Car380 to reactivate
Time: 1043.785 Wash_machine deactivated
```

```
Time: 1043.785 Car380 terminating
------------------------------------------------------------------

End Simulation of Model of Carwash System with Priorities
   date: 9/17/2008 time: 8:21
```

23.3.5 Implementation Of the Carwash Model

The class definitions of the model of the Carwash System with priorities are very similar to the model without priorities. Listing 23.3 shows the OOSimL implementation of the main class, *PCarwash*.

The critical parts of class *PCarwash* are:

- The car queue, *car_queue*, is a priority queue. It is an object of class *Pqueue*
- Arrays are defined and created for the calculations of the performance measures for each car priority
- Several objects of class *Arrivals* are created, one for each car priority

Listing 23.3 OOSimL Implementation of class PCarwash.

```
use all java.io
use java.text.DecimalFormat
use all psimjava

description
A single-server model of a Carwash system with priorities.
Arriving cars (customers) join a priority queue to wait for
service. The server is a Carwash machine that services one
car at a time. Service consists of a complete external wash
of a car.

OOSimL model J. Garrido, Jan 10, 2008
Main class: PCarwash

This class sets up simulation parameters and creates the
relevant objects.
There are four classes of active objects: PCarwash,
     Server, Arrivals, and Car.
There is one passive object, the car_queue of class Pqueue.
The arrivals objects create the various car objects of a
given type that arrive at random intervals.
Every type of car is given a priority and has its own
workload. Random variables: inter-arrival period of a
negative exponential distribution and service period of
a Normal distribution.

File: PCarwash.osl
*/
```

```
public class PCarwash as process is
   private
   object references
      //
      // files for reporting
      define  static statf of class PrintWriter
      define  static tracef of class PrintWriter
   public
   constants
      // number of car types
      define static K = 5 of type integer
   variables
      define static gui_flag of type boolean
      // input car queue size
      define static totalQSize = 40 of type integer
      //
      // simulation period
      define static simPeriod = 1200.0 of type double
      //
      // time to close arrival of cars
      define static close_arrival = 600.5 of type double
      //
      // Workload parameters for every type of customer
      //
      // mean car inter-arrival interval
      define static MeanInterarrival array []
              of type double
      //
      // mean car service interval
      define static MeanServiceDur array [] of type double
      //
      // standard deviation of service interval
      define static StdServiceDur array [] of type double
      //
      // Accumulative variables for every customer type
      //
      // accumulated customer service time
      define static custServiceTime array [] of type double
      // accumulated customer sojourn time
      define static custSojournTime array [] of type double
      // accumulated car waiting time
      define static custWaitTime array [] of type double
      //
      // current number of customers serviced
      define static num_serviced array [] of type integer
      // current number of cars that arrived
      define static num_arrived array [] of type integer
      // current number of cars rejected
      define static num_rejected array [] of type integer
      //
      // Totals
      // accum server idle time
      define static accum_idle = 0.0 of type double
      // accumulated waiting time
```

```
      define static totalWait = 0.0 of type double
      define static totalSojourn = 0.0 of type double
      // total number of cars arrived
      define static num_car of type integer
      // total number of cars serviced
      define static carServiced of type integer
object references
      //
      // Simulation model essential objects
      define static sim of class Simulation
      //
      // Queues for the model
      // queue for arrived waiting cars
      define static car_queue of class Pqueue
      //
      // Classes for the active objects of the model
      define static wash_machine of class Server
      //
      define static genCust array [] of class Arrivals
      define static shop of class PCarwash
      define model of class SimModel
      //
// constructor
function initializer parameters ss of class String is
begin
      call super using ss
endfun initializer
//
function main is
variables
    define j of type integer
begin
    set gui_flag = false
    create MeanInterarrival array [K] of type double
    create MeanServiceDur array [K] of type double
    create StdServiceDur array [K] of type double
    create custServiceTime array [K] of type double
    create custSojournTime array [K] of type double
    create custWaitTime array [K] of type double
    create num_serviced array [K] of type integer
    create num_arrived array [K] of type integer
    create num_rejected array [K] of type integer
    //
    //      highest priority is 0
    set MeanInterarrival[0] = 5.2
    set MeanServiceDur[0] = 4.6
    set StdServiceDur[0] = 0.85
    set MeanInterarrival[1] = 8.5
    set MeanServiceDur[1] = 2.6
    set StdServiceDur[1] = 0.85
    set MeanInterarrival[2] = 14.2
    set MeanServiceDur[2] = 3.0
    set StdServiceDur[2] = 0.85
    set MeanInterarrival[3] = 5.2
```

```
        set MeanServiceDur[3] = 3.5
        set StdServiceDur[3] = 0.85
        set MeanInterarrival[4] = 25.2
        set MeanServiceDur[4] = 2.2
        set StdServiceDur[0] = 0.85
        //
        for j = 0 to K - 1 do
            set custServiceTime[j] = 0.0
            set custSojournTime[j] = 0.0
            set custWaitTime[j] = 0.0
            set num_serviced[j] = 0
            set num_arrived[j] = 0
            set num_rejected[j] = 0
        endfor
        //
        // set-up simulation with an object
        //        of class simulation
        simulation title
            "Model of Carwash System with Priorities"
        // setup files for reporting
        trace file "pcarwtrace.txt"
        statistics file "pcarwstatf.txt"
        //
        // create queues (passive objects)
        create car_queue of class Pqueue using
            "Cust Queue", K, totalQSize
        //
        // Create and start the main active objects of
        //    the model
        create shop of class PCarwash using
            "Car Wash System with Priorities"
        start object shop
    endfun main
    //
    description
        This function is called by the class object with
        interactive I/O
        */
    function pbegin parameters sm of class SimModel is
        variables
            define jin of type integer
            define din of type double
            define j of type integer
        begin
            set gui_flag = true
            create MeanInterarrival array [K] of type double
            create MeanServiceDur array [K] of type double
            create StdServiceDur array [K] of type double
            create custServiceTime array [K] of type double
            create custSojournTime array [K] of type double
            create custWaitTime array [K] of type double
            create num_serviced array [K] of type integer
            create num_arrived array [K] of type integer
            create num_rejected array [K] of type integer
```

```
//
//       highest priority is 0
set MeanInterarrival[0] = 5.2
set MeanServiceDur[0] = 4.6
set StdServiceDur[0] = 0.85
set MeanInterarrival[1] = 8.5
set MeanServiceDur[1] = 2.6
set StdServiceDur[1] = 0.85
set MeanInterarrival[2] = 14.2
set MeanServiceDur[2] = 3.0
set StdServiceDur[2] = 0.85
set MeanInterarrival[3] = 5.2
set MeanServiceDur[3] = 3.5
set StdServiceDur[3] = 0.85
set MeanInterarrival[4] = 25.2
set MeanServiceDur[4] = 2.2
set StdServiceDur[0] = 0.85
//
for j = 0 to K - 1 do
    set custServiceTime[j] = 0.0
    set custSojournTime[j] = 0.0
    set custWaitTime[j] = 0.0
    set num_serviced[j] = 0
    set num_arrived[j] = 0
    set num_rejected[j] = 0
endfor
//
set model = sm
call println of model using
    "Model of Carwash System with Priorities"
// call model.println using
//   "Input workload parameters for Car Wash Model"
// Input parameters
call model.readInt using "Enter queue size (40): "
    return to jin
if jin > 0 then
    set totalQSize = jin
endif
//
set din = model.readDouble
        ("Enter simulation period (1200.0): ")
if din > 0.0 then
    set simPeriod = din
endif
//
call model.readDouble using
    "Enter close time (600.5): "
    return value to din
if din > 0.0 then
    set close_arrival = din
endif
//
//
for j = 0 to K - 1 do
```

```
        call model.readDouble using "Car type " concat j
            concat " Mean inter-arrival period ("
            concat MeanInterarrival[j] concat "): "
            return value to din
        if din > 0.0 then
            set MeanInterarrival[j] = din
        endif
        //
        call model.readDouble using "Car type " concat j
              concat " Mean service period ("
              concat MeanServiceDur[j] concat "): "
    return to din
        if din > 0.0 then
            set MeanServiceDur[j] = din
        endif
        //
        call model.readDouble using "Car type "
            concat j concat " Service time std ("
            concat StdServiceDur[j] concat ": "
      return value to din
        if din > 0.0 then
            set StdServiceDur[j] = din
        endif
      endfor
      //
      // set-up simulation
      simulation title
          "Model of Carwash System with Priorities"
      //
      // Set up report files
      trace file "pcarwtrace.txt"
      statistics file "pcarwstatf.txt"
      //
      // Create  passive objects: queues
      // priority queue with K priorities and
      // totalQSize per priority
      create car_queue of class Pqueue using "CustQ", K,
          totalQSize
      //
      // start main active object in model
      start self
endfun pbegin
//
//
method Main_body is
variables
    define pname of type string
    define machutil of type double
    //
    // formatting strings
    define fmtout1 of type string
    define fmtout2 of type string
    define fmtout3 of type string
    define dispouta of type string
```

```
        define dispoutb of type string
        define j of type integer
        //
object references
        define dfmt of class DecimalFormat
begin
        create genCust array [K] of class Arrivals
        //
        access statistics file
        //
        // create the other active objects of the model
        create wash_machine of class Server
                using "Wash_machine"
        set j = 0
        for j = 0 to K - 1 do
            create genCust[j] of class Arrivals
                using "Arrivals"+j, j, MeanInterarrival[j],
                    MeanServiceDur[j], StdServiceDur[j]
            start object genCust[j]
        endfor
        //
        start object wash_machine
        //
        // display "Workload - car mean inter-arrival: ",
        //      MeanInterarrival, " mean service: ",
        //      MeanServiceDur
        //
        // starting simulation
        start simulation with simPeriod
        //
        for j = 0 to K-1 do
            display "Total cars of type ", j,
                " serviced : ", num_serviced[j]
            statwrite "Total cars of type ", j,
                " serviced : ", num_serviced[j]
            if num_serviced[j] > 0
            then
                statwrite "Car type ", j,
                    " average wait period: ",
                    custWaitTime[j] / num_serviced[j]
                display "Car type ", j,
                    " average wait period: ",
                    custWaitTime[j] / num_serviced[j]
            endif
        endfor
        //
        // set formatting round output to 3 dec places
        create dfmt of class DecimalFormat using "0.###"
        //
        statwrite " "
        display "Total number of cars serviced: ",
            carServiced
        statwrite "Total number of cars serviced: ",
            carServiced
```

```
      if carServiced > 0
      then
        set fmtout1 = call dfmt.format using
            totalWait/carServiced
        display "Car average wait period: ", fmtout1
        statwrite "Total Car average wait period: ",
            fmtout1
        //
        set fmtout2 = call dfmt.format using
            totalSojourn/carServiced
        display
            "Average period car spends in the shop: ",
            fmtout2
        statwrite
            "Average period car spends in the shop: ",
            fmtout2
      endif
      //
      // machine utilization
      set machutil = (simPeriod - accum_idle)/simPeriod
      set fmtout3 = call dfmt.format using machutil
      //
      statwrite "Machine utilization: ", fmtout3
      display "Machine utilization: ", fmtout3
      //
      set disputa = "Cars serviced: " concat
                carServiced concat "\n" concat
                "Avg wait: " concat
                dfmt.format(totalWait/carServiced)
                concat "\n"
      set disputb = disputa concat
                "Mach util: " concat
                dfmt.format
                ((simPeriod-accum_idle)/simPeriod)
                concat "\n" concat
                "Avg time in shop: " concat
                dfmt.format(totalSojourn/carServiced)
      if gui_flag equal true then
        call model.println using disputb
      endif
      exit
    endmethod Main_body
  endclass PCarwash
```

The OOSimL source files for the implementation of this model are stored in files: PCarwash.osl, Arrivals.osl, Server.osl, and Car.osl. These files are all contained in the archive file pcarwash.jar.

23.4 Multi-Server Models with Priorities

The same modifications to the single-server model without priorities that were described in the previous sections, are carried out for the multi-server model without priorities to develop the multi-server model with priorities. The complete multi-server model with priorities is left as an exercise.

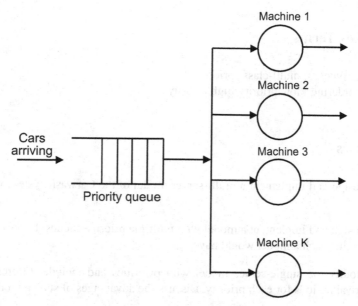

Fig. 23.2 A multi-server queuing model with a priority queue

In the model, a server object removes the customer with the highest priority from the priority queue. If there are several customer objects with the same priority, the one chosen is the one that has been the longest time in the queue (FIFO ordering).

Figure 23.2 shows a multi-server queuing model with a priority queue. Any server object can remove the next customer object from the priority queue.

23.5 Summary

Models of queuing systems with priorities are discussed in this chapter. The priority is an attribute of an active object. The priority is the measure of the relative importance of the active object. The priority affects the ordering of service to customer objects. This also affects the estimation of the waiting period compared to other customers of a different priority. The priority is represented as an integer variable, and the value 0 corresponds to the highest priority.

Models with multiple simple queues, one for each priority, can also be analyzed. More common are the models with a single priority queue. The server selects the next customer with the highest priority to service. If there are several customers with the same priority, the server will provide service using the usual FIFO order as with simple queues.

Other variations to this mechanism are possible, such as the case when there is a server for each priority (or for each group of priorities).

23.6 Key Terms

customer types   multi-class priority
priority ordering   low priority high priority

Exercises

23.1. Design and implement a multi-server model of the Carwash system with priorities.

23.2. Design and implement a model with multiple priority queues. Discuss the advantages that such a model would have.

23.3. Modify the single-server model with priorities and include different mean inter-arrival periods for each priority. Discuss the advantages of such a model.

23.4. Modify the model presented to include different mean service periods for each priority. Discuss the advantages of such a model.

23.5. Extend the single-server model with priorities and include the utilization of the server.

23.6. Extend the multi-server model with priorities and include the utilization of the servers.

23.7. Discuss the fairness of the model with lower-priority customers.

Chapter 24
Standard Resources

24.1 Introduction

Resource management involves the manipulation of resources by the various processes in a model. There are two important types of resources in OOSimL:

1. *Standard resources* that are accessed in a mutually exclusive manner by processes. These resource objects represent a finite pool of resource units and are
   created with the *Res* class.
2. *Detachable resources* that are *produced* and *consumed* by different processes.
   These resource objects represent infinite pools of resource units and are created
   with the *Bin* class.

Resource management of standard resources involves resource allocation to processes, and resource de-allocation from processes. The models that include resource
management also deal with process interactions that are present when processes
compete for resources.

The type of synchronization involved with this process interaction is . Resources
can be held by only one process at a time; the other processes requesting the same
resources must wait.

As mentioned in previous chapters, resources are passive components of a model;
in the software implementation of resource pools are passive objects.

24.2 Resource Manipulation

A system can have several resource types defined, also called resource pools. Each
resource pool can contain one or more resource units or resource items; these resource units can be requested by several processes in the system. A process that
needs a number of resource units from a resource pool follows the following steps:

1. Request a specific number of resource units from resource pool.

2. If there are sufficient resource units available, acquire these; otherwise wait in a hidden queue, which belongs to the resource pool.
3. Use the acquired resource units for a finite interval.
4. Release all or some of the acquired resource units.

Resource units of a specific resource pool can only be acquired by a single process at a time so they are considered mutual exclusive resources. These resource units are acquired and released by the same process.

For every resource pool, there are a specified total number of resource units. When the number of resource units in the resource pool is less than the number requested by a process, the request cannot be granted immediately. In this case, the object is placed in a hidden priority queue and suspended. This waiting process will be reactivated when another process holding resources units (of the same resource pool) releases them.

When the number of resource units is small, there will be a relatively large group of processes waiting to acquire these resource units.

A process can hold some resource units of a resource pool and be requesting units of a different resource pool. The process will usually be competing with other process for these resources.

These resources are acquired in a mutual exclusive manner. Only one process at a time can acquire a particular resource and the type of process synchronization involved is known as mutual exclusion.

24.2.1 Software Implementation of Resources

A resource pool is represented by an object of the resource class *Res*. To manipulate resources, a simulation model needs to define the following sequence of steps:

1. Declare references to resource objects, each representing a resource type or resource pool. These are objects of class *Res*.
2. Create the resource objects, each with a finite number of total resourceunits, this number represents the maximum number of units of the resource pool.
3. In the main body of the process definitions:

    a. Acquire a specific number of resource units of a resource pool.
    b. Use the resource units for a finite time interval.
    c. Release all or part of the resource units acquired.

When a process acquires a number of resource units of a resource pool, the number of available resource units is reduced accordingly. For example, if the initial total number of chairs in a model is 15, then after process P acquires 10 chairs, there will be only 5 chairs left (available). The resource pool is defined with 15 chairs. If another process, Q, requests 7 chairs, it has to wait until process P releases one or more chairs.

After an object releases a number of resource units, a waiting object is reactivated and will attempt again to acquire the number of resource units initially requested. If there are not sufficient resource units available, it will be suspended again and put back into the resource priority queue.

Some internal checks are carried out by the simulation executive. If a process attempts to acquire a number of resource units greater than the maximum defined for that resource pool, an error message is issued and control will return to the process. In a similar manner, when a process attempts to release a number of resource units greater than the number that the process holds, a message is issued and control is returned to the process.

24.2.1.1 Creating Standard Resources

Creating a standard resource pool involves creating an object of class *Res*. This object represents a finite resource pool with a specified number of resource units.

The constructor for creating a resource pool of this class requires the name of the resource pool and the pool size. The pool size defines the total number of available resource units in the resource pool.

The following lines of code declare and create a standard resource pool, *chairs*, with a title "Customer Chairs" and a size of 30 resource units.

```
define chairs of class Res    // declare ref resource pool
...
// create resource pool
create chairs of class Res using "Customer Chairs", 30
```

24.2.1.2 Available Resource Units

The **assign available** statement gets the number of available resource units in the resource pool and assigns this number to the specified variable. The general structure of this statement follows.

assign available units of ⟨ ref_variable ⟩ **to** ⟨ var_name ⟩

The following lines of code get the current number of available resource units in the resource pool *chairs*, which was defined above, and assigns this value to variable *num_res*.

```
define num_res of type integer  // number of resource units
...
assign available units of chairs to num_res
```

24.2.1.3 Acquire Resource Units

The **acquire** statement allows the requesting process to acquire a specified number of units from the specified resource pool. If the resource pool does not have all the requested resource units available, the requesting process is suspended.

Thus, the statement allows the process to acquire a specified number of resource units from a resource pool only if there are sufficient resource units available. The general form of the statement is:

> **acquire** ⟨ int_variable ⟩ **units from** ⟨ ref_variable ⟩
> **request** ⟨ int_variable ⟩ **units from** ⟨ ref_variable ⟩

In the following lines of code, the process attempts to acquire 10 resource units from the resource pool *chairs* (defined above).

```
acquire 10 units from chairs
// execute instructions when resources are acquired
```

24.2.1.4 Release Units of a Resource

This statement releases the specified number of resource units from the process, and returns these to the resource pool. This deallocates the specified number of resource units that the process currently holds. The statement may cause reactivation of any suspended processes that are waiting for resources. One or more of the reactivated processes can then acquire the requested resources units now available, if there are sufficient resource units.

> **release** ⟨ int_variable ⟩ **units of** ⟨ ref_variable ⟩

In the following line of code, a process releases 10 resource units from the resource pool *chairs* (defined above).

```
release 10 units of chairs
```

24.2.2 Using Resources

As mentioned previously, a process will normally acquire a certain number of resource units from a resource pool, use these resource units for a finite time interval, then release the resource units.

The following lines of code show the allocation and de-allocation of resources units by a process, *P1*. This process, *P1*, acquires 10 resource units of *chairs*; it holds the resource units for 6.5 time units; after this interval, it releases the 10 resource units of *chairs*.

```
. . .
acquire 10 units of chairs
hold self for 6.5              // use the resource units
release 10 units of chairs
. . .
```

The process attempts to acquire 10 resource units of *chairs*. If the request for resources of *chairs* is not successful, then the process is automatically suspended and placed in a hidden queue that belongs to object *chairs*. When the process is reactivated, it will again try to acquire the specified number of resource units.

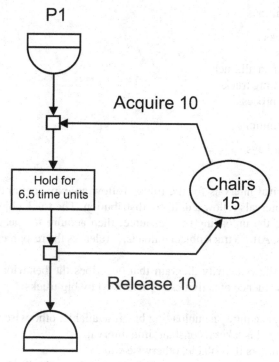

Fig. 24.1 Activity diagram using *chairs* resource pool

When the process is able to acquire 10 resource units of *chairs*, it holds the resource units for 6.5 time units; this represents usage of the resource units for a finite interval. When this interval elapses, the process releases 10 resource units of *chairs* and the process continues with its other activities. Figure 24.1 illustrates the use of the resource pool, *chairs*.

24.3 Model of a Warehouse System

A warehouse receives two types of trucks, small and big, that arrive periodically with goods. Each truck needs an unloading bay to dock and to unload the goods. Small trucks need two workers to unload, big trucks need three workers. The warehouse has a limited number of unloading bays and a limited number of workers. Trucks may need to wait if there are no available unloading bays and/or not sufficient available workers. Each type of truck has a mean arrival rate and a mean unloading time interval. The simulation model of the Warehouse system consists of the following components:

- Process definitions

  - Small trucks
  - Big trucks
  - Arrivals of small trucks
  - Arrivals of big trucks
  - The main process

- Resource definitions

  - Unloading bays
  - Workers

The inter-arrival intervals for the trucks follow an exponential distribution and the unloading intervals follow a uniform distribution. The truck objects acquire one resource unit of the unloading bay resource, then acquire the necessary resource units of workers. After a truck object unloads, it releases the resources units, departs, and terminates.

Figure 24.2 shows activity diagram that describes the behavior of a big truck. The following sequence of activities is performed by big trucks:

1. After arriving, acquire one unloading bay if available, otherwise wait.
2. Dock into bay, this takes a constant time interval.
3. Acquire 3 workers if available, otherwise wait.
4. Unload, takes a random time interval (from a uniform distribution).
5. Release workers.
6. Undock, takes a constant time interval.
7. Release unloading bay.
8. Depart and terminate.

Small trucks perform a similar sequence of activities. The following sequence of activities defines the behavior of small trucks.

1. After arriving, acquire one unloading bay if available, otherwise wait
2. Acquire 2 workers if available, otherwise wait
3. Unload, takes a random time interval (from a uniform distribution)
4. Release workers

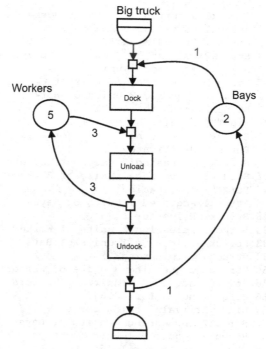

Fig. 24.2 Activity diagram of big truck

5. Release unloading bay
6. Depart and terminate

Listing 24.1 shows the trace listing of the output from a simulation run of the model. The trace in the output shows the relevant events, such as:

- Processes (trucks) start to request resources
- Resources are allocated to the processes
- Other processes start to wait for available resources
- Processes terminate after they have completed all of their activities

Listing 24.1 Trace of a simulation run of the Warehouse model.

```
OOSimL model: Busy Warehouse System
Simulation date: 9/23/2008 time: 14:11
------------------------ TRACE ------------------------------
Time: 0 Warehouse model holds for 625.65
Time: 0 Big T Arrivals  holds for 18.629
Time: 0 Small T Arrivals  holds for 17.151
Time: 17.151 Small T Arrivals  holds for 1.461
Time: 17.151 Struck1 requesting 1 units of Bays
Time: 17.151 Struck1 acquired 1 units of Bays
Time: 17.151 Struck1 requesting 2 units of Workers
```

```
Time: 17.151 Struck1 acquired 2 units of Workers
Time: 17.151 Struck1 holds for 8.264
Time: 18.612 Small T Arrivals  holds for 31.645
Time: 18.612 Struck2 requesting 1 units of Bays
Time: 18.612 Struck2 acquired 1 units of Bays
Time: 18.612 Struck2 requesting 2 units of Workers
Time: 18.612 Struck2 acquired 2 units of Workers
Time: 18.612 Struck2 holds for 6.821
Time: 18.629 Big T Arrivals  holds for 19.638
Time: 18.629 Btruck1 requesting 1 units of Bays
Time: 18.629 Btruck1 deactivated
Time: 25.416 Struck1 releasing 2 units of Workers
Time: 25.416 Struck1 releasing 1 units of Bays
Time: 25.416 Struck1 terminating
Time: 25.416 Btruck1 acquired 1 units of Bays
Time: 25.416 Btruck1 holds for 1.45
Time: 25.433 Struck2 releasing 2 units of Workers
Time: 25.433 Struck2 releasing 1 units of Bays
Time: 25.433 Struck2 terminating
Time: 26.866 Btruck1 requesting 3 units of Workers
Time: 26.866 Btruck1 acquired 3 units of Workers
Time: 26.866 Btruck1 holds for 12.879
Time: 38.268 Big T Arrivals  holds for 6.08
Time: 38.268 Btruck2 requesting 1 units of Bays
Time: 38.268 Btruck2 acquired 1 units of Bays
Time: 38.268 Btruck2 holds for 1.45
Time: 39.718 Btruck2 requesting 3 units of Workers
Time: 39.718 Btruck2 deactivated
Time: 39.745 Btruck1 releasing 3 units of Workers
Time: 39.745 Btruck1 holds for 1.15
Time: 39.745 Btruck2 acquired 3 units of Workers
Time: 39.745 Btruck2 holds for 11.168
Time: 40.895 Btruck1 releasing 1 units of Bays
Time: 40.895 Btruck1 terminating
Time: 44.348 Big T Arrivals  holds for 32.315
Time: 44.348 Btruck3 requesting 1 units of Bays
Time: 44.348 Btruck3 acquired 1 units of Bays
Time: 44.348 Btruck3 holds for 1.45
Time: 45.798 Btruck3 requesting 3 units of Workers
Time: 45.798 Btruck3 deactivated
Time: 50.257 Small T Arrivals  holds for 2.214
Time: 50.257 Struck3 requesting 1 units of Bays
Time: 50.257 Struck3 deactivated
Time: 50.912 Btruck2 releasing 3 units of Workers
Time: 50.912 Btruck2 holds for 1.15
Time: 50.912 Btruck3 acquired 3
. . .
Time: 612.885 Big T Arrivals  holds for 20.089
Time: 612.885 Btruck43 requesting 1 units of Bays
Time: 612.885 Btruck43 acquired 1 units of Bays
Time: 612.885 Btruck43 holds for 1.45
Time: 614.335 Btruck43 requesting 3 units of Workers
Time: 614.335 Btruck43 deactivated
Time: 618.338 Btruck42 releasing 3 units of Workers
```

```
Time: 618.338 Btruck42 holds for 1.15
Time: 618.338 Btruck43 acquired 3 units of Workers
Time: 618.338 Btruck43 holds for 9.807
Time: 619.488 Btruck42 releasing 1 units of Bays
Time: 619.488 Btruck42 terminating
Time: 625.65 Warehouse model holds for 14.283
Time: 628.145 Btruck43 releasing 3 units of Workers
Time: 628.145 Btruck43 holds for 1.15
Time: 629.295 Btruck43 releasing 1 units of Bays
Time: 629.295 Btruck43 terminating
Time: 632.974 Big T Arrivals  holds for 5.943
Time: 632.974 Btruck44 requesting 1 units of Bays
Time: 632.974 Btruck44 acquired 1 units of Bays
Time: 632.974 Btruck44 holds for 1.45
Time: 634.424 Btruck44 requesting 3 units of Workers
Time: 634.424 Btruck44 acquired 3 units of Workers
Time: 634.424 Btruck44 holds for 10.602
Time: 638.918 Big T Arrivals  holds for 4.21
Time: 638.918 Btruck45 requesting 1 units of Bays
Time: 638.918 Btruck45 acquired 1 units of Bays
Time: 638.918 Btruck45 holds for 1.45
Time: 639.933 Small T Arrivals  holds for 3.179
------------------------------------------------------------------

End Simulation of Busy Warehouse System
  date: 9/23/2008 time: 14:11
```

Listing 24.2 shows the listing with the summary statistics of the simulation run. The listing displays resource types used, the random number generators used, the total number of trucks serviced of each type, and the average wait period, for each type.

Listing 24.2 Summary statistics of a simulation run of the Warehouse model.

```
OOSimL model: Busy Warehouse System
Simulation date: date: 9/23/2008 time: 14:11
--------------------STATISTICS REPORT----------------------
------------------------------------------------------------------
Res Bays
Bays usage: 0.8585299019794168
 avg num Bays items used: 1.8061836569706509

% of time of Bays resource usage: 0.9506562620761964
Avg waiting time for Bays: 2.5500048924851084
Avg. num waiting processes: 2.5683087642958395
% of time spent waiting for Bays resources: 0.7695569252035672
------------------------------------------------------------------
Res Workers
Workers usage: 0.6476054685731456
 avg num Workers items used: 3.5306934454374033

% of time of Workers resource usage: 0.9171080392295521
Avg waiting time for Workers: 7.638598375234128
```

```
Avg. num waiting processes: 1.0
% of time spent waiting for Workers resources: 0.3103504064311
------------------------------------------------------------------
Random generator: Small truck Inter-arr
Distribution: Negative exponential
Number of obs: 38
Seed: 15
Mean: 13.1
------------------------------------------------------------------
Random generator: Big truck Inter-arr
Distribution: Negative exponential
Number of obs: 46
Seed: 7
Mean: 14.2
------------------------------------------------------------------
Random generator: Small truck service
Distribution: Uniform
Number of obs: 37
Seed: 0
Lower bound: 5.3
Upper bound: 9.35
------------------------------------------------------------------
Random generator: Big truck service
Distribution: Uniform
Number of obs: 45
Seed: 0
Lower bound: 8.5
Upper bound: 14.5
------------------------------------------------------------------

End Simulation of Busy Warehouse System
date: 9/23/2008 time: 14:11

Total small trucks serviced: 36
Average period small truck spends in warehouse: 24.759
Small truck average wait period: 17.113
Total number of big trucks serviced: 43
Big truck average wait period: 21.189
Avg per btruck in warehouse: 34.101
```

Listing 24.3 shows the source code for class *Btruck*. The complete model implementation of the Warehouse model is stored in the archive file, `wareh.jar`. This archive includes the following source files: `Wareh.osl`, `Sarrivals.osl`, `Barrivals.osl`, `Struck.osl`, and `Btruck.osl`.

Listing 24.3. Code implementation of class Btruck of the Warehouse model.

```
use all psimjava
description
    A model of a busy warehouse system
    Small and big trucks constantly arrive to a warehouse to
    unload goods. Each truck needs an unloading bay to dock
    and start unloading. Big trucks need three workers and a
```

```
      constant time interval for docking and undocking. Trucks
      may need to wait for an available unloading bay and/or
      wait for available workers.
      Both types of trucks have different mean arrival rates
      and different mean unloading periods.
      The warehouse has 2 unloading bays and 5 workers.

      OOSimL model, J. Garrido, September 2008.

       class:   Btruck
       File:    Btruck.osl
       This class defines the behavior of big trucks

*/
public class Btruck as process is
  private
  constants
     define DOCK_INTERV = 1.45 of type double
     define UNDOCK_INTERV = 1.15 of type double
  variables
     define truckNum of type integer     // Truck number
     define arrivalTime of type double   // arrival time
     define service_dur of type double   // unloading interv
     define bname of type string
  //
  public
  function initializer parameters btname of type string,
              unload_dur of type double is
  begin
    call super using btname
    set truckNum = Wareh.get_bnumArr()
    assign simulation clock to arrivalTime
    set service_dur = unload_dur      // unloading interval
    set bname = btname
  endfun initializer
  //
  function get_arrivalT return type double
  is begin
    return arrivalTime
  endfun get_arrivalT
  //
  function get_serv_dur return type double is
  begin
    return service_dur
  endfun get_serv_dur
  //
  function Main_body is
    variables
      define start_wait of type double  // starts wait
      define wait_p of type double      // wait interval
      define bsojourn of type double    // total interval
      define simclock of type double
    begin
      // setb the start wait time for this truck
```

```
        assign simulation clock to start_wait
        //
        display bname, " request unloading bay at ", start_wait
        // tracewrite bname, " request unloading bay "
        // process will wait for an unload bay
        //
        acquire 1 units from Wareh.bays          // 1 unloading bay
        //
        assign simulation clock to simclock
        display bname, " acquired unloading bay at: ", simclock
        //
        // docking
        hold self for DOCK_INTERV
        //
        display bname, " requesting 3 workers at ", simclock
        //
        // process will wait until 2 workers become available
        //
        acquire 3 units from Wareh.workers    // 3 workers
        //
        assign simulation clock to simclock
        display bname, " acquired workers at: ", simclock
        //
        // wait period for this truck
        set wait_p = get_clock() - start_wait
        // accumulate truck wait interval
        call Wareh.accumBWait using wait_p    // accumulate wait
        //
        // now the unloading service of the truck
        hold self for service_dur        // unloading interval
        //
        // service completed, release workers
        //
        release 3 units of Wareh.workers
        //
        // undock
        hold self for UNDOCK_INTERV
        //
        // ok, now release the bay
        release 1 units of Wareh.bays
        //
        // increment num big trucks serviced
        call Wareh.incr_bigTserv

        // total time in warehouse: bSojourn
        set bsojourn = get_clock() - arrivalTime
        // accumulate sojourn time
        call Wareh.accum_Bsojourn using bsojourn
        //
        assign simulation clock to simclock
        display bname, " terminates at ", simclock
        terminate self     //terminates itself
    endfun Main_body
endclass Btruck
```

24.4 Allocating Resources with Priorities

In the model of the Warehouse system, the processes compete for mutual exclusive access to resources, all with the same default priority (priority 0). In larger models, processes may have different priorities.

A process that is assigned a lower priority than the default, needs to use a priority higher than zero.

Assigning a higher priority to a process affects the behavior of the simulation model because processes are placed by priority in the hidden resource queue when they need to wait for resources. Priority with value zero corresponds to the highest priority. Processes with higher priority will be given preference in the allocation of resources.

24.5 Deadlock

When competing with each other for several resources, a set of processes may reach a state of deadlock. Processes that have already acquired one or more resources and are requesting other resources, may have to wait indefinitely.

Every process in the set waits until another process releases the resources that it needs. The processes are actually waiting for each other.

The simulation language and libraries do not automatically avoid, prevent, or detect deadlock. The model designer has to apply one of many techniques for preventing or avoiding deadlock that are explained in specialized literature.

24.6 Summary

Standard resource manipulation involves basic resource synchronization with mutual exclusive resources. A resource type in a simulation model is defined as a resource pool with an initial number of available resource units of that resource type. Every resource pool is created as an object of the *Res* library class. The resource units can only be held by one process at a time. The process needs to acquire the resources, use the resources for some finite interval of time, and then release all or part of the number of resources held. When a process is waiting for available resources, it is suspended and placed (by priority) in a hidden queue owned by the resource pool.

Priorities in processes are important in allocating resources. Another important concept is the notion of deadlock. This may occur if the order of the allocation of resources of different types to set of processes is not carefully selected. Deadlock is a condition of indefinite waiting for resources that other processes hold but will not release because they are also waiting for other resources.

Exercises

24.1. Modify the model of the Carwash system using resources. Change the server to a resource instead of an active process. Retain the nature of arrival rates and service times. Run the simulation for the same period of system with priorities. What advantages does it have to have the Carwash machine as a resource? Discuss.

24.2. Modify the model of the busy Warehouse system to induce deadlock. Why does deadlock now occur?

24.3. Assume that in exercise 1 there are additional resources for the cars: workers. How would you allocate these resources?

24.4. Modify Exercise 24.3 to use optional resources, that is, resources that will only be acquired if they are available. Is there any advantage in using optional resources?

24.5. Modify the model of the busy Warehouse, by introducing higher priority to the big trucks. Run several simulations with the same workloads and analyze the different performance measures.

24.6. A simple port system provides two piers and three tugs for arriving ships. The resource types are the piers and the tugs. There are two types of processes, big ships, and small ships. The ships arrive at the port to unload their cargo. A ship cannot dock if it cannot acquire the appropriate number of tugs and a pier. To undock and leave, a ship needs to acquire a tug.

Several ships of each type arrive to the port to unload their cargo. The ships arrive, dock, unload, and leave. The small ships need one pier and one tug to dock after they arrive. The big ships need one pier and two tugs to dock. After the ships unload, all ships need one tug to depart.

24.7. Modify the model in the previous exercise to include big ships having a higher priority.

Chapter 25
Detachable Resources

25.1 Introduction

Detachable resources behave in a different manner compared to the standard resources. Objects of *detachable resources* are *infinite containers* created with an initial number of resource units. The resource container has no upper limit in the number of resource units in it. With these resources another type of process synchronization is involved, the producer-consumer resource *synchronization*.

25.2 Infinite Containers

A process can add more resource units and another process can remove resource units. A process will not normally return the resource units taken from the container. Some processes behave as producers of resource items, other process behave as consumers.

A producer generates resource units that are placed into the resource container and the consumer takes resource units from the container.

The consumer process is suspended if there are no resource units available in the resource container. The producer process increases the number of available resource units and the consumer process decreases the number of resource units in the resource container.

This handling of detachable resources involves a type of *synchronization* between the producer process and the consumer process. The simplest type of synchronization is in the form of *cooperation* between the consumer and producer processes.

J.M. Garrido, *Object Oriented Simulation: A Modeling and Programming Perspective*,   331
DOI: 10.1007/978-1-4419-0516-1_25,
© Springer Science + Business Media, LLC 2009

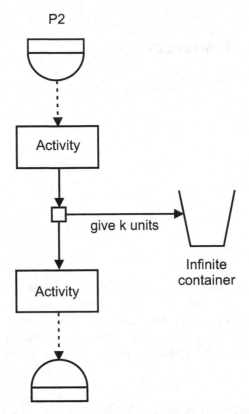

Fig. 25.1 A producer process and a detachable resource container

25.3 Producer and Consumer Processes

A producer process generates resource items and this activity takes a finite interval of time. The process then places or *gives* the resource items into a resource container. Figure 25.1 shows a simplified activity diagram that illustrates a producer process placing k resource items into a container. The process will never have to wait because the resource object is an infinite container.

A consumer process *takes* a number of resource items from a resource container and then spends some finite interval of time using these items. Figure 25.2 shows a consumer process that takes k resource items from a resource container.

If the number of available resource items in the resource container is not sufficient for the consumer's request, the consumer process is suspended (and placed in a hidden queue that belongs to the resource container object). The consumer process will attempt again to take the specified number of resources when it is reactivated, until it finally gets the requested resource items.

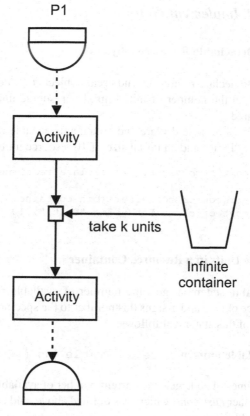

Fig. 25.2 Activity diagram for a consumer process

25.4 Implementing Detachable Resources

The following steps are carried out to implement a detachable resource container in a simulation model.

1. Declare the reference to the resource container object of class *Bin*.
2. Create the resource container with a title and an initial number of resource items.
3. A producer process:

    a. Spends a finite interval to produce a number of resource items.
    b. Places, or gives, a number of resource items into the resource container.

4. A consumer process:

    a. Removes, or takes, a number of resource items from the resource container.
    b. Spends a finite interval of time to use (consume) the resource items.

25.4.1 OOSimL Implementation

25.4.1.1 Create Detachable Resource Objects

Class *Bin* is used to declare references and create objects of a detachable resource container. A title and the number of initial number resource units in the resource container are required.

The following lines of code declare and create a detachable resource container, *cust_cont*, with title "Parts" and an initial size of 10 resource units.

```
define cust_cont of class Bin // declare resource container
...
// create the resource container (bin container)
create cust_cont of class Bin using "Parts", 10
```

25.4.1.2 Available Units in a Resource Container

The **assign available** statement gets the number of available resource units in a detachable resource object, and assigns this number to the specified integer variable. The general form of this statement follows.

> **assign available units of** ⟨ ref_variable ⟩ **to** ⟨ var_name ⟩

The following lines of code gets the current number of available resource units in the resource container *cust_cont*, which was defined above, and assigns this number to the integer variable *num_units*.

```
define num_units of type integer
...
assign available units of cust_cont to num_units
```

25.4.1.3 Take Units from a Resource Container

A process can remove a specified number of units from the detachable resource object using the **take** statement. If there are sufficient units in the resource container, the process takes these units and continues normally. When the operation completes, the number of resource units in the resource container is decreased by the number of resource items taken by the process.

If there are not sufficient resource units available, the process is suspended and waits for available resource units. The general form of the **take** statement follows.

> **take** ⟨ int_variable ⟩ **units from** ⟨ ref_variable ⟩

The following lines of code allow a process to take 10 resource units from the *cust_cont* container (defined above).

```
take 10 units from cust_cont
// execute after resource units are taken
```

25.4.1.4 Give Resource Units to a Resource Container

A process uses the **give** statement to insert (or give) a specified number of resource units to a detachable container object. This places a specified number of resource units into the container. The number of units in the container is then updated. The general form of the statement follows.

> **give** ⟨ int_variable ⟩ **units to** ⟨ ref_variable ⟩

In the following lines of code, a process places 8 resource units, which is stored in integer variable *num_units*, into the *cust_cont* resource container (defined above).

```
define num_units of type integer
...
set num_units = 8
...
give num_units units to cust_cont
```

25.4.2 Producer Process

In the following statements, the behavior of a basic producer process is implemented. This is shown in Figure 25.1. The resource container was declared and created with name *steel_bolts*.

```
hold self for produce_items  // interval to produce items
give k units to steel_bolts  // deposit k items into container
```

In the code above, the producer process spends *produce_items* time units to produce the resource items. After this time interval has elapsed, the producer process gives two items to the resource container.

25.4.3 Consumer Process

The following lines of code implement the basic behavior of a consumer process, as shown in Figure 25.2.

```
// attempt to remove items from resource container
take k units from steel_bolts
hold self for consume_items  // time interval to consume items
. . .
```

If there are not sufficient items in the resource container, the consumer process is suspended and placed in the hidden queue of the resource object. If there are sufficient items available in the resource container, the consumer continues normally and spends a time interval consuming the items. The number of items in the container is reduced accordingly.

A suspended consumer process is reactivated when it is at the head of the resource queue and another process has given items to the resource container. When this happens, the consumer process again tests if it can take two items from the resource container.

25.5 A Machine Parts-Replacement System

There are several machines in a shop, each having a part that fails periodically. The part that fails needs to be removed from the machine, and a replacement part installed, if available. This removal and replacement of parts is carried out by a repairman. The parts that fail are to be repaired by the repairman, who also has other jobs to carry out when not repairing parts.

In this model, there are two process definitions, *Machine* and *Repairman*; these are implemented as OOSimL classes. Several machine objects and one repairman object are created.

The model also includes two different resource containers, which are implemented as objects of class *Bin*. These resource containers are:

- The parts that fail, *fault_parts*;
- The replacement parts, *rep_parts*. These are the parts that have been repaired.

The machine processes are producers of damaged parts; they give items to the *fault_parts* resource container. The machine processes are also consumers of replacement parts; they take items from the *rep_parts* resource container. Figure 25.3 shows a simplified activity diagram of the machine process with the two resource containers.

The repairman process is a consumer of damaged parts; it takes items from the *fault_parts* resource container. The repairman process is also a producer of replacement parts; it gives items to the *rep_parts* resource container.

Listing 25.1 shows the listing of the results summary of a simulation run with this model. The output listing includes the resource container usage and performance metrics; these are average machine up period, the average down period, the machine utilization, and the repairman utilization.

Listing 25.1 Summary results of a simulation run of the model.

```
OOSimL model: Machine Parts Replacement System
Simulation date: date: 9/28/2008 time: 11:34
Mean oper. interval: 162.5 mean repair interval: 13.3
-------------------STATISTICS REPORT-----------------
```

Machine

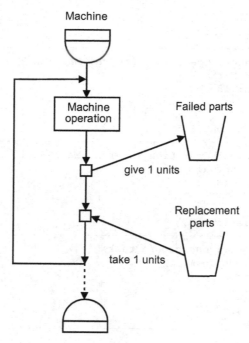

Fig. 25.3 Activity diagram of the machine process

```
-----------------------------------------------------------
Replacement parts
Number of completed operations: 51
Max items: 15
Avg num available items: 13.850104111136883

-----------------------------------------------------------
-----------------------------------------------------------
Fault parts
Number of completed operations: 51
Max items: 3
Avg num available items: 0.7108392461027906


-----------------------------------------------------------
-----------------------------------------------------------
Random generator: repair interval
Distribution: Normal
Number of obs: 51
Seed: 25
Mean: 13.3
Standard deviation: 0.5
-----------------------------------------------------------
Random generator: Operation interval Machine 3
Distribution: Normal
Number of obs: 18
Seed: 19
```

```
Mean: 162.5
Standard deviation: 6.5
-------------------------------------------------------
Random generator: Operation interval Machine 2
Distribution: Normal
Number of obs: 18
Seed: 13
Mean: 162.5
Standard deviation: 6.5
-------------------------------------------------------
Random generator: Operation interval Machine 1
Distribution: Normal
Number of obs: 18
Seed: 7
Mean: 162.5
Standard deviation: 6.5
-------------------------------------------------------
Random generator: background task
Distribution: Uniform
Number of obs: 67
Seed: 0
Lower bound: 28.45
Upper bound: 62.3
-------------------------------------------------------

End Simulation of Machine Parts Replacement System
  date: 9/28/2008 time: 11:34

Total machines serviced: 3
Average down period: 15.299999999998931
Average up period: 2782.15476170466
Average machine utilization: 0.7273607220142901
```

Listing 25.2 shows the trace output of the simulation run. The listing shows the various time events, mainly when each process starts to wait for a requested part and when it gets the part.

Listing 25.2 Trace output of a simulation run of the model.

```
OOSimL model: Machine Parts Replacement System
Simulation date: 9/28/2008 time: 11:34
------------------------- TRACE ----------------------------
Time: 0 Mean oper. interval: 162.5 mean repair interval: 13.3
Time: 0 Machine Shop holds for 3825
Time: 0 Machine 1 to oper for 167.9938394270824
Time: 0 Machine 1 holds for 167.994
Time: 0 Machine 2 to oper for 173.4387407155666
Time: 0 Machine 2 holds for 173.439
Time: 0 Machine 3 to oper for 171.1538128332344
Time: 0 Machine 3 holds for 171.154
Time: 0 Repairman to perform background task
Time: 0 Repairman holds for 53.208
Time: 53.208 Repairman to perform background task
```

```
Time: 53.208 Repairman holds for 41.747
Time: 94.955 Repairman to perform background task
Time: 94.955 Repairman holds for 55.054
Time: 150.009 Repairman to perform background task
Time: 150.009 Repairman holds for 50.081
Time: 167.994 Machine 1 failed
Time: 167.994 Machine 1 holds for 0.45
Time: 168.444 Machine 1 gives 1 of Fault parts
Time: 168.444 Replacement parts available: 15
Time: 168.444 Machine 1 requesting 1 of Replacement parts
Time: 168.444 Machine 1 took 1 of Replacement parts
Time: 168.444 Machine 1 holds for 0.45
Time: 168.894 Machine 1 took replacement
Time: 168.894 Machine 1 to oper for 168.43369516189736
Time: 168.894 Machine 1 holds for 168.434
Time: 171.154 Machine 3 failed
Time: 171.154 Machine 3 holds for 0.45
Time: 171.604 Machine 3 gives 1 of Fault parts
Time: 171.604 Replacement parts available: 14
Time: 171.604 Machine 3 requesting 1 of Replacement parts
Time: 171.604 Machine 3 took 1 of Replacement parts
Time: 171.604 Machine 3 holds for 0.45
Time: 172.054 Machine 3 took replacement
Time: 172.054 Machine 3 to oper for 157.22493327498918
Time: 172.054 Machine 3 holds for 157.225
Time: 173.439 Machine 2 failed
Time: 173.439 Machine 2 holds for 0.45
Time: 173.889 Machine 2 gives 1 of Fault parts
Time: 173.889 Replacement parts available: 13
Time: 173.889 Machine 2 requesting 1 of Replacement parts
Time: 173.889 Machine 2 took 1 of Replacement parts
Time: 173.889 Machine 2 holds for 0.45
Time: 174.339 Machine 2 took replacement
Time: 174.339 Machine 2 to oper for 159.86357967388378
Time: 174.339 Machine 2 holds for 159.864
Time: 200.09 Repairman num of faulty parts 3
Time: 200.09 Repairman requesting 1 of Fault parts
Time: 200.09 Repairman took 1 of Fault parts
Time: 200.09 Repairman to repair part
Time: 200.09 Repairman to repair task for 13.40529040458385
Time: 200.09 Repairman holds for 13.405
Time: 213.496 Repairman done repairing
Time: 213.496 Repairman gives 1 of Replacement parts
Time: 213.496 Repairman num of faulty parts 2
Time: 213.496 Repairman requesting 1 of Fault parts
. . .
Time: 2843.673 Repairman took 1 of Fault parts
Time: 2843.673 Repairman to repair part
Time: 2843.673 Repairman to repair task for 13.620773138276915
Time: 2843.673 Repairman holds for 13.621
Time: 2857.294 Repairman done repairing
Time: 2857.294 Repairman gives 1 of Replacement parts
Time: 2857.294 Repairman to perform background task
Time: 2857.294 Repairman holds for 43.982
```

```
Time: 2901.276 Repairman to perform background task
Time: 2901.276 Repairman holds for 58.623
Time: 2959.899 Repairman to perform background task
Time: 2959.899 Repairman holds for 52.357
Time: 3012.256 Repairman to perform background task
Time: 3012.256 Repairman holds for 36.656
Time: 3048.912 Repairman to perform background task
Time: 3048.912 Repairman holds for 41.792
Time: 3090.705 Repairman to perform background task
Time: 3090.705 Repairman holds for 41.374
Time: 3132.079 Repairman to perform background task
Time: 3132.079 Repairman holds for 28.584
Time: 3160.662 Repairman to perform background task
Time: 3160.662 Repairman holds for 57.878
Time: 3218.54 Repairman to perform background task
Time: 3218.54 Repairman holds for 57.038
Time: 3275.578 Repairman to perform background task
Time: 3275.578 Repairman holds for 32.777
Time: 3308.355 Repairman to perform background task
Time: 3308.355 Repairman holds for 47.549
Time: 3355.905 Repairman to perform background task
Time: 3355.905 Repairman holds for 42.427
Time: 3398.332 Repairman to perform background task
Time: 3398.332 Repairman holds for 54.187
Time: 3452.519 Repairman to perform background task
Time: 3452.519 Repairman holds for 47.558
Time: 3500.077 Repairman to perform background task
Time: 3500.077 Repairman holds for 49.724
Time: 3549.801 Repairman to perform background task
Time: 3549.801 Repairman holds for 55.71
Time: 3605.511 Repairman to perform background task
Time: 3605.511 Repairman holds for 44.614
Time: 3650.125 Repairman to perform background task
Time: 3650.125 Repairman holds for 28.934
Time: 3679.059 Repairman to perform background task
Time: 3679.059 Repairman holds for 48.797
Time: 3727.856 Repairman to perform background task
Time: 3727.856 Repairman holds for 59.229
Time: 3787.085 Repairman to perform background task
Time: 3787.085 Repairman terminating
End Simulation of Machine Parts Replacement System
  date: 9/28/2008 time: 11:34
```

Listing25.3 shows the implementation of class *Machine*. The source files with implementations for all classes are stored in archive file `preplace.jar`. This archive includes files: `Preplace.osl`, `Machine.osl`, and `Repairman.osl`.

Listing 25.3 Source code with implementation of class Machine.

```
use all psimjava
description
  A model of machine parts replacement system.
  Several machines in a shop each have a part that fails
```

periodically. The part that fails needs to be removed from
the machine, and a replacement part, if available, installed.
The parts that fail are to be repaired by a repairman, who
also have other jobs to carry out when not repairing parts.

OOSimL model, J. Garrido, September 2008.
This class defines behavior of Machine objects

```
*/
class Machine as process is
private
variables
    define machineNum of type integer    // machine number
    define mean_oper of type double       // operation interval
    define st_dev of type double          // standard deviation
    define simclock of type double        // current sim time
    define removal_per = 0.45 of type double
    define replace_per = 0.45 of type double
    define start_wait of type double    // start to wait
    define wait_p of type double        // wait interval
    define total_oper of type double
    define mname of type string           // name of machine
object references
    define oper_rand of class Normal    // random generator
public
 function initializer parameters pname of type string,
       oper_dur of type double, std of type double
 is
begin
    call super using pname
    set mean_oper = oper_dur
    set st_dev = std
    create oper_rand of class Normal
        using "Operation interval " concat pname,
        mean_oper, st_dev
endfun initializer
//
function Main_body is
variables
    define operation_per of type double // operation interval
    define opercmp of type double        // completion time

    define rep_flag = true of type boolean
begin
    set mname = get_name()
    set total_oper = 0.75 * Preplace.simPeriod
    assign simulation clock to simclock
    while simclock < total_oper and rep_flag do
      // display mname," starting at ", simclock
      // tracewrite mname," starting"
      assign random value from oper_rand to operation_per
      display mname, " to oper for ", operation_per,
          " at ", simclock
      tracewrite mname, " to oper for ", operation_per
      //
```

```
        // completion of operation
        set opercmp = simclock + operation_per
        if ( opercmp < total_oper)
        then
            hold self for operation_per      // operation interval
            // part failed
            assign simulation clock to simclock
            display mname, " failed at ", simclock
            tracewrite mname, " failed"
            //
            // remove faulty part and replace
            call remov_rep
            //
            // now compute this wait period
            set wait_p = simclock - start_wait
            add wait_p to Preplace.adown           // accumulate wait
            // accumulate operation intervals
            add operation_per to Preplace.aserv
        else
            set rep_flag = false
        endif
    endwhile
    display mname, " terminating at: ", simclock
    terminate self
endfun Main_body
//
function remov_rep is
variables
        define removcmp of type double    // removal completion
        define availrep of type integer   // available rep parts
begin
        // now remove and replace part
        //
        assign simulation clock to simclock
        set start_wait = simclock
        set removcmp = simclock + removal_per
        if  removcmp < total_oper
        then
            hold self for removal_per            // removal of part
            assign simulation clock to simclock
            display mname, " requesting replacement at ",
simclock
            //
            // pace in container the damaged part to repair
            give 1 units to Preplace.fault_parts           //
            // process will try until replacement available
            assign available units of Preplace.rep_parts
              to availrep
            display "Rep parts available: ", availrep
            tracewrite "Replacement parts available: ", availrep
            //
            take 1 units from Preplace.rep_parts
            //
            hold self for replace_per
```

```
        assign simulation clock to simclock
        display mname, " took replacement at: ", simclock
        tracewrite mname, " took replacement"
      endif
   endfun remov_rep
 endclass Machine
```

25.6 Summary

Detachable resource objects behave as infinite containers, in which items are placed in and taken from. Basic process interaction that appears is process cooperation and is described in the form of producer-consumer synchronization.

The processes that use detachable resource containers are usually called producer and consumer processes. A process that attempts to take items from a detachable resource container will be suspended if there are no resource items available (or not a sufficient number of such items) in the resource container. The suspended process will be reactivated when another object (producer) gives items to the resource container and this process is at the head of the resource queue. These resource containers are useful to simulate inter-process communication and other process interactions.

25.7 Exercises

1. Modify the Parts-replacement model so that it would have several repairmen.
2. Modify the Parts-replacement model to include machine objects with different priorities.
3. Extend the Parts-replacement model that includes an additional stage to deliver the damage part from the machine to the repairman.
4. In Exercise 3, consider that the delivery of damaged parts and the return of repaired parts needs the availability of carts to carry the parts.
5. Modify Exercise 3 to include different machine parts that fail at different times. Run the simulation model and identify the difference in performance with respect to the exercises above.

Chapter 26
Synchronous Process Cooperation

26.1 Introduction

Synchronous cooperation results among two or more processes when executing a
joint activity during a finite time interval called the *cooperation interval*. For the
processes to carry out the joint activity, the simultaneous participation of the processes is required during the time interval of cooperation. At the end of this joint
activity, the processes will continue independently with their individual activities.

  This chapter discusses the principles of synchronous cooperation among processes, and presents a case study with a simulation model that implements synchronous communication among a set of sender and receive processes.

26.2 Joint Process Activities

In order for two processes to take part in a joint activity, one of the processes takes a
more active role in the interaction and designated as the *master*; the other process is
designated as the *slave* during the cooperation interval. The master is the dominant
process and the slave behaves subordinated to the master process during the joint
activity.

  When the interaction starts, the slave process is suspended until the end of the
cooperation interval. The master process then reactivates the slave process, and the
two processes will continue their own independent activities. When the slave process is not available, the master process has to wait and is suspended until a slave
process becomes available.

  Figure 26.1 illustrates the master and slave processes cooperating in a joint activity. The figure shows the partial timelines of the two processes. The slave process
becomes subordinated to the master process during the interval of cooperation.

J.M. Garrido, *Object Oriented Simulation: A Modeling and Programming Perspective*,
DOI: 10.1007/978-1-4419-0516-1_26,
© Springer Science + Business Media, LLC 2009

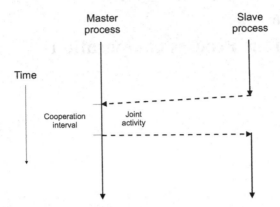

Fig. 26.1 Interaction of master and slave processes

26.3 Synchronization Mechanism

The synchronization mechanism needed for the process cooperation discussed is provided by objects of class *Waitq*, known as cooperation objects. These objects support the cooperation of multiple slave processes and multiple master processes. Every cooperation object has two hidden queues: the slave queue and the master queue.

At the beginning of the interaction, the slave processes are suspended and placed in the slave queue until the end of the cooperation interval. A master process then reactivates a slave process. At the end of the cooperation interval, the processes will continue their own independent activities. When one of or more of the slave processes are not available, a master process has to wait suspended and placed in the master queue.

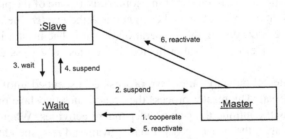

Fig. 26.2 Cooperation of master and slave processes with a cooperation object

A slave process that requests cooperation with a master process, executes the **wait** statement. A master process that requests cooperation with a slave process, executes the **cooperate** statement. Figure 26.2 is a UML diagram that shows the process cooperation between a master process and a slave process using a cooperation object of class *Waitq*.

Figure 26.3 shows the simulation activity diagram of two processes, P1 and P2, cooperating in a joint activity. Process P1 is the slave and process P2 is the master process. The two processes start with their own individual activities (*Act.1a* and *Act.2a*) then they initiate the cooperation by using the facilities provided by the cooperating object of class *Waitq*. Process P1 gets suspended by the cooperating object. After executing the joint activity, process P2 reactivates process P1. From this point on, both processes continue with their independent activities, *Act.1b* and *Act.2b*.

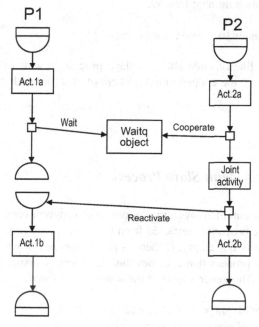

Fig. 26.3 Activity diagram with cooperation of master and slave processes

26.3.1 Creating Cooperation Objects in OOSimL

Cooperation objects are created with class *Waitq*. The objects are created and initialized with a title and an optional maximum number of priorities to use. Cooperation objects have two internal priority queues, one for the *master* processes and one for the *slave* processes.

The following lines of code declare a cooperation object, *coopt_cust*, and create the object with title "Channel A", and with the default number of priorities.

```
define coopt_cust of class Waitq
...
create coopt_cust of class Waitq using "Channel A"
```

26.3.2 Wait to Cooperate

The **wait** statement places current process in the slave queue of the cooperation
object and suspends it to wait for a master process. This allows a slave process
to cooperate with a master process, when there is a master process available. The
general form of this statement follows.

> **wait for master in** ⟨ ref_variable ⟩

The following line of code allows a slave process to wait to cooperate with a
master process using the cooperation object *coopt_cust* (defined above).

```
wait for master in coopt_cust     // wait for master process
...
```

26.3.3 Cooperate with Slave Process

The **cooperate** statement allows a master process to attempt cooperation with slave
processes. A slave process is retrieved from the slave queue of the cooperation object, if this queue is not empty. If there is no slave process available in the slave
queue, the master process that executes this statement is suspended and placed in
the master queue. The general form of the statement follows.

> **cooperate with slave** ⟨ ref_variable ⟩
> **of class** ⟨ cl_name ⟩ **in** ⟨ ref_variable ⟩

The following lines of code allow a master process to attempt cooperation with
a slave process using the *coopt_cust* synchronization object. When the cooperation
becomes possible, a slave process is removed from the slave queue, the master process continues executing normally. Otherwise, the process is suspended to wait for
a slave process.

```
define custobj of class Customer
...
cooperate with slave custobj of class Customer in coopt_cust
// execute when a slave is found
```

26.3.4 Length of Slave Queue

The **assign length** statement assigns the length (number of processes) in the slave queue to a specified variable. This value represents the number of slave processes waiting on the cooperation (synchronization) object. The general form of the statement follows.

> **assign length of slave queue** ⟨ ref_variable ⟩ **to** ⟨ var_name ⟩

The following lines of code gets the number of slave processes waiting in the *coopt_cust* object defined above and stores the value in variable *num_slaves*.

```
define num_slaves of type integer
...
assign length of slave queue coopt_cust to num_slaves
```

26.3.5 Length of Master Queue

The **assign length** statement gets the length of the master queue (i.e., the number of master processes waiting on the cooperation object), and assigns it to the specified variable. The general form of the statement follows.

> **assign length of master queue** ⟨ ref_variable ⟩
> **to** ⟨ var_name ⟩

The following lines of code get the number of master processes waiting in master queue of the cooperation object *coopt_cust* defined above, and store this integer value into variable *num_master*.

```
define num_master of type integer
...
assign length of master queue coopt_cust to num_master
```

26.4 Cooperation with Several Slaves

A master process can cooperate in a joint activity with several slave objects. The master process creates a separate queue to place the slave processes. For example, a master process that needs to cooperate with N slave processes defines and creates a queue to place each reference to slave process.

The following code shows N slave processes that cooperate in a joint activity with the master process. The slave processes are placed in queue, *s_queue*, during the cooperation. This queue is owned by the master process. The duration of the cooperation interval is stored in the variable *coop_int*. At the end of the cooperation interval, the master process removes each slave process and reactivates it. The master process then performs its own activities. The passive object *waitq_obj* of class *Waitq*, is defined in the main class of the model.

```
constants
   define N = 25 of type integer
variables
   define numslaves of type integer    // number of slaves
object references
   define s_queue of class Pqueue       // priority queue
   define slave_ref of class Slave
   . . .
   set numslaves = 0
   create s_queue = of class Pqueue using "Slave queue"
   . . .
   while numslaves < N do
      cooperate with slave slave_ref of class Slave
           in waitq_obj
      insert slave_ref into s_queue      // enqueue
           into slave queue
      increment numslaves
   endwhile
   //
   // carry out joint activity
   hold self for coop_int         // cooperation interval
   // now release slave processes
   for j = 0 to N-1 do
      remove slave_ref of class Slave from s_queue
      reactivate slave_ref now
   endfor
   . . .
```

26.5 Synchronous Process Communication

A synchronous communication of two processes occurs when a sender process and a receiver process are engaged in a joint activity of *data transfer*. Because this is synchronous communication, both processes need to participate simultaneously during the interval of cooperation.

A sender process attempts to send a message and is suspended if the receiver process is not willing to receive the message at that time. In the same manner, a receiver process is suspended if it attempts to receive a message but the sender is not available to cooperate at the same time. A *channel* is the means of communication between the sender and the receiver processes.

Figure 26.4 shows a UML communication diagram that illustrates direct communication between a sender process and a receiver process. As mentioned previously, the synchronization occurs when executing a specific communication task or activity in the sender simultaneously with a communication activity in the receiver. The channel is used as a carrier of the message in transfer from the sender process to the receiver process.

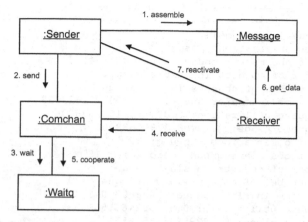

Fig. 26.4 UML diagram with synchronous communication of two processes

After the cooperation interval, the receiver process (master) reactivates the sender process (slave), and from this time on, each process continues with its own independent activities.

26.6 Process Cooperation Model

The simulation model explained is an implementation of the objects shown in Figure 26.4 that shows the interaction among five objects, of which only two are active objects, the sender and the receiver processes. The cooperation object of class *Waitq* implements the mechanism that controls the interaction of the sender and receiver processes. This cooperation object is used by the channel, implemented as an object of class *Comchan*. The data sent by the sender process and received by the receiver process is assembled into an object of class *Message*.

The simulation model consists of five pairs of sender and receiver processes and is implemented with five classes written with OOSimL. There is a channel for each pair of sender and receiver. The source files are: Scomm.osl, Sender.osl, Receiver, Comchan, Message. These source files are archived in the file scomm.jar, which also includes the output listings of a sample simulation run.

Listing 26.1 shows the listing of the results summary of a simulation run with this model. The output listing includes performance metrics such as: the average wait times for the sender and receiver processes and the total number of messages successfully sent and received, and the channel utilization.

Listing 26.1 Summary results of a simulation run of the model.

```
OOSimL model: Synchronous communication with channels
Simulation date: date: 10/7/2008 time: 14:36
-------------------STATISTICS REPORT--------------------
-----------------------------------------------------------
Wait queue: synChannel4
Number of observations master q: 59
Number of obs master queue  zero wait: 44
Max number of objects in master queue: 1
Average number of objects in master queue: 0
Average time in master queue: 16.14204921623553
Master queue utilization: 0.09458231962638006
Master queue usage: 0.09458231962638006
Number of observations slave q: 59
Number of obs slave queue  zero wait: 15
Max number of objects in slave queue: 1
Average number of objects in slave queue: 0
Average time in slave queue: 24.8603104133925
Slave queue utilization: 0.5729524665586553
Slave queue usage: 0.5729524665586553
-----------------------------------------------------------
Wait queue: synChannel3
Number of observations master q: 44
Number of obs master queue  zero wait: 33
Max number of objects in master queue: 1
Average number of objects in master queue: 0
Average time in master queue: 14.959279939894998
Master queue utilization: 0.06427815599173632
Master queue usage: 0.06427815599173632
Number of observations slave q: 44
Number of obs slave queue  zero wait: 11
Max number of objects in slave queue: 1
Average number of objects in slave queue: 0
Average time in slave queue: 39.1784255397218
Slave queue utilization: 0.6733791889639684
Slave queue usage: 0.6733791889639684
-----------------------------------------------------------
Wait queue: synChannel2
Number of observations master q: 50
Number of obs master queue  zero wait: 35
Max number of objects in master queue: 1
Average number of objects in master queue: 0
Average time in master queue: 13.991424961906587
Master queue utilization: 0.08198100563617142
Master queue usage: 0.08198100563617142
Number of observations slave q: 50
Number of obs slave queue  zero wait: 15
Max number of objects in slave queue: 1
Average number of objects in slave queue: 0
Average time in slave queue: 31.532534115764385
Slave queue utilization: 0.6158698069485231
Slave queue usage: 0.6158698069485231
-----------------------------------------------------------
Wait queue: synChannel1
```

```
Number of observations master q: 60
Number of obs master queue  zero wait: 36
Max number of objects in master queue: 1
Average number of objects in master queue: 0
Average time in master queue: 13.581375576776347
Master queue utilization: 0.12732539603227827
Master queue usage: 0.12732539603227827
Number of observations slave q: 60
Number of obs slave queue  zero wait: 24
Max number of objects in slave queue: 1
Average number of objects in slave queue: 0
Average time in slave queue: 25.551580670991093
Slave queue utilization: 0.5988651719763538
Slave queue usage: 0.5988651719763538
------------------------------------------------------------
Wait queue: synChannel0
Number of observations master q: 46
Number of obs master queue  zero wait: 35
Max number of objects in master queue: 1
Average number of objects in master queue: 0
Average time in master queue: 12.631481116210853
Master queue utilization: 0.05427589542121851
Master queue usage: 0.05427589542121851
Number of observations slave q: 46
Number of obs slave queue  zero wait: 11
Max number of objects in slave queue: 1
Average number of objects in slave queue: 0
Average time in slave queue: 39.66874996934699
Slave queue utilization: 0.7127978510117037
Slave queue usage: 0.7127978510117037
------------------------------------------------------------
Random generator: Consume interval4
Distribution: Negative exponential
Number of obs: 59
Seed: 61
Mean: 42.75
------------------------------------------------------------
Random generator: Produce data interval4
Distribution: Negative exponential
Number of obs: 60
Seed: 5
Mean: 13.25
------------------------------------------------------------
Random generator: Consume interval3
Distribution: Negative exponential
Number of obs: 44
Seed: 49
Mean: 42.75
------------------------------------------------------------
Random generator: Produce data interval3
Distribution: Negative exponential
Number of obs: 45
Seed: 4
Mean: 13.25
```

```
------------------------------------------------------------
Random generator: Consume interval2
Distribution: Negative exponential
Number of obs: 50
Seed: 37
Mean: 42.75
------------------------------------------------------------
Random generator: Produce data interval2
Distribution: Negative exponential
Number of obs: 51
Seed: 3
Mean: 13.25
------------------------------------------------------------
Random generator: Consume interval1
Distribution: Negative exponential
Number of obs: 60
Seed: 25
Mean: 42.75
------------------------------------------------------------
Random generator: Produce data interval1
Distribution: Negative exponential
Number of obs: 61
Seed: 2
Mean: 13.25
------------------------------------------------------------
Random generator: Consume interval0
Distribution: Negative exponential
Number of obs: 46
Seed: 13
Mean: 42.75
------------------------------------------------------------
Random generator: Produce data interval0
Distribution: Negative exponential
Number of obs: 47
Seed: 1
Mean: 13.25
------------------------------------------------------------
Random generator: Comm int Channel4
Distribution: Normal
Number of obs: 59
Seed: 55
Mean: 3.45
Standard deviation: 0.75
------------------------------------------------------------
Random generator: Comm int Channel3
Distribution: Normal
Number of obs: 44
Seed: 43
Mean: 3.45
Standard deviation: 0.75
------------------------------------------------------------
Random generator: Comm int Channel2
Distribution: Normal
Number of obs: 50
```

```
Seed: 31
Mean: 3.45
Standard deviation: 0.75
-------------------------------------------------------------
Random generator: Comm int Channel1
Distribution: Normal
Number of obs: 60
Seed: 19
Mean: 3.45
Standard deviation: 0.75
-------------------------------------------------------------
Random generator: Comm int Channel0
Distribution: Normal
Number of obs: 46
Seed: 7
Mean: 3.45
Standard deviation: 0.75
-------------------------------------------------------------

End Simulation of Synchronous communication
    date: 10/7/2008 time: 14:36

Sender0 wait interval: 1824.7625
Receiver0 wait interval: 0138.9463
Sender1 wait interval: 1533.0948
Receiver1 wait interval: 0325.9530
Sender2 wait interval: 1576.6267
Receiver2 wait interval: 0209.8714
Sender3 wait interval: 1723.8507
Receiver3 wait interval: 0164.5521
Sender4 wait interval: 1466.7583
Receiver4 wait interval: 0242.1307
Average sender wait: 1625.0186
Average receiver wait: 0216.2907
```

Listing 26.2 shows a partial listing of the trace of a simulation run with this model.

Listing 26.2 Trace output of a simulation run of the model.

```
OOSimL model: Synchronous communication with channels
Simulation date: 10/7/2008 time: 14:36
----------------------- TRACE -----------------------------
Time: 0 Input Parameters:
Time: 0 Simulation period: 2560.0
Time: 0 Receiver mean consume interval: 42.75
Time: 0 Sender mean produce interval: 13.25
Time: 0 Number of rec/sender processes: 5
Time: 0 Synchronous Communication holds for 2560
Time: 0 Message No. 0 Computer Science sender
    Sender0 rec Receiver0
Time: 0 Sender0 holds for 17.392
Time: 0 Receiver0 attempting comm via Channel0
```

```
Time: 0 Receiver0 coopt with synChannel0
Time: 0 Message No. 1 Information Systems sender
   Sender1 rec Receiver1
Time: 0 Sender1 holds for 17.405
Time: 0 Receiver1 attempting comm via Channel1
Time: 0 Receiver1 coopt with synChannel1
Time: 0 Message No. 2 Kennesaw State University sender
   Sender2 rec Receiver2
Time: 0 Sender2 holds for 17.401
Time: 0 Receiver2 attempting comm via Channel2
Time: 0 Receiver2 coopt with synChannel2
Time: 0 Message No. 3 1000 Chastain Road sender
   Sender3 rec Receiver3
Time: 0 Sender3 holds for 17.379
Time: 0 Receiver3 attempting comm via Channel3
Time: 0 Receiver3 coopt with synChannel3
Time: 0 Message No. 4 Kennesaw, GA sender
   Sender4 rec Receiver4
Time: 0 Sender4 holds for 17.374
Time: 0 Receiver4 attempting comm via Channel4
Time: 0 Receiver4 coopt with synChannel4
Time: 17.374 Sender4 attempting to communicate via
   chan Channel4
Time: 17.374 Sender4 wait on synChannel4
Time: 17.374 Receiver4 holds for 4.745
Time: 17.379 Sender3 attempting to communicate via
   chan Channel3
Time: 17.379 Sender3 wait on synChannel3
Time: 17.379 Receiver3 holds for 3.79
Time: 17.392 Sender0 attempting to communicate via
   chan Channel0
Time: 17.392 Sender0 wait on synChannel0
Time: 17.392 Receiver0 holds for 4.084
Time: 17.401 Sender2 attempting to communicate via
   chan Channel2
Time: 17.401 Sender2 wait on synChannel2
Time: 17.401 Receiver2 holds for 4.567
Time: 17.405 Sender1 attempting to communicate via
   chan Channel1
Time: 17.405 Sender1 wait on synChannel1
Time: 17.405 Receiver1 holds for 4.449
Time: 21.169 Sender3 to reactivate
Time: 21.169 Receiver3 received message 3 via
   channel Channel3
Time: 21.169 Receiver3 received 1000 Chastain Road from
   sender: Sender3
Time: 21.169 Receiver3 holds for 55.886
Time: 21.169 Sender3 sent message # 3
Time: 21.169 Message No. 5 1000 Chastain Road sender
   Sender3 rec Receiver3
   . . .
Time: 2539.37 Receiver0 attempting comm via Channel0
Time: 2539.37 Receiver0 coopt with synChannel0
Time: 2542.24 Sender1 to reactivate
```

```
Time: 2542.24 Receiver1 received message 257 via
   channel Channel1
Time: 2542.24 Receiver1 received Information Systems from
   sender: Sender1
Time: 2542.24 Receiver1 holds for 109.153
Time: 2542.24 Sender1 sent message # 257
Time: 2542.24 Message No. 262 Information Systems sender
   Sender1 rec Receiver1
Time: 2542.24 Sender1 holds for 0.385
Time: 2542.625 Sender1 attempting to communicate via
   chan Channel1
Time: 2542.625 Sender1 wait on synChannel1
Time: 2549.441 Sender0 attempting to communicate via
   chan Channel0
Time: 2549.441 Sender0 wait on synChannel0
Time: 2549.441 Receiver0 holds for 3.201
Time: 2552.643 Sender0 to reactivate
Time: 2552.643 Receiver0 received message 260 via
   channel Channel0
Time: 2552.643 Receiver0 received Computer Science from
   sender: Sender0
Time: 2552.643 Receiver0 holds for 13.07
Time: 2552.643 Sender0 sent message # 260
Time: 2552.643 Message No. 263 Computer Science sender
   Sender0 rec Receiver0
Time: 2552.643 Sender0 holds for 1.691
Time: 2554.334 Sender0 attempting to communicate via
   chan Channel0
Time: 2554.334 Sender0 wait on synChannel0
Time: 2554.677 Sender3 attempting to communicate via
   chan Channel3
Time: 2554.677 Sender3 wait on synChannel3
Time: 2560 Synchronous Communication holds
   for 115.127
Time: 2565.712 Receiver0 deactivated
Time: 2604.223 Receiver3 deactivated
Time: 2651.393 Receiver1 deactivated
Time: 2654.566 Receiver4 deactivated
Time: 2675.127 Receiver2 deactivated
--------------------------------------------------------------

End Simulation of Synchronous communication with channels
   date: 10/7/2008 time: 14:36

Time: 2675.127 Sender0 terminating
Time: 2675.127 Receiver0 terminating
Time: 2675.127 Sender1 terminating
Time: 2675.127 Receiver1 terminating
Time: 2675.127 Sender2 terminating
Time: 2675.127 Receiver2 terminating
Time: 2675.127 Sender3 terminating
Time: 2675.127 Receiver3 terminating
Time: 2675.127 Sender4 terminating
Time: 2675.127 Receiver4 terminating
```

Listing 26.3 shows the implementation of class *Sender* of the simulation model.

Listing 26.3 Source code of class *Sender*.

```
use all java.io
use all psimjava
description
   Synchronous communication (direct comm)
   J. Garrido, September 2008

Process synchronous communication with OOSimL
Sender process directly communicates with a receiver process
to transfer a message through a channel.
This model uses an array of sender and array of receiver
processes. A waitq object for the rendezvous represents a
channel for each pair of processes.

File: Sender.osl
*/
class Sender as process is
 private
 variables
    define mean_prod of type double    // interval produce mess
    define idnum of type integer       // sender id number
    define wait_int of type double     // sender wait interval
    define sender_wait of type double  // total sender wait
    define startw of type double       // time of start waiting
    define simclock of type double     // current sim time
    define sname of type string        // name of sender process
 object references
    define smsg of class Message       // message to send
    define produc of class NegExp      // period to produce mess
    define rec_proc of class Receiver  // receiver object
    define lchan of class Comchan      // ref to channel object

 public
 function initializer parameters sname of type string,
     sendnum of type integer, mean_prod of type double
 is
 begin
    call super using sname
    set idnum = sendnum                // sender id number
    //
    // random number generator for
    // interval to produce data
    create produc of class NegExp using
         "Produce data interval"
         concat idnum, mean_prod, idnum+1
    set sender_wait = 0.0
    //

    display sname, " created"
```

```
endfun initializer
//
function get_wait return type double is
begin
    return sender_wait
endfun get_wait
//
// assemble a message with contents
function assemble parameters contents of type string,
            rec of class Receiver
is
begin
    create smsg of class Message using contents
    call smsg.set_sender using self     // sender
    call smsg.set_rec using rec         // receiver
    //
    display "Message No. ", smsg.get_messnum(), " ",
        smsg.get_data(), " sender ", get_name(), " rec ",
        rec.get_name()
    tracewrite "Message No. ", smsg.get_messnum(), " ",
        smsg.get_data(), " sender ", get_name(), " rec ",
        rec.get_name()
endfun assemble
//
//
function Main_body is
variables
    define produce_per of type double // int produce data

object references
    define lchan of class Comchan       // ref to channel
begin
    set sname = call get_name
    set lchan = Scomm.channel[idnum]
    assign simulation clock to simclock
    while simclock < Scomm.simperiod do
      // display sname, " to generate msg at ", simclock
      //
      //
      // complete setting up the channel
      set rec_proc = Scomm.rec_obj[idnum]    // receiver
      // call lchan.set_sender using self
      // call lchan.set_rec using rec_proc
      //
      // assemble data for receiver process rec_proc
      call assemble using Scomm.data[idnum], rec_proc
      //
      // generate random interval to produce item
      assign random value from produc to produce_per
      //
      hold self for produce_per       // interval produce msg
      //
      assign simulation clock to simclock
      set startw = simclock              // start to wait
```

```
        //
        display sname, " attempting to communicate via chan ",
            lchan.get_chname(), " at ", simclock
        tracewrite sname, " attempting to comm via chan ",
            lchan.get_chname()
        //
        call send using lchan, smsg  // wait to send message
        //
        assign simulation clock to simclock
        display sname, " sent message # ", smsg.get_messnum(),
            " at ", simclock
        tracewrite sname, " sent message # ",
            smsg.get_messnum()
        //
        set sender_wait = sender_wait + wait_int
    endwhile
    // display sname, " terminating at ", simclock
    suspend self // terminate in main class
endfun Main_body
//
function send parameters mchan of class Comchan,
              lmsg of class Message is
variables
    // communication interval
    define comm_int of type double
begin
    //
    // display sname, " to comm via ", synchan.get_name()
    // display sname, " sending msg with data: ",
    //         lmsg.get_data()
    //
    set startw = simclock
    //
    // send message through the channel
    // communicate with receiver
    call mchan.send using lmsg
    //
    // get communication interval for channel
    set comm_int = call mchan.get_commint
    // display sname, " comm interval: ", comm_int,
    //         " chan: ", mchan.get_chname()
    //
    //
    // display sname, " communicated chan: ",
    //         synchan.get_name()
    //
    assign simulation clock to simclock
    // wait interval
    set wait_int = (simclock - startw) - comm_int
    //
    endfun send
endclass Sender
```

26.7 Summary

The synchronization based on process cooperation occurs when two or more processes engage in a joint activity. This synchronization mechanism is implemented with a cooperation object of class *Waitq*. This cooperation involves an interaction between a master process and one or more slave processes.

When a slave process requests cooperation with a master process, the slave process is suspended and placed in a slave queue until a master object becomes available and performs the joint activity for the time interval of cooperation. Then the master process reactivates the slave process. When master process requests cooperation with a slave process but there is no slave process available, the master process is suspended and placed in the master queue.

26.8 Questions

1. Change the simulation model of the synchronized communication and include object priorities. Make the highest-priority senders synchronize with the first receiver, then the second highest-priority senders with the second receivers, and so on. Determine the same performance measures (average customer cooperating time and average customer waiting time) but by priorities. What advantages and limitations does adding priorities have in the model? Are there any other relevant performance measures to consider?

2. A ferry takes trucks from mainland to a nearby island. Only one truck can be loaded on the ferry at a time. Every truck must get to the island, deliver goods, and then return to the mainland. If there is no truck waiting, the ferry must wait for the crossing trip. Consider the crossing interval as the period of cooperation between the truck object and the ferry object. The mean inter-arrival period for trucks is 8.5 time units, and follows an exponential distribution. The crossing interval follows a normal distribution with mean 7.2 time units and a standard deviation of 0.8 time units. Compute relevant performance measures.

3. The ferry in the previous problem can take up to eight cars and no trucks. Use similar workload as in the previous problem. Compute relevant performance metrics.

4. Several on-line terminals are connected to a server machine through a front-end processor, in an information retrieval system. Customers who request service join a queue at every terminal. Every customer in a terminal sends a query and then waits for a reply from the system. The front-end processor polls every terminal in turn to copy its query to a buffer pool. This pool has capacity to store five queries. The front-end processor has to wait at that terminal if there is no buffer available. The server processor gets the query from the buffer and then places the reply on the same buffer. The reply is sent directly to the corresponding terminal from the buffer. The customer ends the transaction as soon as he or she receives the reply. Determine the relevant performance measures. The timing data are:

- Customer inter-arrival period: negative exponential distribution with a mean equal to three time units;
- Period to type query: uniform distribution with a range from five to eight time units;
- Interval for query processing by server: uniform distribution with a range from three to five time units. Query transfer query to buffer: constant equal to two time units;
- Interval for query transfer from query: constant equal to two time units;
- Polling interval (for every terminal): constant equal to one time unit;
- Interval for customer to examine reply: uniform distribution with range from five to seven time units.

5. Modify the model of the information retrieval system to include customer priorities.

Chapter 27
Conditional Waiting

27.1 Introduction

Conditional waiting is another type of synchronization among processes; this synchronization suspends one or more processes waiting for a given condition to become true. A process is suspended in a hidden queue known as a condition queue, if the condition is not true. The process is later reactivated to continue and carry out some activities, which often include acquiring resources. This synchronization mechanism is known as conditional waiting.

27.2 Using Conditional Waiting

With conditional waiting, the processes involved use the synchronization mechanism implemented in a synchronization conditional object that suspends and later reactivates the interacting processes.

The synchronization object evaluates the specified condition on behalf of a process. If the condition is not true, the process is suspended by the synchronization object and placed in the condition queue. The suspended processes are held in the condition queue that belongs to the synchronization object. Another process, which changes the parameters of the condition, will signal the synchronization object and it reactivates any waiting processes.

Figure 27.1 illustrates this type of synchronization with a simulation activity diagram that shows two processes interacting in a conditional wait. Process *P1* executes a conditional wait and evaluates a condition, process *P2* sends a signal to reactivate process *P1* if it had been suspended.

When processes in a group are each attempting to acquire several resources, the processes should normally request the resource units only when all these resources are available.

J.M. Garrido, *Object Oriented Simulation: A Modeling and Programming Perspective*,
DOI: 10.1007/978-1-4419-0516-1_27,
© Springer Science + Business Media, LLC 2009

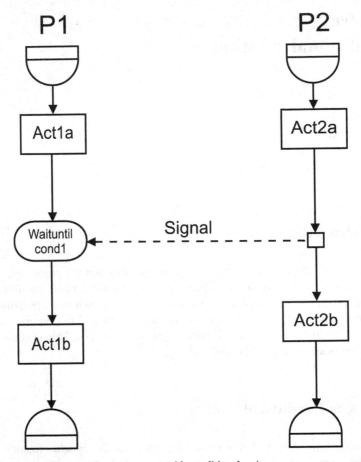

Fig. 27.1 Activity diagram of two processes with conditional wait

This set of processes must synchronize on a conditional wait object. If the condition is not true, the process is suspended and placed by priority in the conditional queue of the synchronization object. Another process that currently holds resources will signal the synchronization object when it releases resources, and one or more processes are reactivated. The processes that are reactivated will reevaluate the condition again.

For the problem described, conditional wait mechanism is very useful because it prevents a process from tying up resources that will not be used until the following condition is met: all the resources requested by the process are available.

27.3 Conditional Waiting with OOSimL

The conditional waiting synchronization is handled by conditional objects of class *Condq*. These objects implement the synchronization mechanism for the processes to evaluate the specified condition and wait if the condition is not true. These conditional objects can suspend processes and place them in their conditional queue by priority. Figure 27.2 shows a UML communication diagram with two processes synchronizing with a conditional wait object.

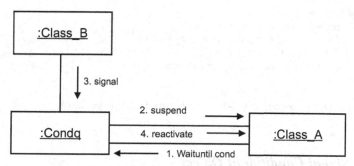

Fig. 27.2 UML communication diagram of two processes with conditional wait

27.3.1 Creating Conditional Objects

To create a conditional object of class *Condq*, the **create** statement is used with the title and the optional number of priorities to use. The default number of priorities is 250.

The following lines of code declare and create a conditional object with title "Customer Cond" and with the default number of priorities.

```
define cond_cust of class Condq
...
create cond_cust of class Condq using "Customer Cond"
```

27.3.2 Wait Until Condition

The **waituntil** statement causes the executing process to check the specified condition and if it is false, the process is suspended. The condition specified is a boolean expression. The suspended process is placed in the hidden priority queue that belongs to the conditional object. When the process is reactivated, it should re-evaluate the condition. If the condition is true, the executing process continues normally. The **waituntil** statement should be part of the body of a loop that will repeatedly evaluate the condition until it is true.

    waituntil ⟨ condition_var ⟩ **in** ⟨ ref_variable ⟩

The following lines of code allow a process that references a condition *mcond* and synchronizes with a *Condq* object, *cond_cust* (created above).

```
define mcond of type boolean
...
set mcond = false
while mcond not equal true do
      // evaluate boolean expression
      set mcond = (att1 > 3 ) and (att2 <= att1)
      waituntil mcond in cond_cust
endwhile
//
// continue executing when the condition is true
```

27.3.3 Signal Conditional Object

The **signal** statement is executed by a process that has caused changes in the parameters of the condition. Execution of this statement removes the process or processes waiting at the head of the queue, and reactivates them. When a process resumes execution, it will re-evaluate the condition and may be suspended again.

    signal to ⟨ ref_variable ⟩

The following line of code allows a process to signal the *Condq* object, *cond_cust* created above.

```
signal to cond_cust
```

27.3.4 Length of Conditional Queue

The **assign length** statement, gets the number of processes waiting in the conditional queue of the specified *Condq* object, and assigns it to the specified integer variable.

In the following lines of code, the current process gets the number of processes waiting in the conditional queue of object *cond_cust* (defined above) and assign this number to variable *cond_num*.

```
define cond_num of type integer
...
assign length of cond_cust to cond_num
```

27.4 The Port System

Ships loaded with goods arrive at a port to unload their cargo. To dock on a pier, ships request two tugboats and a pier. Docking, unloading, undocking each requires a finite interval. To leave, each ship requests one tugboat. If the resources are not available, ships have to wait. Ships are allowed to dock only if two tugboats are available and the tide is not low. The tide changes every 13 hours, and lasts for 4 hours. Ships have to wait until the following condition is true: the tide is high and there are at least two tugboats available. This condition must be true before proceeding to acquire the tugboats and then attempting to dock.

27.4.1 Implementing The Simulation Model

Ships arrive at a port.

In this model, there are two types of resources: tugboats and piers. The tide is modeled as a process; the other type of process corresponds to the ships. For the Port system, the timings involved are:

- Docking time is constant: 32.5 minutes.
- Unloading follows a distribution: mean time is 74.0 minutes with a standard deviation of 8.0 minutes.
- Undocking time interval is constant: 25.0 time units.
- Inter-arrival time follows an exponential distribution with mean of 26.0 minutes.

Listing 27.1 shows the summary results of a simulation run of the model of the Port system with conditional wait.

Listing 27.1 Summary results of a simulation run of the model of the Port System.

```
OOSimL model: Port System with Conditions
Simulation date: date: 10/13/2008 time: 9:16
-------------------STATISTICS REPORT------------------------
------------------------------------------------------------
Res Piers
Piers usage: 0.6376500973465851
 avg num Piers items used: 1.785644671385981

% of time of Piers resource usage: 0.7141959512601732
Avg waiting time for Piers: 17.874743688929094
Avg. num waiting processes: 2.012810719010603
% of time spent waiting for Piers resources: 0.631501448467481
------------------------------------------------------------
Res Tugboats
Tugs usage: 0.2760416666666667
 avg num Tugboats items used: 1.9601688113785887

% of time of Tugboats resource usage: 0.4224763679499517
```

```
-------------------------------------------------------------
Condition queue: Dock cond queue
Number of observations: 36
Number of obs with zero wait: 25
Maximum number of processes in queue: 2
Average number of processes in queue: 0
Average time in queue: 49.96801256600297
Cond queue utilization: 0.25452399069150144
-------------------------------------------------------------
Random generator: Ship inter-arrival
Distribution: Negative exponential
Number of obs: 25
Seed: 7
Mean: 46.45
-------------------------------------------------------------
Random generator: Unload interval
Distribution: Normal
Number of obs: 25
Seed: 13
Mean: 24.5
Standard deviation: 3.85
-------------------------------------------------------------


End Simulation of Port System with Conditions
  date: 10/13/2008 time: 9:16

Total number of ships that arrived: 25
Average wait period: 121.499
```

Listing 27.2 shows the trace of a simulation run of the model of the Port system with conditional wait.

Listing 27.1 Trace of a simulation run of the model of the Port System.

```
OOSimL model: Port System with Conditions
Simulation date: 10/13/2008 time: 9:16
------------------------ TRACE -----------------------------
Time: 0 Port with Conditions holds for 1760.5
Time: 0 Arrivals  holds for 60.939
Time: 0 Tide holds for 240
Time: 60.939 Arrivals  holds for 64.239
Time: 60.939 Ship1 requesting 1 units of Piers
Time: 60.939 Ship1 acquired 1 units of Piers
Time: 60.939 Ship1 waits until condition true
Time: 60.939 Ship1 Testing tide: false
Time: 60.939 Ship1 waituntil Dock cond queue
Time: 60.939 Ship1 deactivated
Time: 125.178 Arrivals  holds for 19.889
Time: 125.178 Ship2 requesting 1 units of Piers
Time: 125.178 Ship2 acquired 1 units of Piers
Time: 125.178 Ship2 waits until condition true
Time: 125.178 Ship2 Testing tide: false
```

```
Time: 125.178 Ship2 waituntil Dock cond queue
Time: 125.178 Ship2 deactivated
Time: 145.068 Arrivals  holds for 105.707
Time: 145.068 Ship3 requesting 1 units of Piers
Time: 145.068 Ship3 deactivated
Time: 240 Tide signal with Dock cond queue
Time: 240 Ship1 to reactivate
Time: 240 Tide holds for 540
Time: 240 Ship1 Testing tide: true
Time: 240 Ship1 waituntil Dock cond queue
Time: 240 Ship2 to reactivate
Time: 240 Ship1 no wait on Dock cond queue
Time: 240 Ship1 continues
Time: 240 Ship1 requesting 2 units of Tugboats
Time: 240 Ship1 acquired 2 units of Tugboats
Time: 240 Ship1 holds for 22.5
Time: 240 Ship2 Testing tide: false
Time: 240 Ship2 waituntil Dock cond queue
Time: 240 Ship2 deactivated
Time: 250.775 Arrivals  holds for 57.208
Time: 250.775 Ship4 requesting 1 units of Piers
Time: 250.775 Ship4 deactivated
    . . .
Time: 1293.308 Ship25 waits until condition true
Time: 1293.308 Ship25 Testing tide: true
Time: 1293.308 Ship25 waituntil Dock cond queue
Time: 1293.308 Ship25 no wait on Dock cond queue
Time: 1293.308 Ship25 continues
Time: 1293.308 Ship25 requesting 2 units of Tugboats
Time: 1293.308 Ship25 acquired 2 units of Tugboats
Time: 1293.308 Ship25 holds for 22.5
Time: 1315.808 Ship25 releasing 2 units of Tugboats
Time: 1315.808 Ship25 signal with Dock cond queue
Time: 1315.808 Ship25 holds for 27.277
Time: 1317.32 Ship24 requesting 1 units of Tugboats
Time: 1317.32 Ship24 acquired 1 units of Tugboats
Time: 1317.32 Ship24 holds for 14.625
Time: 1331.945 Ship24 releasing 1 units of Tugboats
Time: 1331.945 Ship24 releasing 1 units of Piers
Time: 1331.945 Ship24 signal with Dock cond queue
Time: 1331.945 Ship24 departing
Time: 1331.945 Ship24 terminating
Time: 1343.085 Ship25 requesting 1 units of Tugboats
Time: 1343.085 Ship25 acquired 1 units of Tugboats
Time: 1343.085 Ship25 holds for 14.625
Time: 1357.71 Ship25 releasing 1 units of Tugboats
Time: 1357.71 Ship25 releasing 1 units of Piers
Time: 1357.71 Ship25 signal with Dock cond queue
Time: 1357.71 Ship25 departing
Time: 1357.71 Ship25 terminating
Time: 1560 Tide holds for 240
Time: 1760.5 Port with Conditions holds for 39.5
Time: 1800 Tide signal with Dock cond queue
Time: 1800 Tide holds for 540
```

```
-----------------------------------------------------------------
End Simulation of Port System with Conditions
   date: 10/13/2008 time: 9:16
```

Note that the dynamic behavior of tide is modeled as a process and it changes the condition. Every time two events occur: the tide changes from low to high and the tide changes from high to low, the condition changes. This process executes the **signal** statement with the *Condq* object, whenever the event of the tide changing from low to high occurs.

When a ship process releases resources, this event may also cause a change of the condition. The process executes the **signal** statement.

Listing 27.3 shows the source code class *Ship*. The classes of this model are stored in files: `Cport.osl`, `Arrivals.osl`, `Ship.osl`, and `Tide.osl`.

Listing 27.3 Source code of class Ship of the model of the Port System.

```
use all psimjava

description
 Port System with conditional waiting
 OOSimL model, J. Garrido, April 2008.

   Main class: Cport
   File: Ship.osl


Ships arrive at a port and unload their cargo. Ships request
2 tugboats and a pier. To leave the ships request 1 tugboat.
The activities of a ship, docking, unloading, and leaving,
have a finite period of duration.
If the resources are not available, ships have to wait.

Condition: Ships are only allowed to dock if 2 tugboats are
available and the tide is not low.
The tide changes every 12 hours. The low tide lasts
 for 4 hours. The tide is modeled as a process.

This system is similar to an operating system in which
processes have conditional waiting, using conditional
variables in monitors.

Activity of a ship object:
1. conditional wait for tugboats and low tide
2. dock
3. unload
4. undock
5. leave (terminate)

Assumptions:
1. dock interval is constant
2. undock interval takes about 65% of dock interval
*/
```

```
public class Ship as process  is
 private
 variables
    define startw of type double        // ship start wait
    define unload of type double        // unload interval
    define simclock of type double      // current simul time
    define shipname of type string
 object references
    define static ctide of class Tide
 public
 variables
    define shipnum of type integer      // ship number
    //
    //       Function implementations of class Ship
    //
 function initializer parameters shname of type string,
         unloadper of type double is
 begin
    call super using shname
 display shname, " unloadper: ", unloadper
    set unload = unloadper
    set shipnum = Cport.numarrivals      // ship number
    assign simulation clock to simclock
    display shname, " created at time: ", simclock
    set shipname = shname
 endfun initializer
  //
 function Main_body is
 variables
    define wait_per of type double       // wait interval
    define doc_per of type double        // dock interval
    define tugsavail of type integer     // tug boats available
    define mcond = false of type boolean // condition tide
 begin
    set doc_per = 22.5                    // constant dock period
    //
    assign simulation clock to simclock
    set startw = simclock                 // start time to wait
    //
    display shipname, " requests pier at: ", simclock
    //
    // attempt to acquire pier
    acquire 1 units from Cport.piers
    //
    set simclock = get_clock()
    display shipname, " acquired pier at time: ", simclock
    // wait for high tide and 2 tugboats
    display shipname, " waits until condition true at: ",
        simclock
    tracewrite shipname, " waits until condition true"
    //
    set mcond = false
    while mcond not equal true do
        set mcond = call Cport.tugs_low_tide // eval condition
```

```
        display shipname, " Testing tide: ", mcond,
                " at: ", simclock
        tracewrite shipname, " Testing tide: ", mcond
        //
        waituntil mcond in Cport.dockq
        //
        set simclock = get_clock()
endwhile
//
display shipname, " continues at: ", simclock
tracewrite shipname, " continues"
//
// wait for available tugboats
assign available units of Cport.tugs to tugsavail
display "Number of available tugboats: ", tugsavail
//
acquire 2 units from Cport.tugs // acquire tugboats
//
set simclock = get_clock()
display shipname, " acquires 2 tugboats at: ", simclock
//
set wait_per = simclock - startw   // wait interval
add wait_per to Cport.acc_wait     // accumulate wait
//
// ship now will dock
hold self for doc_per                    // dock interval
//
release 2 units of Cport.tugs
//
set simclock = get_clock()
display shipname, " releases tugs, signaling dockq at: ",
        simclock
//
signal to Cport.dockq
//
// ship will now unload
display shipname, " with unloading interval: ", unload
//
hold self for unload             // take time to unload
assign simulation clock to simclock
display shipname, " requesting tugboat at: ", simclock
//
set startw =  simclock           // start to wait again
//
acquire 1 units from Cport.tugs
//
set simclock = get_clock()
//
display shipname, " acquires 1 tugboat at ", simclock
//
set wait_per = simclock - startw
add wait_per to Cport.acc_wait
//
// undock
```

```
        hold self for (0.65*doc_per)      // time to undock
        //
        release 1 units of Cport.tugs     // release the tugboat
        //
        set simclock = get_clock()
        display shipname, " releases tugboat at: ", simclock
        //
        release 1 units of Cport.piers    // release the pier
        //
        signal to Cport.dockq             // signal condition
        //
        display shipname, " departing at: ", simclock
        tracewrite shipname, " departing"
        terminate self                    // terminate this ship
    endfun Main_body
endclass Ship
```

27.5 Summary

The synchronization mechanism with conditional waiting is another form of process interaction. A process that depends on a specified condition to carry out some activities uses a conditional wait mechanism. For example, if a process attempts to acquire various resources of different types, it will evaluate a condition and wait if the condition is not true.

The process executes the **waituntil** statement. The process is suspended and placed in a conditional queue, if the condition is not true. An object of class *Condq* is used as the passive object with the synchronization mechanism.

Another process executes the **signal** statement using the same *Condq* object. Executing this statement reactivates the process at the head of the queue. This conditional priority queue belongs to the *Condq* object. The reactivated process evaluates its condition again and continues normally if the condition is true. A simulation model of the Port system is presented.

27.6 Exercises

1. Modify the model of the Port system and include another type of ship, which requires more resources.
2. Modify the model of the Port system so ships can evaluate a second condition before undocking. This condition tests if there are sufficient tugs for undocking and if the tide is not low.
3. Discuss how you can use the conditional wait mechanism to improve the overall performance of the model of the synchronous communication system described in Chapter 10.

4. Develop a simulation model in which deadlock occurs. Modify the model using the conditional wait mechanism to prevent the occurrence of deadlock.
5. Develop a simulation model of a traffic intersection. Cars arrive at the intersection with an exponential distribution and the traffic light remains in green and red for a finite period. The conditions should be based on all possible alternatives for the cars arriving into the intersection.
6. Discuss how you can implement the conditional wait mechanism without using objects of class *Condq*. What are the main limitations and advantages of this alternative?

Chapter 28
Interrupts

28.1 Introduction

Simulation models often include one or more processes that interrupt the normal sequence of activities of other processes. An interrupt is a form of process interaction. In a simple scenario, a process interrupts the current activity of a second process. This causes the interrupted process to stop temporarily its current operation and perform a certain task immediately. The first process is the *interrupting* process and the second is the *interrupted* process. This chapter describes the notion of interruptions, the interrupt mechanisms, and presents two simulation models that include interrupts.

28.2 Basic concepts of Interruptions

The interruption is a signal sent by a process to another process. The process receiving the signal reacts by stopping its normal sequence of operations and performing a special task or activity known as the *interrupt routine*, which may include suspending itself.

The interrupted process, if it had been suspended on interruption, is restarted at some later time by the interrupting process or by a different process. The interrupted process will then resume its activities from the point of interruption.

The use of interrupts is often associated with priorities. For example, in a simulation model with multiple types of customers, a customer process with a high *priority* will interrupt the current activity of another process that has a lower priority.

Another example of systems with interrupts is a system with machine breakdowns. In the simulation model, a special process will interrupt the normal operation of a machine after it has been operating for some operational time interval.

The existence of interruptions in a model is known as preemption. The behavior of a system is considered *preemptive* if it includes interruptions. Preemption is very

J.M. Garrido, *Object Oriented Simulation: A Modeling and Programming Perspective*,
DOI: 10.1007/978-1-4419-0516-1_28,
© Springer Science + Business Media, LLC 2009

important in a large group of practical applications, and in developing large and complex systems.

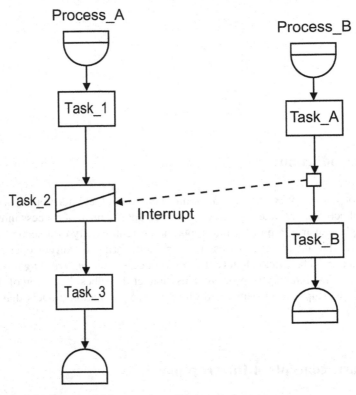

Fig. 28.1 Activity diagram with interrupting and interrupted processes

Figure 28.1 shows an activity diagram with an interrupting process and an interrupted process. In this diagram, the interrupted process is not suspended.

28.3 Handling Interrupts

A simple way to describe how the interrupting mechanism works is as follows:

1. The interrupting process sends a signal to the interrupted process.
2. The interrupted process:

   a. Stops the execution of its current activity and performs a special activity in response to the interrupt signal. This activity is known as an *interrupt routine*.
   b. Suspends itself, if necessary.

3. At some later point in time, the interrupting process (or some other process) reactivates the interrupted process.
4. The interrupted process resumes the activity it was originally executing from the point of interruption.

The interrupted process executes an interrupt routine as a result of the interrupt signal sent by the interrupting process. This interrupt routine includes operations such as releasing resources, computing the remaining time for the current activity, sending a message (or alarm) to some output device, and possibly suspending itself.

The interrupt routine can change some of the conditions within the process so that it will perform a different sequence of activities, instead of suspending itself.

The interrupted process may include several interrupt routines. The decision of which interrupt routine to execute depends on the *interrupt level*, which is sent by the interrupting process. Usually, the interrupt level depends on the priority of the interrupting process.

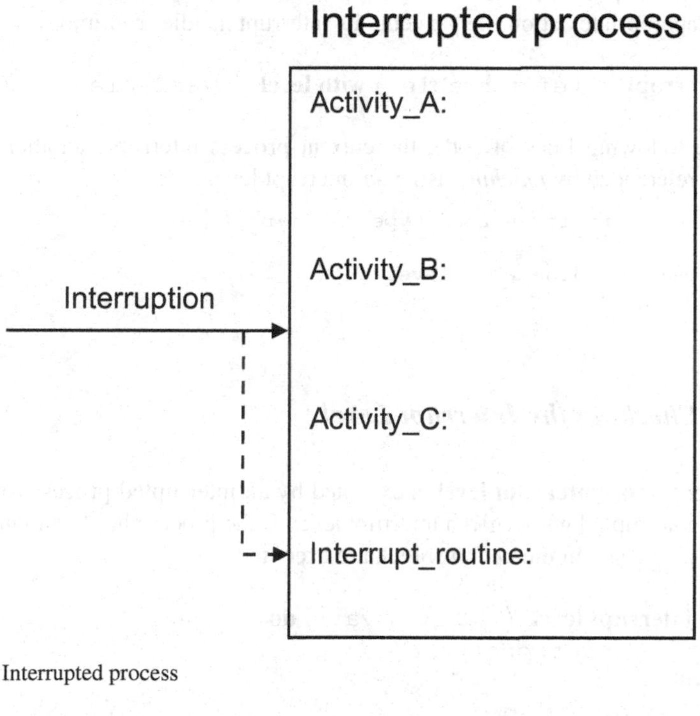

Fig. 28.2 Interrupted process

Figure 28.2 shows the activities of an interrupted process object. The process is interrupted at the *interrupt point*, while executing *Activity_B*. Execution then transfers to the interrupt routine.

A typical and simple example of a model with interruptions is a system with machine breakdowns. Several machines are operational until there is a fault in one

or more machines. After the breakdown, a machine remains unavailable for a finite
time interval of repair. A machine breakdown can be modeled as an unpredictable
and external event.

The process modeling the breakdown agent is a process that interrupts the machine process, which reacts by stopping its operations. The machine process then
waits suspended for a finite interval, the repair interval. When the repair interval has
elapsed, the breakdown process restarts the machine process.

In some simulation models, the use of *priorities* results in a more flexible and
powerful interrupt interaction. A process can only interrupt another process if this
second one has a lower priority than the interrupting process.

28.4 Interrupts using OOSimL

The **interrupt** statement sends an interrupt signal to the specified process using a
specified interrupt level. The interrupted process is rescheduled immediately so it
can take appropriate action (i.e., execute its interrupt handler routine).

interrupt ⟨ `ref_variable` ⟩ **with level** ⟨ `variable` ⟩

In the following lines of code, the current process interrupts another process,
which is referenced by *machine* using an interrupt level of 2.

```
define interr_lev = 2 of type integer
...
interrupt machine with level interr_lev
...
```


28.4.1 Checking the Interrupt Level

The statement **on interrupt level** is executed by an interrupted process to check if
has been interrupted with a given interrupt level. If the process has been interrupted,
then the statements in the *actions* block are executed.

on interrupt level ⟨ `int_lev_var` ⟩ **do**
        ⟨ `actions` ⟩
enddo

In the following lines of code, the interrupted process checks if it has been interrupted with interrupt level 5. If an interrupt has occurred with interrupt level 5, the
process executes the sequence of statements in its interrupt handling routine.

```
on interrupt level 5 do
    ...      // statements to be executed
enddo
```

28.4.2 Get the Interrupt Level Status

The **assign interrupt level** statement gets the status of the specified interrupt level of the process. The value returned is 1 if the interrupt level specified has been set. The value is zero if the process has not been interrupted with this interrupt level, or the interrupt level has been cleared.

If the interrupt level is not specified, this statement gets the lowest interrupt level of the calling process. This value is zero if the process has not been interrupted, or the flag has been cleared.

> **assign interrupt level** ⟨ int_lev_var ⟩
>   [**of** ⟨ ref_var ⟩] **to** ⟨ var_lev ⟩

In the following lines of code, the current process stores the status of interrupt level 2 and stores it in variable *varlev2*.

```
set lintlev = 2
...
assign interrupt level lintlev to varlev2
```

28.4.3 Get Remaining Time

The **assign remaining** statement gets the remaining interval left from time the process was interrupted. This time value is useful if the interrupted process was carrying out some task for a specified time interval when it was interrupted. When the process resumes execution (gets rescheduled), it will continue executing for the remaining time interval.

> **assign remaining time to** ⟨ variable ⟩

The following lines of code in the interrupted process, store the remaining period in variable *rem_period*.

```
set intlev = 2
on interrupt level intlev do
   assign remaining time to rem_period
   ...
enddo
```

28.4.4 Clear Interrupt Levels

The **clear interrupt** statement clears the specified interrupt level or all the interrupt levels of the process. This statement is normally used in the interrupt handling routine. The clauses in brackets are optional. If the level clause is not present, all interrupt levels are cleared.

> **clear interrupt** [**level** ⟨variable ⟩] [**of** ⟨ ref_variable ⟩]

The following lines of code in the interrupted process, clear all the interrupt levels.

```
set intlev = 2
on interrupt level intlev do
   assign remaining time to rem_period
   clear interrupt      // clear all interrupt levels
   ...                  // interrupt handling
enddo
```

The following lines of code in the interrupted process clear the interrupt level specified by *intlev*.

```
set intlev = 2
on interrupt level intlev do
   assign remaining time to rem_period
   clear interrupt level intlev // clear interrupt level
   ...                  // interrupt handling
enddo
```

28.5 Carwash Model with Interrupts

Previously, a model of single-server Carwash system was discussed. The previous model now is extended with interruptions. Each Car process has a priority. Cars arrive and join a car priority queue to wait for service.

An arriving car may find the machine is busy; it then interrupts the busy machine if the priority of the car being serviced is lower than the arriving car. In simpler terms, a car with a high priority can interrupt the service of a lower priority car. The machine adopts the priority of the car it is servicing.

The processes in the model are: several arrivals, the cars, and the machine processes. The arrivals processes are the source of cars; the cars are the customers and the machines are the servers. Priorities are assigned to the customers on arrival. There are two queues: the customer input queue, the interrupted customer queue. These are priority queues. The components of the model are:

- A machine that services the cars, the customers
- Several customers arriving at random times

- K different arrivals processes, one for every priority
- A priority queue for arriving customers with different priorities.
- A priority queue for interrupted customers.

Figure 28.3 shows the general structure of the Carwash model with interrupts.

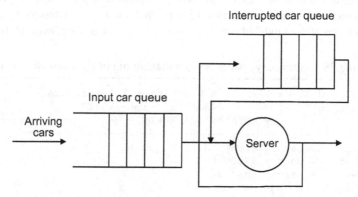

Fig. 28.3 Model of the Carwash system with interrupts

The customer queue and the interrupted customer queue in the model are priority queues, with K different priorities. The required data for the single-server model with interruptions is:

- The number of priorities, K
- The mean inter-arrival interval for the customers: this can be the same for all priorities or can be different for every priority
- The mean service interval for the customers: it can be the same for all priorities or can be different for every priority
- The total simulation period.

The general behavior for this model can informally be described by the following sequence of operations:

1. Customers arrive with a given priority and a service interval.
2. The arriving customer joins the customer priority queue. If the queue is full, the customer leaves the system.
3. The server removes the customer with the highest possible priority from the queue. The server provides service to the customer for a finite time interval, which is the service interval for the customer.
4. If the server is busy, an arriving customer process performs the following actions:

   a. Checks if the server is servicing a customer with lower priority
   b. If so, the arriving customer interrupts the customer being served, with the appropriate interrupt level

5. The arriving customer receives service from the server
6. After the service has been completed, the customer leaves the system.

The interrupted customer is suspended and placed into the interrupted customer queue. The arrivals processes each create new customer arrivals at random times and assign a random service period for a given priority.

The performance measures are the average customer sojourn time and the average customer wait time by priorities. Listing 28.1 shows the summary results of a simulation run of the model of the single-server Carwash system with interrupts.

Listing 28.1 Summary results of a simulation run of the Carwash System.

```
OOSimL model: Carwash with Priorities & Interrupts
Simulation date: date: 10/30/2008 time: 10:23
-------------------STATISTICS REPORT--------------------
--------------------------------------------------------
Priority queue: Interrupted cust queue
Capacity of queue: 1750000
Number of observations: 36
Max number of objects in queue: 3
Average number of objects in queue: 1
Average time in queue: 25.41059347513295
Queue utilization: 0.6900346909282424
Queue usage: 0.5646798550029544
--------------------------------------------------------
Priority queue: Cust Queue
Capacity of queue: 200
Number of observations: 588
Max number of objects in queue: 145
Average number of objects in queue: 69
Average time in queue: 1.7979991963670754
Queue utilization: 0.8590960352622246
Queue usage: 0.4783297862059306
--------------------------------------------------------
Random generator: Inter-arrival type 4
Distribution: Negative exponential
Number of obs: 29
Seed: 55
Mean: 25.2
--------------------------------------------------------
Random generator: Inter-arrival type 3
Distribution: Negative exponential
Number of obs: 122
Seed: 43
Mean: 5.2
--------------------------------------------------------
Random generator: Inter-arrival type 2
Distribution: Negative exponential
Number of obs: 35
Seed: 31
Mean: 14.2
--------------------------------------------------------
```

```
Random generator: Inter-arrival type 1
Distribution: Negative exponential
Number of obs: 75
Seed: 19
Mean: 8.5
--------------------------------------------------------
Random generator: Inter-arrival type 0
Distribution: Negative exponential
Number of obs: 120
Seed: 7
Mean: 5.2
--------------------------------------------------------
Random generator: Service Period type 4
Distribution: Normal
Number of obs: 29
Seed: 61
Mean: 2.2
Standard deviation: 0.0
--------------------------------------------------------
Random generator: Service Period type 3
Distribution: Normal
Number of obs: 122
Seed: 49
Mean: 3.5
Standard deviation: 0.85
--------------------------------------------------------
Random generator: Service Period type 2
Distribution: Normal
Number of obs: 35
Seed: 37
Mean: 3.0
Standard deviation: 0.85
--------------------------------------------------------
Random generator: Service Period type 1
Distribution: Normal
Number of obs: 75
Seed: 25
Mean: 2.6

Standard deviation: 0.85
--------------------------------------------------------
Random generator: Service Period type 0
Distribution: Normal
Number of obs: 120
Seed: 13
Mean: 4.6
Standard deviation: 0.85
--------------------------------------------------------

End Simulation of Carwash with Priorities & Interrupts
date: 10/30/2008 time: 10:23

Total cars of type 0 serviced : 120
Car type 0 average wait period: 9.200917741221392
```

```
Total cars of type 1 serviced : 69
Car type 1 average wait period: 240.13592412242014
Total cars of type 2 serviced : 35
Car type 2 average wait period: 441.03131013419136
Total cars of type 3 serviced : 41
Car type 3 average wait period: 773.7085282961636
Total cars of type 4 serviced : 29
Car type 4 average wait period: 704.5033058486074

Total number of cars serviced: 294
Total Car average wait period: 290.008
Average period car spends in the shop: 286.163
Machine utilization: 0.994
```

Listing 28.2 shows the trace results of a simulation run of the model of the Single-server Carwash system with interrupts.

Listing 28.2 Trace of a simulation run of the Carwash System.

```
OOSimL model: Carwash with Priorities & Interrupts
Simulation date: 10/30/2008 time: 10:23
------------------------ TRACE ------------------------------
Time: 0 Arrivals0 holds for 6.822
Time: 0 Arrivals1 holds for 11.208
Time: 0 Arrivals2 holds for 18.667
Time: 0 Arrivals3 holds for 6.76
Time: 0 Arrivals4 holds for 32.927
Time: 0 Wash_machine deactivated
Time: 6.76 Arrivals3 holds for 9.962
Time: 6.76 Car1 priority 3 arrives
Time: 6.76 Car1 enqueued into Cust Queue
Time: 6.76 Wash_machine to reactivate
Time: 6.76 Car1 deactivated
Time: 6.76 Car1 dequeued from Cust Queue
Time: 6.76 Wash_machine begins service of Car1 type 3
Time: 6.76 Wash_machine holds for 3.812
Time: 6.822 Arrivals0 holds for 7.191
Time: 6.822 Car2 priority 0 arrives
Time: 6.822 Car2 enqueued into Cust Queue
Time: 6.822 Wash_machine interrupted by Car2
Time: 6.822 Car2 deactivated
Time: 6.822 Service of Car1 interrupted
Time: 6.822 Car1 enqueued into Interrupted cust queue
Time: 6.822 Wash_machine clears interrupt levels
Time: 6.822 Car2 dequeued from Cust Queue
Time: 6.822 Wash_machine begins service of Car2 type 0
Time: 6.822 Wash_machine holds for 6.03
Time: 11.208 Arrivals1 holds for 3.771
Time: 11.208 Car3 priority 1 arrives
Time: 11.208 Car3 enqueued into Cust Queue
Time: 11.208 Car3 deactivated
Time: 12.852 Wash_machine completed service of Car2
```

```
Time:  12.852 Car2 to reactivate
Time:  12.852 Car3 dequeued from Cust Queue
Time:  12.852 Wash_machine begins service of Car3 type 1
Time:  12.852 Wash_machine holds for 2.779
Time:  12.852 Car2 terminating
Time:  14.014 Arrivals0 holds for 2.227
Time:  14.014 Car4 priority 0 arrives
Time:  14.014 Car4 enqueued into Cust Queue
Time:  14.014 Wash_machine interrupted by Car4
Time:  14.014 Car4 deactivated
Time:  14.014 Service of Car3 interrupted
Time:  14.014 Car3 enqueued into Interrupted cust queue
  . . .
Time:  1035.45 Car319 to reactivate
Time:  1035.45 Car327 dequeued from Cust Queue
Time:  1035.45 Wash_machine begins service of Car327 type 4
Time:  1035.45 Wash_machine holds for 2.2
Time:  1035.45 Car319 terminating
Time:  1037.65 Wash_machine completed service of Car327
Time:  1037.65 Car327 to reactivate
Time:  1037.65 Car348 dequeued from Cust Queue
Time:  1037.65 Wash_machine begins service of Car348 type 4
Time:  1037.65 Wash_machine holds for 2.2
Time:  1037.65 Car327 terminating
Time:  1039.85 Wash_machine completed service of Car348
Time:  1039.85 Car348 to reactivate
Time:  1039.85 Car366 dequeued from Cust Queue
Time:  1039.85 Wash_machine begins service of Car366 type 4
Time:  1039.85 Wash_machine holds for 2.2
Time:  1039.85 Car348 terminating
Time:  1042.05 Wash_machine completed service of Car366
Time:  1042.05 Car366 to reactivate
Time:  1042.05 Car374 dequeued from Cust Queue
Time:  1042.05 Wash_machine begins service of Car374 type 4
Time:  1042.05 Wash_machine holds for 2.2
Time:  1042.05 Car366 terminating
Time:  1044.25 Wash_machine completed service of Car374
Time:  1044.25 Car374 to reactivate

Time:  1044.25 Car380 dequeued from Cust Queue
Time:  1044.25 Wash_machine begins service of Car380 type 4
Time:  1044.25 Wash_machine holds for 2.2
Time:  1044.25 Car374 terminating
Time:  1046.45 Wash_machine completed service of Car380
Time:  1046.45 Car380 to reactivate
Time:  1046.45 Wash_machine deactivated
Time:  1046.45 Car380 terminating
------------------------------------------------------------------

End Simulation of Carwash with Priorities & Interrupts
 date: 10/30/2008 time: 10:23
```

Listing 28.3 shows the OOSimL code for class *Server* in the model for the Carwash system with interrupts. The files with the source code are: `Server.osl`, `PCarwash.osl`, `Arrivals.osl`, and `Cars.osl`. These are stored in the archive file `intcarwash.jar`

Listing 28.3 Source code of class *Server* of the Carwash model.

```
use all psimjava
description
    OOSimL model of the Carwash system with interrupts
    and priorities

    J Garrido, September 2008

    This class defines the server object, which
     is the carwash machine. It takes the car at the head of
    the queue and services the car. When the machine
    completes service of the car, it gets another car from
    the queue.
    If the queue is empty, it goes into its idle state
*/
class Server as process is
  private
  variables
      define custpriority of type integer
      define interrupt_flag of type boolean
  object references
      define currentCustomer of class Car // current customer
      define interrupt_queue of class Pqueue
  //
  public
  function initializer parameters name of type string is
  begin
      call super using name
      // display name, " created at: ", simclock
      set interrupt_flag = false
      create interrupt_queue of class Pqueue
          using "Interrupted cust queue"
  endfun initializer
  //
  function Main_body is
  variables
    define startIdle of type double
    define idle_period of type double        // idle period
    define simclock of type double           // simulation ime
    define cname of type string              // name attribute
  begin
    set cname = get_name()
    assign simulation clock to simclock
    display cname, " starting main body at ", simclock
    //
    while simclock < PCarwash.simPeriod do
      if PCarwash.car_queue is empty and
```

```
            interrupt_queue is empty
        then
            // queue is empty
            // starting time of idle period
            set startIdle = get_clock()
            display cname, " goes idle at ", simclock
            suspend self          // suspend server
            //
            // reactivated by a car object
            // queue must now be nonempty
            display cname, " reactived"
            set simclock = get_clock()
            set idle_period = simclock- startIdle

            add idle_period to PCarwash.accum_idle
            display cname, " reactivated at " + simclock
        endif
        call serviceCustomer    // service the car
    endwhile
    terminate self
endfun Main_body
//
function serviceCustomer is
variables
    define startTime of type double
    define service_per of type double
    define objname of type string
    define ccustname of type string
    define ccustservt of type double
    define simclock of type double
    define int_lev of type integer
    define rem_time of type double
    define lpriority of type integer
object references
    define lcar of class Car
begin
    set int_lev = 1
    if interrupt_queue is not empty and
        PCarwash.car_queue is not empty
    then
        // get copy of customer at head of interrupt queue
        set currentCustomer = cast class Car
            call interrupt_queue.objcopy
        assign priority of currentCustomer to custpriority
        // get copy customer from head of waiting queue
        set lcar = cast class Car
            call PCarwash.car_queue.objcopy
        assign priority of lcar to lpriority

        // compare the priorities of the two customers
        if lpriority < custpriority then
            remove currentCustomer of class Car
                from PCarwash.car_queue
        else
```

```
              remove currentCustomer of class Car
                   from interrupt_queue
          endif
     else
          if PCarwash.car_queue is not empty then
             // get customer from head of input car queue
             remove currentCustomer of class Car
                   from PCarwash.car_queue
          else
             if interrupt_queue is not empty then
                remove currentCustomer of class Car
                      from interrupt_queue
             endif
          endif
     endif // interrupt_flag
          //
     assign priority of currentCustomer to custpriority
     set objname = get_name()
     set ccustname = currentCustomer.get_name()
     // get cust service time
     set ccustservt = currentCustomer.get_serv_dur()
     assign simulation clock to startTime // service start
     if currentCustomer.get_pend() then
             display objname, " resumes service of: ",
                    ccustname, " at: ", startTime, " for ",
                    ccustservt
             tracewrite objname, " resumes service of ",
                    ccustname, " type ", custpriority
     else
             display objname, " begins service of: ",
                    ccustname, " at: ", startTime, " for ",
                    ccustservt
             tracewrite objname, " begins service of ",
                    ccustname, " type ", custpriority
     endif
        //
        // accumulate waiting time for this customer (car)
        // and accumulate for the cust priority
        add (startTime - currentCustomer.get_arrivalT()) to
                PCarwash.custWaitTime[custpriority]
        //
        // accumulate total wait time
        add (startTime - currentCustomer.get_arrivalT()) to
                PCarwash.totalWait
        //
        set service_per = currentCustomer.get_serv_dur()
        hold self for service_per
        //
        set interrupt_flag = false
        //
        assign simulation clock to simclock
        // was process interrupted?
        on interrupt level int_lev do
           display "Service of ", ccustname, " interrupted at: ",
```

```
              simclock
         tracewrite "Service of ", ccustname, " interrupted "
         // insert current customer into interrupted car queue
         insert currentCustomer into interrupt_queue
         assign remaining time to rem_time
         // update customer remaining service time interval
         call currentCustomer.change_servp using rem_time
         call currentCustomer.change_arrival
         call currentCustomer.set_pend
         clear interrupt
         set interrupt_flag = true
         return
    enddo
    //
    add (simclock - startTime) to
        PCarwash.custServiceTime[custpriority]
    display objname, " completes service of: ", ccustname,
        " at: ", simclock
    tracewrite objname, " completed service of ",
        ccustname
    reactivate currentCustomer now    // let car continue
  endfun serviceCustomer
  //
  function get_ctype return type integer is
  begin
      return custpriority
  endfun get_ctype
endclass Server
```

28.6 The Machine Breakdowns Model

A machine can become unavailable as a result of a mechanical failure or an external interrupt for maintenance or for another reason. It is very common in this type of modeling to use the average values for mean time between failures (MTBF) and mean time to repair (MTTR). The appropriate probability distributions are also used.

The model of the Machine Breakdowns system is another simulation model with interrupts. Several machines (objects of class Machine) in a shop each have a part that fails periodically. The damaged part needs to be removed from the machine and a replacement part installed. The parts that fail are to be repaired by a repairman (an object of class Repairman), who also has other jobs to carry out when not repairing parts.

When a part of a Machine process fails, the following sequence of operations is performed by the Machine process:

1. Remove the damaged part, this takes a finite time interval.
2. Place the damaged part in a *Bin* object of damaged parts, for the repairman to pick up.

3. Interrupt the Repairman process, if it is carrying out background jobs. When interrupted, the Repairman process proceeds to repair the damaged parts submitted by the Machine process(s).
4. If possible, take a replacement part from the replacement Bin object. If there are no replacement parts available, suspend to wait for one.
5. Install the replacement part, this takes a finite time interval.
6. Repeat the previous steps.

The following sequence of operations is carried out by Repairman process:

1. Check if there are parts in the *Bin* object of damaged parts. If there is one or more damaged parts in the *Bin* object:

   a. Take a damaged part.
   b. Repair the damaged part; this takes a random and finite time interval.
   c. Place the repaired part in the *Bin* object for repaired parts.

2. If there are no damaged parts in the *Bin* object:

   a. Carry out some background job for a random and finite time interval.
   b. If interrupted, store remaining interval for service of the job.
   c. If there is a background job pending, continue from point of interruption.

3. Repeat the operations.

After a Repairman process has repaired all outstanding damaged parts, it resumes any background job that may have been interrupted. The performance measures computed by the model are: average machine down period, average machine up period, and average machine utilization.

28.7 Summary

Interruptions are events sent to a process, which cause the process to stop temporarily the normal sequence of activities and resume at a later time. The interruptions in processes are normally associated with the process priorities (i.e., a high priority process would need to interrupt a lower priority process).

The interrupt facility is based on the interrupting process sending a synchronization signal to the interrupted process. This second process decides what task to perform when it senses an interruption and, depending on the level of interrupt, can execute one of several interrupt routines.

At the end of an interrupt routine, the interrupting process object usually suspends itself. Some time after, the interrupted process object may be allowed to resume its normal activities, to continue from the point of interruption, or to restart its activities (from the beginning). In the first case study described in this chapter, all interrupted process objects are allowed to resume their activities. For this, the interrupting or the interrupted process object, maintains a time variable with the period left to complete the current operation.

The presence of interruptions in a simulation model constitutes another form of process interaction. The concepts are important in developing large and complex systems.

28.8 Key Terms

interrupted process	interrupting process	interrupt level
signal	interrupt routine	remaining time
preemption	interrupt point	priority
MTBF	MTTR	machine downtime

Exercises

28.1. Modify the model of the Machine Breakdowns system. Include an external agent that interrupts the normal operation of machines. Compare the traces of the two models. Discuss advantages and disadvantages of this design.

28.2. Study the model of the Carwash system with preemption. Observe the trace of several simulation runs. Change the selection criteria for the interrupted processes. The machine process must now remove a car from the interrupted car queue and only when it is empty will the machine process remove a from the input car queue. Compare the trace of simulation runs of the two models.

28.3. Modify the model of the Carwash system (with preemption) and change the selection criteria for the interrupted processes. The new selection assumes that of the several customer processes with the same priority, the one to interrupt is the one with the least recent starting time (the oldest process object within the priority group).

28.4. A computer system uses a round robin scheduling discipline, a preemptive scheduling. Processes arriving into the ready queue are assigned a service period (randomly with an exponential distribution). The server process carries out service to the processes for only a fixed finite interval, called the *time quantum*. Interrupted processes are placed back into the ready queue. A process may need to cycle several times before completing its required service. Design and implement the model and determine the average waiting time, average sojourn time, and the percentage of time the server is not idle (the server utilization). Run the simulation model several times. Change the time quantum and again run the simulation several times.

28.5. Modify exercise 28.4 and include job priorities. Run the simulation model several times. Change the model again and assign higher priority to the jobs that have been inside the system for the longest period.

Chapter 29
Input Analysis and Specification

29.1 Introduction

Developing a simulation model involves structuring modeling and quantitative modeling. The first consists of designing the logical aspects of the model; the second modeling includes the specification of:

- The types of input variables, deterministic or random
- The probability distributions that random input variables follow
- Estimation of the input parameters.

If the real system exits, for which a simulation model is being developed, then the input data should be collected and analyzed and the model inputs can be specified in the model in a valid and realistic manner. If the real system does not yet exist or no data is available, careful and reasonable assumptions need to be taken to formulate the input specifications of the model.

One of the first steps in the data collection is determining what data is required, which depends on the model scope and the detail level decided on previously. Then data is collected by reviewing existing files and documentation, conducting interviews, direct observations, and taking assumptions, and other activities.

The analysis and interpretation of data is necessary for deciding their suitability of use in the simulation model then developing a representation of the data. The tests on data are performed for data independence (randomness), homogeneity, and stationarity. After data have been tested, it should be converted to a form that can be useful for simulation.

Most modern integrated simulation software systems include tools for statistical analysis of data. However, the use of more standard and widely known statistical tools is recommended such as: SAS, SPSS, and Minitab. Spreadsheet programs such as MS Excel contain the Data Analysis tool, which is fairly powerful and sufficient for most common statistical analysis tasks.

J.M. Garrido, *Object Oriented Simulation: A Modeling and Programming Perspective*, 393
DOI: 10.1007/978-1-4419-0516-1_29,
© Springer Science + Business Media, LLC 2009

29.2 Types of Input Variables

The two basic types of input quantities are deterministic and random quantities. On occasions, it may be difficult to decide whether a quantity is deterministic or random. Sensitivity analysis can help to decide whether a quantity is deterministic or random. This analysis studies the impact of changes in data on the simulation results.

When an input quantity in a real system exhibits some variability, then it is modeled as a random variable whose behavior is defined by a probability distribution. A probability distribution describes the range of possible values that a random variable can attain and the probability that the value of the random variable is within any (measurable) subset of that range.

If the simulation model is being developed for a system that does not yet exist or no data is available about an existing system, careful and reasonable assumptions have to be taken in specifying the input data. Failure to choose the appropriate probability distribution can affect the accuracy of the simulation results.

29.3 Representing Data

There are several techniques to represent the data for use in the simulation model. The recommended technique is to select a theoretical probability distribution that best fits the data. Another technique is to use an empirical distribution that characterizes the data.

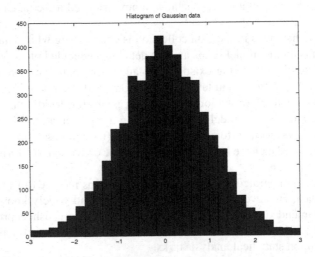

Fig. 29.1 A histogram of a frequency distribution

A histogram is a chart of tabulated frequencies, shown as bars. It shows what proportion of cases fall into each of several groups. The groups are usually specified as non-overlapping intervals of some variable. The categories (bars) must be adjacent.

A histogram of the frequency distribution of the data is usually constructed first. A fitness test is next carried out to check whether one of the theoretical distributions fits the data. Figure 29.1 shows a histogram of a frequency distribution with 30 groups or classes.

29.3.1 Probability Distributions

The *probability density function*, $f(x)$ is defined as the derivative of the cumulative distribution function, $F'(x)$. It follows that $F(x)$ can also be derived from the integral of $f(x)$. Then the probability that the random variable X has a value in the interval (a,b) is calculated by:

$$P(a < X < b) = F(b) - F(a) = \int_a^b f(x).$$

The cumulative distribution functions are useful for calculating probabilities, and probability density functions are useful for calculating expected values (average values of the random variables).

Probability distributions are either *discrete* or *continuous*. A probability distribution is called discrete if its cumulative distribution function only increases in jumps, i.e., a probability distribution is discrete if there is a finite or countable set whose probability is 1. A discrete distribution has a finite set of values that can be drawn from a range.

A continuous distribution has an infinite set of possible values within a range. A continuous distribution describes probabilistic properties of a random variable which takes on a continuous (not countable) set of values. The probability associated with any particular value of a continuous distribution is null. Therefore, continuous distributions are normally described in terms of probability density, rather than probability.

The most common probability distribution functions for simulation modeling are:

- Uniform
- Negative exponential
- Normal
- Triangular
- Binomial
- Geometric
- Poisson
- Weibull
- Gamma

• Erlang

29.3.2 The Uniform Distribution

The Uniform distribution is one of the most fundamental continuous distributions to use, and in simulation, it is the basic distribution to generate random numbers. It specifies that every value between the given lower and upper limits is equally likely to occur. It is used when only the bounds of a random variable are known. Given a as the lower limit of the random variable X, and b as the upper limit, the probability density function is given by:

$$f(x) = \frac{1}{b-a}.$$

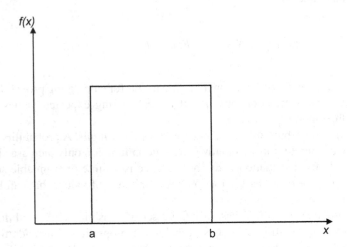

Fig. 29.2 A Uniform probability distribution

The mean of the random variable X is $(a+b)/2$. The variance of the random variable X is given by: $(b-a)^2/12$. If the random variable is discrete, it has only a finite number of values, each with the same probability. Figure 29.2 shows a uniform probability distribution function.

29.3.3 The Triangular Distribution

The triangular distribution is defined by three values: minimum, mode, and maximum. This continuous distribution is sometimes used as a first approximation and applicable when estimates of the minimum, maximum, and the most likely values are available.

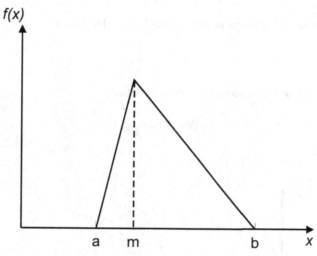

Fig. 29.3 A Triangular probability distribution

Figure 29.3 shows a Triangular probability distribution function. The triangular distribution is defined by:

$$f(x) = \begin{cases} \frac{2(x-a)}{(m-a)(b-a)} , & \text{when } a \leq x \leq m \\ \frac{2(b-x)}{(b-m)(b-a)} , & \text{when } m \leq x \leq b \\ 0 , & \text{otherwise} \end{cases}$$

The mean of the random variable X is $(a+b+m)/3$. The variance of the random variable X is given by: $(a^2 + b^2 + m^2 - ab - am - bm)/18$.

29.3.4 The Exponential Distribution

The negative exponential distribution is a continuous distribution that has only one parameter, λ that specifies the mean. The distribution is defined by:

$$f(x) = \begin{cases} \lambda e^{-\lambda x} , & \text{when } x \geq 0 \\ 0 , & \text{otherwise} \end{cases}$$

This distribution describes a type of experiment with successes that occur at some rate λ. A random variable X is the period until the next success. Since the distribution is continuous, a success can occur at any instant of time between 0 and ∞. The probability that the next success will occur at the instant equal to or less than x is given by:

$$P[X \leq x] = F(x) = 1 - e^{-\lambda x}.$$

The expected value of the random variable X is defined as:

$$E[X] = \frac{1}{\lambda}.$$

The variance of the random variable X is defined as:

$$\text{Var}[X] = \frac{1}{\lambda^2}.$$

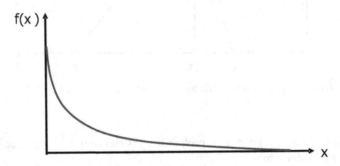

Fig. 29.4 A negative exponential probability distribution

Figure 29.4 shows a negative exponential distribution function. The exponential distribution has the memory-less property. If the sequence of trials with the experiment has been in progress for some time τ, the probability that it will continue for some additional period y is independent of τ.

This distribution is usually applied in processes such as customer inter-arrival times and equipment or machinery time to failure.

29.3.5 The Normal Distribution

The normal distribution is sometimes called the Gaussian distribution. This continuous distribution is used to describe phenomena that vary in a symmetrical manner from the mean.

The Normal distribution has a probability density function given by:

$$f(x) = \frac{1}{\sigma\sqrt{2\pi}} e^{-(x-\mu)^2/2\sigma^2}.$$

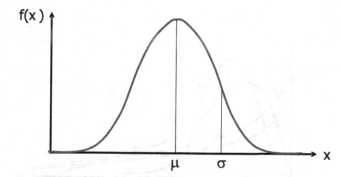

Fig. 29.5 A Normal probability distribution

The random variable X has mean μ and variance σ^2. When $\mu = 0$ and $\sigma = 1$, the function is called the unit normal distribution or standard Normal distribution. The sum of several independent random variables is approximately normally distributed. Figure 29.5 shows a Normal probability distribution function.

The normal distribution is used for processes that are known to have a symmetric distribution and for which the mean and standard deviation can be estimated. The distribution is also applied when the Central Limit Theorem holds, i.e., quantities that are sums of other quantities. This is useful for determining the properties of the resulting probability distribution when combining several random sub-processes.

29.3.6 The Weibull Distribution

The Weibull distribution is a continuous distribution bounded on the lower side. This distribution is usually applied in describing times to complete some tasks and time to failure of equipment or machinery. Figure 29.6 shows a Weibull probability distribution function.

The distribution has a probability density function given by:

$$f(x) = \begin{cases} \alpha \beta^{-\alpha} x^{\alpha-1} e^{-(x/\beta)^\alpha}, & \text{if } x > 0 \\ 0, & \text{otherwise} \end{cases}$$

The random variable X has mean:

$$\frac{\beta}{\alpha} \Gamma\left(\frac{1}{\alpha}\right), \text{where } \Gamma \text{ is the Gamma function.}$$

The variance is defined by:

$$\frac{\beta^2}{\alpha} \left\{ 2\Gamma\left(\frac{2}{\alpha}\right) - \frac{1}{\alpha}\left[\Gamma\left(\frac{1}{\alpha}\right)\right]^2 \right\}$$

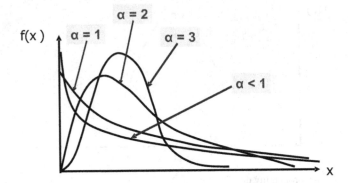

Fig. 29.6 A Weibull probability distribution

29.3.7 The Bernoulli Distribution

The Bernoulli is a discrete distribution that deals with the random occurrence with two possible outcomes. It is used to derive other discrete distributions.

The distribution is defined by:

$$F(x) = \begin{cases} 0, & \text{if } x < 0 \\ 1 - p, & \text{if } 0 \le x < 1 \\ 1, & \text{if } 1 \le x \end{cases}$$

The mean is p, and the variance is $p(1-p)$.

29.3.8 The Geometric Distribution

The geometric distribution is a discrete distribution. It is used to describe occurrences with two possible outcomes success and failure. The experiment assigns to failure the probability p (therefore $q = 1 - p$ is the probability of success). The experiment is repeated a number of times under identical conditions. This series of experiments is called a sequence of Bernoulli trials. The random variable X is the number of trials made until the occurrence of the first success. The probability that the random variable X has a value equal to or less than x is determined by:

$$F(x) = \sum_{n=0}^{x} (1-p)p^n = 1 - p^{x+1}.$$

The expected value of the random variable X is defined as:

$$E[X] = p/(1-p).$$

The variance of the random variable X is defined as:

$$\text{Var}[X] = p/(1-p)^2.$$

This distribution has the *memory-less* property. If after x trials, a success has not occurred, the probability that at least l additional trials are required is independent of x.

29.3.9 The Binomial Distribution

The binomial is a discrete distribution. It is used to describe occurrences in which there are two possible outcomes, success and failure. A random variable X is the number of successes in the first n trials. Given that the probability of a success is p, the probability that a given set of x trials result in successes (and a set of $n-x$ result in failures is q) is given by:

$$(1-p)^x p^{n-x}.$$

The probability that x successes occur from all possible combinations of n trials and x successes is:

$$P[x] = \binom{n}{k}(1-p)^x p^{n-x}.$$

The cumulative distribution function for the Binomial distribution is:

$$F(x) = \sum_{m=0}^{x} \binom{n}{k}(1-p)^x p^{n-x}.$$

The expected value of the random variable X is defined as:

$$E[X] = n(1-p).$$

The variance of the random variable X is defined as:

$$\text{Var}[X] = np(1-p).$$

29.3.10 The Poisson Distribution

The Poisson is a discrete distribution. It defines the number of events that occur in an interval of time when the events occur at a constant rate, λ.

It is commonly used to represent the number of arrivals over a given interval. A success in this type of experiment can also represent the completion of service, the response by a user. For a fixed period of time T, the probability of x successes is given by the expression:

$$\frac{(\lambda T)^x}{x!}e^{-\lambda T},$$

and the cumulative distribution is defined as:

$$F[x] = \sum_{n=0}^{x} \frac{(\lambda T)^x}{x!}e^{-\lambda T}.$$

The mean (expected) value and the variance of the random variable X are both equal to λ.

29.4 Testing Selected Distributions

After selecting a probability distribution, it must be tested on how well its represents the data. The objective is to check if a distribution is accurate enough for the intended purpose of the simulation model.

Several procedures and statistical hypothesis tests are available to check a distribution:

- Density/Histogram Overplots
- Frequency comparisons
- Distribution Function Difference Plots
- Probability Plots
- Goodness-of-Fit Tests
- Chi-square Tests
- Kolmogorov-Smirnov Tests

29.5 Summary

A cumulative distribution function defines the probability that a random variable, X, does not exceed a real value, x. These functions can be discrete or continuous. It is discrete if the distribution function changes value only at discrete points $x_1, x_2, \ldots$ of the random variable; otherwise, it is continuous. The most common distribution functions are the binomial, geometric, Poisson, exponential, uniform, and normal. A stochastic process is a set of random variables as functions of time.

The random events in a simulation model are generated using some probability distribution. These distribution functions have to be carefully selected.

The results of a simulation run are presented as a trace, which is the sequence of all the events their times of occurrence, and the summary statistics. The summary statistics must reflect must reflect the characteristics of the stochastic system being modeled.

Systems that exhibit some dependency in their state changes are modeled as Markov models. In these systems, the next state depends on the sequence of previous states. For some of the practical models considered in this book, the amount of time spent in any state is memory-less, and has an exponential distribution.

Exercises

29.1. Consider an experiment of throwing three dice. What is the sample space defined for this experiment? Suppose a success is defined as 5-2-6, what is the probability of the success event? What type of probability distribution does the experiment follow? What random variable would you associate with this experiment?

29.2. In a Poisson process, the number of job arrivals to be processed by the CPU is very important. How many different types of probability distributions would you consider for this process? Which are these distributions? Why consider more than one distribution? How do these distributions deal with time?

29.3. Explain the reason(s) why the density function cannot represent probabilities.

29.4. Consider again the experiment described in question (1) above. How do the conditions of the problem change if the throw of the second die depends on the result of the throwing of the first die? Take any relevant assumptions.

29.5. A data communication system transfers binary data from a sender station to a receiver station. Errors occur when sending a 1 with probability 0.03, and when sending a 0 with probability 0.07. The sender sends a 1 with probability 0.55. Determine the probability of the receiver receiving a 1 correctly.

Chapter 30
Simulation Output Analysis

30.1 Introduction

The goal in analyzing output data from running a simulation model is to make a valid statistical inference about the initial and long-term average behavior of the system based on the sample average from N replicate simulation runs.

Output Analysis is the analysis of data generated by a simulation run to predict system performance or compare performance of two or more system designs. In stochastic simulations, multiple runs are always necessary. The output of a single run can be viewed as a sample of size 1.

Output analysis is needed because output data from a simulation exhibits random variability when random number generators are used. i.e., two different random number streams will produce two sets of output which (probably) will differ. The statistical tool mainly used is the *confidence interval* for the mean.

For most simulations, the output data are correlated and the processes are non-stationary. The statistical (output) analysis determines:

- The estimate of the mean and variance of random variables, or
- The number of observations required to achieve a desired precision of these estimates.

30.2 Performance Measures

The output data of simulation models are used to help evaluate the *performance measures* of a system.

Normally, the other basic data output from a simulation run is called the trace. This contains the values of the random variables, the times of occurrence of these values (events), and all other data about the state of the system being modeled.

The performance measures or summary statistics reflect the characteristics of the stochastic process being modeled.

J.M. Garrido, *Object Oriented Simulation: A Modeling and Programming Perspective*,
DOI: 10.1007/978-1-4419-0516-1_30,
© Springer Science + Business Media, LLC 2009

The most common measures used to represent the results of simulation runs are:

- The mean (or average), which gives the fundamental characteristic of the data
- The standard deviation, the most common index of dispersion to summarize variability of the data
- A frequency plot, or histogram, the simplest way to represent distribution of the data.

The mean and the standard deviations can be computed by accumulating values of the random variable while the simulation run is carried out.

30.3 Comparing Sample Data

To obtain reliable *estimates* of the performance measures of interest, certain statistical analysis of the collected data has to be carried out. Two of these analysis methods are:

- Point estimation, which is single value of the sample data of interest;
- Interval estimation, which is a pair of values, $[l, u]$, of the sample data; also called the confidence interval.

With interval estimation, the desired parameter to be estimated lies between the two values, l and u, that define the interval with a given probability. Both point and interval estimations are needed for meaningful data interpretation. It is useful to have the confidence interval be short, and the desired quantity found in the interval with a high probability.

For example, the sample mean, $\bar{x}$, is an approximation (estimate) of the population mean, μ. If there is a finite number, n, of samples, then there are n estimates of the mean. Since it is not feasible to obtain the exact value of the population mean, one approach to follow is to find the probability that the population mean is within a certain interval $[l, u]$. This probability is expressed as:

$$P[l \le \mu \le u] = 1 - q.$$

The interval $[l, u]$ is called the *confidence interval*, and the value $1 - q$ is called the confidence coefficient. The method consists in finding the bounds for the interval, and finding the probability that the population mean (μ) is within that interval.

Simulations results depend on two types of input. First, the system parameters also called the configuration parameters; for example, the number of servers. Second, the workload parameters that are random samples from the various probability distributions; for example, inter-arrival and service periods.

It is important to differentiate between the effects of variations of the random samples and the effects of the configuration parameters. Otherwise, the interpretation of the results will not be correct.

To obtain improved accuracy of the estimates of performance measures, variance reduction methods are used.

30.4 Statistical Inference

Statistical Inference is a set of methods to assist a decision maker to draw conclusions about a population from a specific sample. There are two major groups of methods:

- Hypothesis testing, which is used in decision making
- Estimation, which involves establishing a degree of accuracy associated with a point estimate.

Point estimates are quantities that are characteristics of a population/distribution, such as μ and σ^2, and are called parameters. Generally these population parameters are unknown, so these parameters can be estimated from a sample. Since this estimate a parameter by a single number, this process is referred to as *point estimation*. For example, $\bar{X}$ is an estimate of μ and S^2 is an estimate of σ^2.

When making statistical inferences about the population mean, the goal is to make a valid statistical inference about the value of the mean, μ, based on the value of the sample estimate, $\bar{X}$.

30.4.1 Confidence Intervals

A *Confidence Interval* is an interval estimate for a parameter that specifies a level of confidence that provides a way of quantifying imprecision. The goal of a confidence interval procedure is to form an interval, with endpoints determined by the sample, that will contain, or "cover" the target parameter with a pre-specified (high) probability called the *confidence level*.

The Central Limit Theorem (CLT) states that as we increase the number of samples $(N \geq 30)$, the distribution of the means will be approximately normally distributed. To apply the CLT:

- Each single run of a stochastic simulation model can be considered a single sample.
- Each independent model replication, where replications are performed using different random number streams, produces another sample point.

30.4.2 Calculating A Confidence Interval

A $100(1 - \alpha)$ percent confidence interval, for $0 < \alpha < 1$, of the mean is a range of values running from a lower bound to an upper bound wherein we can be $100(1 - \alpha)$ percent confident that the true population mean falls. The quantity α is sometimes called the *significance level*. For example, for a 95% confidence, $\alpha = 0.05$. The following formula is used to compute the confidence interval.

$$\bar{X} \pm t_{n-1,1-\alpha/2}\sqrt{\frac{S^2}{n}}$$

In the formula:

$\bar{X}$ is the sample mean

n is the number of replications

S_n is the sample standard deviation

$t_{n-1,1-\alpha/2}$ is the value from the t-distribution table

For a confidence interval, the level of precision can be calculated where the number of independent replications is known a priori.

To use confidence intervals with specified precision, the number of replications necessary can be computed to obtain a specified level of precision. This procedure uses a half-length of a $100(1-\alpha)$ percent confidence interval.

The number of replicates to run is calculated based on how accurate you want the sample average from your replicates to be. The accuracy is a measure of how close the sample average is to the true long-term average performance of the system. The following formula is used for calculating the number of replicates to run.

$$N = \left(\frac{t_{n-1,1-\alpha/2}\, S_n}{e}\right)^2$$

In the formula:

N is the number of replications to run

n is the number of replications already made in a pilot run

S_n is the standard deviation from the n pilot replications

e is the desired accuracy in the sample mean

$t_{n-1,1-\alpha/2}$ is the value from the t-distribution table

30.5 Terminating and Non-terminating Runs

A terminating simulation run is carried out to study the behavior of a system over a particular time interval. For example, the behavior of a database server during the *peak period* of the day. A non-terminating simulation run is carried out to study the steady-state or long-term average behavior of a system.

30.5.1 Analyzing Terminating Simulations

In a terminating simulation run, the simulation starts at a defined state and ends when the simulation reaches some other defined state or time. The majority of service systems are modeled as terminating systems.

Analyzing terminating simulations involve carrying out several simulation runs using different seeds for the random number generations. Data is gathered for successive time intervals during the simulation period.

30.5.2 Analyzing Non-terminating Simulations

In a non-terminating simulation, the long-term average behavior of a system is analyzed. In this analysis, an adequate length of the simulation period needs to be calculated. The simulation runs then are performed to gather data for the statistical analysis of the steady-state behavior of the system.

Non-terminating simulation runs begin with a warm-up, or transient, state and gradually moves to a steady state.

30.6 Summary

Output analysis involves gathering the output data from running a simulation model and making valid statistical inferences about the initial and long-term average behavior of the system. This analysis is based on the samples from several replicate simulation runs.

The output data from a simulation exhibits random variability when random number generators are used. i.e., two different random number streams will produce two sets of output which (probably) will differ. For most simulations, the output data are correlated and the processes are non-stationary. The statistical tool mainly used is the *confidence interval*.

Chapter 31
Model Validation

31.1 Introduction

Validation of a simulation model provides assurance or confidence that the model is sufficiently adequate and appropriate for use according to the purpose of the model. Validation deals with ensuring that the model closely represents the real system. This should address the concerns of users that the model and results of its simulation runs are acceptable within certain range specified by the purpose of the model.

Verification of the simulation model deals with ensuring that the model is correctly implemented. If a model has not been validated, it is unlikely that it will be used in a real-world setting.

In order for a model to be acceptable, the model should be thoroughly verified and validated before use. This chapter presents an overview of several concepts and techniques for verification and validation of simulation models.

31.2 Verification Techniques for Simulation Models

During the formulation of the conceptual model in model development, a set of assumptions is taken (about the real system). Verification addresses the question of whether the model implements these assumptions correctly. Debugging and low-level testing are some of the techniques used for verification. Formal methods are a more detailed and mathematical set of methods.

Object-oriented modeling and programming provide enhancements to modularity and information hiding and improve developing and debugging large and complex programs and simulation models. Some of the advantages offered by object-orientation were discussed in previous chapters. Object-orientation helps and enhances the debugging of software that implements simulation models.

J.M. Garrido, *Object Oriented Simulation: A Modeling and Programming Perspective*,
DOI: 10.1007/978-1-4419-0516-1_31,
© Springer Science + Business Media, LLC 2009

31.2.1 Simulation Traces

The *trace* of a simulation run is a list of the sequence of sequence of events that occur when a simulation model is executed. The trace listings help verify the model. These allow the modeler to check the correctness of the model implementation. The trace facility of simulation models should provide selective tracing, the user would be able to select the level of detail in the trace.

Graphical outputs of simulation runs help in summarizing the traces and in displaying indication of the behavior of the model. For example, the graph that displays the length of the queue of customer arrivals. This type of information helps in debugging the model implementation.

31.2.2 Simulation Tests

Several tests are available for simulation runs. Results for all these tests should be carefully analyzed and documented. Some of these tests are:

- The *seed independence* test. In this test, the results of simulation runs are compared with different seed values. The results should be similar.
- The *parameter test* or *continuity test*. In this test, several simulation runs are carried out for each set of input parameter values. For small changes in the input, small changes in the output should be expected.
- *Degeneracy tests*. These tests check that the simulation runs of the model exhibit good behavior for extreme values of simulation parameters. These extreme cases are the allowed bounds (upper and lower) for the various parameters.
- *Consistency tests*. These tests check that the simulation runs generate similar results for input values of parameters that have similar effects. For example, various values of input parameters could produce the same or similar workload on the model.

31.3 Validation of Simulation Models

Validation attempts to answer the question of whether the *assumptions* about the real system are correct. However, a simulation model is an approximation of a real system. Users of the simulation model expect these assumptions to be as close to reality as possible. The model could be invalid in that the assumptions taken are not realistic.

A model is valid for some particular purpose, i.e., under certain specific assumptions. Validation is model dependent; the techniques used in one model may not be applicable to another model.

A great part of the validation effort is concerned with comparing observations about the real system with observations from the simulation model.

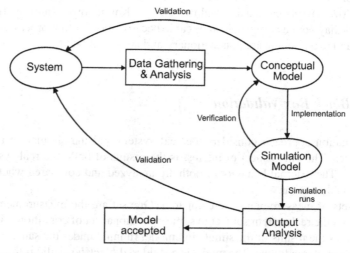

Fig. 31.1 Validation and verification in model development

Figure 31.1 illustrates verification and validation as part of the model development process. After the model has been accepted as valid, it can be used for conducting experiments, for making inferences about the system represented, and for decision-making.

Validation can be considered at various levels of the model development process.

- At the level of the conceptual model, *conceptual model validity* provides assurance that the assumptions made in specifying the conceptual model are correct.
- At the level of the simulation model, *operational validity* provides assurance that the outputs of simulation runs of the model are sufficiently accurate according to the purpose of the model.
- *Data validity* provides assurance that the data used in model development and conducting experiments is adequate and correct.

31.3.1 General Validation Approach

Validation of a simulation model involves analyzing:

- Assumptions about the real system
- Values of the input parameters and their distributions
- Simulation results.

Using expert knowledge is the most common way to validate the simulation model. Experts compare results of simulation runs with measurements of the real system. This test is sometimes called *results validation*.

The comparison analysis may use classical statistical tests, such as: t-test, Mann-Whitney, two-sample chi-square, and two-sample Kolmogorov-Smirnov. However, these tests may not be completely applicable because most output processes of simulations and real systems are non-stationary and auto-correlated.

31.3.2 Black Box Validation

This validation approach considers the real system and the simulation model as black boxes. The only aspect of interest is the results of both, the real system and the model. The external behavior of both are analyzed and compared whether they are acceptably similar.

Two sets of measurements are compared. One set are the measurements of the output from the real system subject to some operational set of conditions. The other set measures the results of the simulation model running under the same (or almost the same) set of conditions. The model is considered *black box* valid if the results of both observations are very close to each other.

An important technique compares the simulation model and the real system by inputting the model with historical system input data, which was used on inspections of the real system. This technique is called *historical data validation*.

Methods of statistical inference are used carefully to analyze the comparison and draw conclusions about the validity of the model. This is relevant when the observations are used to test some hypothesis.

There are two general types of validation errors. Errors of the first type occur when a valid model is wrongly rejected. This can result because there is a percentage of error in the statistical inference as used to test a hypothesis.

The errors of the second type occur when a hypothesis that is false is taken as true, or an invalid model is taken as valid. Another type of validation error occurs when the people carrying out the tests ask the wrong questions.

31.3.3 White Box Validation

White box validation considers the structure and internal behavior of the real system and the simulation model as known. With black box validation, the main concern is on external behavior and the predictive nature of the simulation model.

The behavior of the simulation model depends mainly on the probability distribution chosen for the random variables. These represent uncertain behavior of the system and implemented in the simulation model. The selection of these distributions can be a very difficult task.

The internal behavior of the model depends on logical rules. These rules should follow the rules that influence the internal behavior of the real system. It is convenient that this type of rule checking is carried out before the model is fully implemented. It is also important to validate the dynamic behavior of the system, not only of its individual components. The trace is a good source for this part of the validation process.

31.4 Summary

Verification of a simulation model assures that the simulation model be completely tested, for correct implementation. Validation assures that the simulation model is an accurate representation of the real system. End users expect to be verified and validated. There are several techniques that guide the modeler to achieve a reasonable degree of verification and validation.

Appendix A
Configuring Tools and Compiling OOSimL Programs

This appendix describes the procedures for configuring the appropriate software development tools and using the OOSimL compiler for developing OOSimL programs.

A.1 The OOSimL Compiler

The OOSimL compilation is a two-phase process. The first phase involves a translation into an equivalent Java source program, the second phase involves the corresponding Java translation to Java byte-code. The OOSimL compiler software, a sample model, and documentation are available from the OOSimL Web page:

    http://science.kennesaw.edu/~jgarrido/oosiml.html

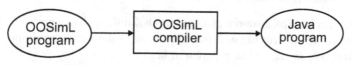

Fig. A.1 First phase of compilation of an OOSimL program

The first phase of the compilation is illustrated in Figure A.1. The second phase of compilation involves compiling the corresponding Java program and use of the Java compiler. Figure A.2 shows what is involved in compilation of a source program in Java. The Java compiler, which is provided by Sun Microsystems, checks for syntax errors in the source program and then translates it into a program in byte-code, which is the program in an intermediate form.

Note that the Java bytecode is not dependent on any particular platform or computer system. This makes the bytecode very portable from one machine to another.

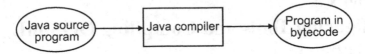

Fig. A.2 Compiling a Java source program

Figure A.3 shows how to execute a program in bytecode. The Java virtual machine (JVM), which is another software tool from Sun Microsystems, carries out the interpretation of the program in bytecode.

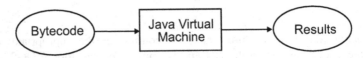

Fig. A.3 Executing a Java program

The next sections introduce and explain how to configure and use the OOSimL compiler with several software development environments. Currently, there are three general procedures used for developing programs and simulation models with the OOSimL compiler. These procedures are:

1. Working with the jGRASP integrated development environment (IDE).
2. Developing the simulation model with the Eclipse integrated environment.
3. Working in a DOS window.

The OOSimL compiler software consists of two main components: an executable program, `oosiml.exe`, and the run-time library, `oosimlib.jar`. The compiler has the following functions:

1. Syntax checking of a source program in OOSimL; a list of errors is displayed and written to an error file with the same name as the source program
2. Generation of an equivalent program in Java

The first general step for installing the software is to create a folder and then to store the relevant files in the folder. As mentioned previously, the two essential files are: the OOSimL compiler, which is an executable program called `oosiml.exe`, and the runtime library, `oosimlib.jar`.

A.2 Developing Models with The jGRASP Environment

jGRASP is a relative flexible and easy-to-use light environment to develop Java and OOSimL programs. The jGRASP tool needs to be configured so that it will execute

the OOSimL compiler when the user issues the Compile command. The jGRASP
software can be downloaded from:

```
http://www.jgrasp.org
```

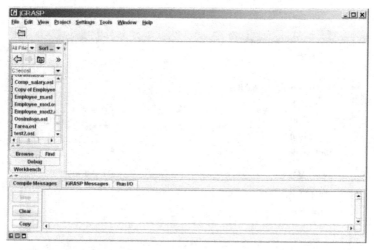

Fig. A.4 The jGRASP main window

The following steps provide a guide for configuring OOSimL to work with
jGRASP.

1. Place the OOSimL compiler in an appropriate directory, such as `c:\eoosl`.
2. Start jGRASP; the main window appears on the screen as shown in Figure A.4.
3. On the Settings menu, select Compiler Settings.
4. Choose Workspace; a new window appears with title: Settings for Workspace.
   On Language option, select Plain Text.
5. Click the New button.
6. A new dialog window appears on the screen with the title: `User Compiler`
   `Environment` (Plain Text). On the top bar of the window, type: `OOSIML`
   `Compiler`. Figure A.5 shows this window.
7. On the Compile row, type: `OOSIML %FILE`.
8. On the directory column, type: `C:\eoosl`, or any other folder that contains the
   OOSimL compiler.
9. Click the Save button.
10. Click the OK button.
11. Back on the Settings for workspace window, click on the line `User: OOSimL`
    `Compiler`. Figure A.6 shows this window.
12. Click the Use button.

The following steps are used to configure jGRASP for using the libraries,
`oosimlib.jar` and `acm.jar`.

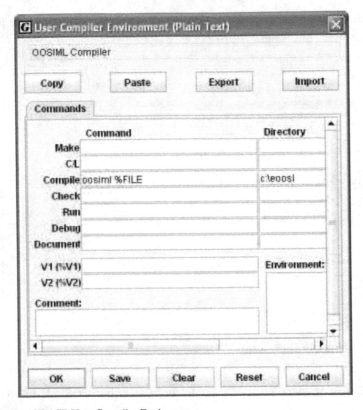

Fig. A.5 The jGRASP User Compiler Environment

1. Click on the Settings menu in the main jGRASP menu bar.
2. Select PATH/CLASSPATH then Workspace.
3. Select CLASSPATH. Figure A.7 shows the window with the current settings for CLASSPATH.
4. Click on the New button to add a new search path.
5. On the new window that appears, type c:\eoosl\oosimlib.jar. Then click on the Ok button. This assumes that this library is located in the c:\eoosl directory. Figure A.8 shows this window.
6. Click on the New button to add another search path.
7. On the new window that appears, type c:\eoosl\acm.jar. Then click on the Ok button. This assumes that this library is located in the c:\eoosl directory. Figure A.8 shows this window.

The following sequence of steps is used for compiling OOSimL programs with jGRASP.

1. Start jGRASP.

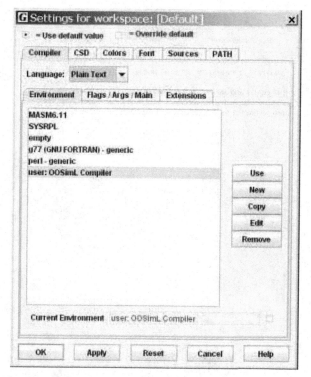

Fig. A.6 The jGRASP Settings for the OOSimL compiler workspace

2. The jGRASP main window appears on the screen, as shown in Figure A.4. On the left pane, select the folder where the OOSimL program files are located.
3. Click the File menu, and select Open.
4. In the Open File, type `osl` in the File Extension text-box (far right side), and press the Enter key.
5. Select the file to open and click the Open button.
6. The source file (with extension `osl`) appears on the screen. Edit the file and save, if necessary.
7. Click the Compiler menu and select Compile or click the button with the green cross.
8. On the bottom pane of the screen, all the messages appear, including any compiler error messages. If there are no errors, the message `No syntax errors found` appears as the last message.
9. Edit the file if any errors were found.
10. Save the file and recompile, if necessary.
11. To close the file, click the File menu and select Clear.

After the OOSimL compilation, the corresponding Java program must be compiled with the Java compiler. The following sequence of steps is used to compile and execute a Java program.

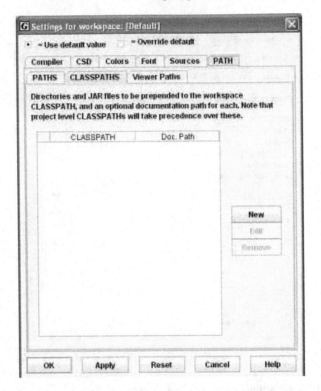

Fig. A.7 The jGRASP Settings for PATH and CLASSPATH

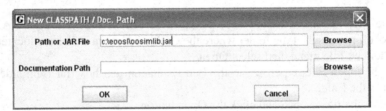

Fig. A.8 The jGRASP window for adding a search path

1. Click the File menu and select Open.
2. Select `java` for the type of file.
3. Select the desired Java file.
4. Click the Compiler menu and select Compile, or click the button with the green cross.
5. The bottom window will display jGRASP: Operation complete.
6. Click the Run selection, or click the button with the red man running.
7. If necessary, type the appropriate input data values required by the program when it executes.

A.3 Using The Eclipse Platform

The Eclipse platform is an open extensible IDE for developing programs in Java, C++, and various other programming languages. Eclipse has been developed for several Operating Systems platforms, such as Linux, MS Windows, Mac OS X, and others. The platform is composed of the Workbench, the Workspace, and other components. The Workbench is the desktop development environment; it is a tool that integrates the creation, management, and navigation of workspace resources. Eclipse uses the workspaces to store the user projects.

Each Workbench window contains one or more perspectives, which contain views and editors and control what appears in certain menus and tool bars. A Workbench consists of:

- Perspectives
- Views
- Editors

A perspective is a group of views and editors in the Workbench window. One or more perspectives can exist in a single Workbench window. A view is a visual component within the Workbench. It is normally used to navigate a hierarchy of resources in the Workbench, or display properties for the active editor. Modifications made in a view are saved immediately.

An editor is also a visual component within the Workbench. It is used to edit or browse a resource. The visual presentation might be text or a diagram. Editors are launched by clicking on a resource in a view. Some features are common to both views and editors. These can be active or inactive, but only one can be active at any one time. The active part is the target for common operations like cut, copy and paste. If an editor tab is not highlighted it indicates the editor is not active, however views may show data based on the last active editor. The Eclipse software can be downloaded from:

```
http://www.eclipse.org
```

A.4 Configuring Eclipse for OOSimL Models

After installing the Eclipse Platform, start Eclipse by double-clicking on the Eclipse icon on the desktop. The next few steps should be followed to appropriately configure Eclipse for developing OOSimL simulation models. Select a folder for the Eclipse workspace. On the File menu, select Switch Workspace, then select Other. The following window shows on the screen.

Set the folder where the projects with source files are located. All the OOSimL and Java source files will be placed in a Java project. For example, assuming that the Java projects are located in the parent folder C:\eoosl, type this path then click the OK button. Eclipse loads immediately the workspace. Figure A.9 shows the Eclipse Workspace launcher for setting the workspace to a desired location.

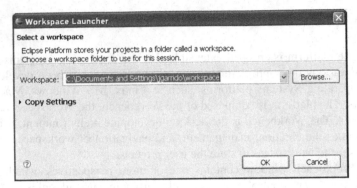

Fig. A.9 The Workspace launcher of Eclipse

A.4.1 Setting Eclipse for Editing OOSimL Source Files

The following two steps will enable the user to edit and compile OOSimL programs, which have an `osl` extension. Select the Window menu and select Preferences. The following window shows on the screen.

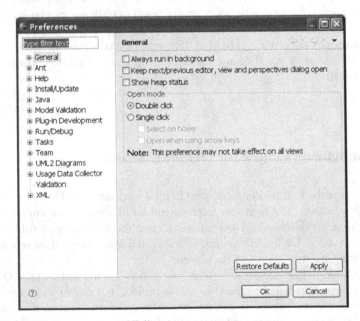

Fig. A.10 The Preferences menu of Eclipse

Figure A.10 shows the Preferences menu of Eclipse. On the left pane of this window, expand the tree on General, then expand Editors. Select File Associations.

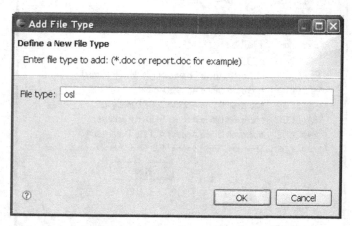

Fig. A.11 Adding the `osl` extension in Eclipse File Association

On the upper right-hand side of the Preferences window, click the Add button. The Add File Type window appears. Add the *osl* extension by typing `*.osl` for the File Type, as shown on the Figure A.11. Click the OK button to close this window. Click the OK button again to close the Preferences window.

The following steps will associate the *osl* file extension with the Eclipse editor. With the Windows Explorer, locate a folder with OOSimL source files. On the Tools menu, select Folder Options. Figure A.12 shows the Windows Explorer with Folder Options.

To create a new file extension and associate it with a text editor, click on the New button and type `osl` on the Create New Extension window that appears on the screen. Click the Advanced button and select Text Document. Figure A.13 shows the Create New Extension window.

Now Eclipse can open an OOSimL file and use its editor to write and modify the OOSimL source files. For example, from the Eclipse File menu select Open File in the folder of project *eoosl3*. On the new window that appears, select a file from a folder with OOSimL source files.

The OOSimL file (`MBarber.osl`) is opened and it shows in the editor area of the Eclipse platform. Figure A.14 shows the selected file, `MBarber.osl`, in the editor area.

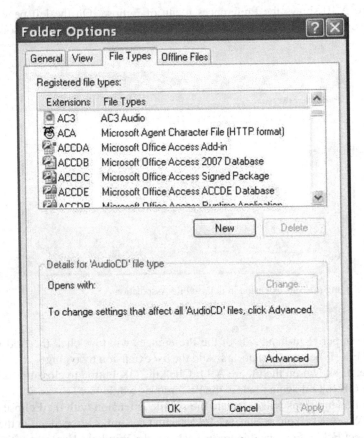

Fig. A.12 Setting the Windows Explorer for setting Folder Options

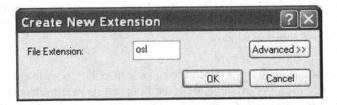

Fig. A.13 Windows Explorer for setting Create New Extension

A.4.2 Configuring Eclipse for the OOSimL Compiler

The following steps will configure Eclipse to use the OOSimL compiler as an external tool. Figure A.15 shows the External Tools Configurations window.

1. In the Run menu, select External Tools

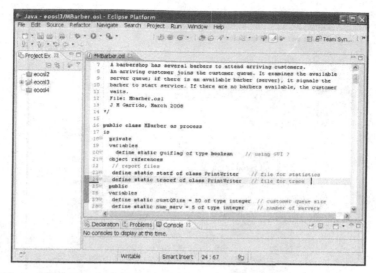

Fig. A.14 An OOSimL source file in the Eclipse editor area

2. Select External Tools Configurations
3. In the new window that appears, type the name, "OOSimL Compiler"
4. For the Location, click on the button Browse File System
5. Select the executable file: oosiml.exe
6. On the Argument, select file prompt
7. Click the Apply button
8. Click the Close button.

For compiling an OOSimL program, activate the Run menu from the top tool bar and select "OOSimL Compiler". Another way to start the OOSimL compiler is to click on the corresponding button on the second top bar.

A.4.3 Developing OOSimL Simulation Models with Eclipse

As mentioned previously, all OOSimL and Java source files should be stored in a Java project. To develop a simulation model, a Java project must first be created with Eclipse. The OOSimL source files are then created within this project. A Java project is used because the OOSimL compiler generates the corresponding Java class after compiling an *.osl file.

To create a new Java project, activate the File menu on the top tool bar, select New, select Project, and then select Java Project. Figure A.16 shows the Project Wizard window that appears on the screen.

Fig. A.15 External Tools Configuration in Eclipse

Inside the New Project window, expand the Java subtree and select Java Project. Click the Next button at the bottom of the window. Type a name for the project and click the Finish button. Automatically a Java Perspective is opened for the project.

A project will normally contain more than one source file, each representing a class implementation. The source files can be created and edited or can be imported from another folder if these files already exist. To create a new source file in a project, click the project name, activate the File menu on the top tool bar, select New then select File. Type the name of the file and click on the Finish button.

To import an existing file, click on the name of the project, click on the File menu, then select Import. On the Import window, expand the General tree and select File System. Click on the Next button. On the new window click the Browse button to find the source directory of the file to import. Select the file(s) to import and click on the Finish button.

All OOSimL source files should be compiled in any given project. To compile an OOSimL source file, select External Tools on the Run menu, select "OOSimL Compiler". Indicate the source file name to compile. Figure A.17 shows the bottom pane of the window with the result of the OOSimL compilation of the `Carwash.osl` source file of project *eoosl2*.

The next step sets the additional libraries required to build the project by setting the options in the build path for a Java project. Activate the Project menu and select

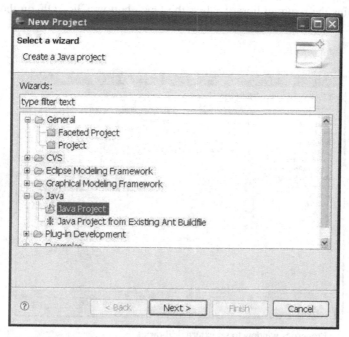

Fig. A.16 Selecting a Project Wizard in Eclipse

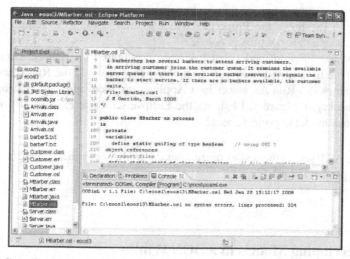

Fig. A.17 Compilation of an OOSimL source file in Eclipse

Properties. Select Java Build Path and open the Libraries tab. Click on the Add External JARs button. On the JAR Selection window, search and select the JAR file

that contains the required library. Click the Open button. Click OK on the current
window.

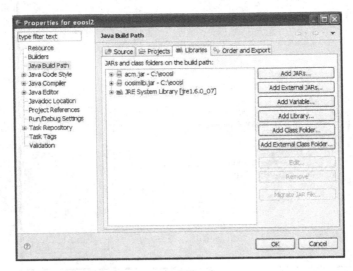

Fig. A.18 The Properties window to set external libraries

Figure A.18 shows the Properties window after adding the required library,
oosimlib.jar, to the project *eoosl2*.

To run a simulation model that has been configured on Eclipse, click on the
project name in the Eclipse Project Explorer pane. Activate the Run menu on the
top tool bar, select Run As, select Java Application, then select the matching item
(default package). Figure A.19 shows the Eclipse screen after a simulation run of
the Carwash model in project *eoosl2*.

Figure A.20 shows the results of running the multi-server Barbershop simulation
model in project *eoosl3*.

A.5 Developing Models in a DOS Window

In a DOS window, any text editor can be used to enter a new program in OOSimL or
to modify an existing OOSimL program. Two good editors for developing OOSimL
and Java programs are Notepad++ and the DOS Editor. For editing and using the
OOSimL compiler in a DOS window, complete the following steps:

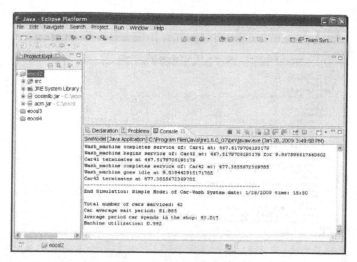

Fig. A.19 Running the carwash simulation model in Eclipse

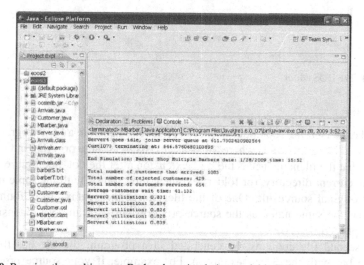

Fig. A.20 Running the multi-server Barbershop simulation model in Eclipse

1. Start and open a DOS window. You can do this by clicking the Start button and then selecting Run. In the Run window, type the word `command` and click the OK button.
2. Change the directory to the one where your files are stored. Use the CD command in DOS.
3. Start the DOS editor. Figure A.21 shows a DOS window with the editor.
4. Type and edit the source program (e.g., `Tarea.osl`) with the DOS editor. Note that the source files have the `.osl` extension.

Fig. A.21 The DOS editor

5. Invoke the OOSimL compiler to check syntax and generate a Java program. Type `oosiml Tarea.osl`, where `Tarea.osl` is the source program in OOSimL. Note that the filename needs the `osl` extension after the dot. See Figure A.22.

6. In the current directory, (or folder) two new files appear with the same name as your original source file. One of the files stores the syntax errors found. This file has the same name as the source program but with an `err` extension; for example, `Tarea.err`.

7. The second file contains the generated Java program; the file has the same name but with the `java` extension. For example, if your source program is `Tarea.osl`, then the Java program created is `Tarea.java`.

8. Use the Java compiler to compile the Java program (e.g. `Tarea.java`) generated by the OOSimL compiler.

9. Use the Java virtual machine (JVM) to execute the compiled program. When starting execution, enter the input data to the program, if needed.

10. Return to the Windows desktop by typing `exit` while in DOS.

In step 2 (in a DOS window), to change the directory to the one where you have the source programs, type the following command: `cd\`, and then press the Enter key. If the directory with your source programs is called `eoosl`, on the next line type `cd eoosl` and then press the Enter key; this changes to the directory called

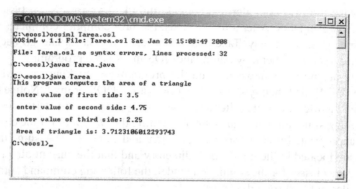

Fig. A.22 The DOS window

eoosl. To get a list of the files in the current directory, type dir and then press Enter.

To start the DOS editor, type edit at the command prompt then press the Enter key. After the editor starts and if you are typing a new source program, start typing line by line; press the Enter key at the end of every line. When you have completed entering the text, click on the File menu and select the Save as option. Type the name of the file (program name). It must start with a capital letter, and have a .osl extension. For example, Tarea.osl. Figure A.21 shows the DOS editor with some text lines already entered. To exit the DOS editor, click the File menu, and then select Exit.

To compile (step 5 above) an OOSimL source program called Tarea.osl, type oosiml Tarea.osl and then press the Enter key. After a few seconds, you will see a message on the screen. In this case, File Tarea.osl, no syntax errors, lines processed: 32. The window in Figure A.22 shows these commands.

The OOSimL compiler generates two new files with the same name as the original source program. The first file is the corresponding Java program. The other file created contains the syntax errors that the OOSimL compiler detected. The first part of the name of this file is the same as the source file but with the .err appended. For example, after compiling the Tarea.osl source program, the Java file generated is tarea.java and the error file produced is called Tarea.err.

The error file generated by the OOSimL compiler shows all the syntax errors detected in the source program. These are indicated with the line number and column number where they appear. If there are no errors detected, then the last line of this text file includes the message no syntax errors. The total number of lines read is also shown

In summary, after invoking the OOSimL compiler, the new files that appear on the current directory are Tarea.osl, Tarea.java, and Tarea.err. You can check this with the dir command in DOS. You can also check the date with Windows Explorer.

To invoke the Java compiler and compile the file `Tarea.java`, type `javac Tarea.java` in DOS. After a few seconds, the Java compiler completes and displays error messages, if any. Take note of the error messages and go back to the DOS editor to correct them, by editing the OOSimL source program.

If there are no error messages, run the program by invoking the Java Virtual Machine (JVM), and then type `java Tarea` at the DOS prompt. Notice that you don't need the file extension. After a few seconds, your program starts execution.

Compiling simulation programs, involve setting the *classpath* for the compiler to find the appropriate libraries, `oosimlib.jar` and `acm.jar`. Assume that these libraries are located in the `c:\eoosl` directory and that the current directory contains the Java classes for the simulation model, the following command compiles all the Java files in the current directory.

```
javac -classpath c:\eoosl\oosimlib.jar;c:\eoosl\acm.jar *.java
```

The following command will start execution of the simulation model, assuming that the main class is named *SimModel*.

```
java -classpath c:\eoosl\acm.jar;
             c:\eoosl\oosimlib.jar;. SimModel
```

Appendix B
Overview of Basic Probability Theory

B.1 Introduction

The basic principles of probability theory are presented and random variables are discussed. Random numbers are then introduced. Only the relevant concepts of random number usage are explained, which are necessary in developing simulation models. Probability and statistics are essential for selecting the appropriate probability distributions and random number generation and for other aspects in the construction of simulation models.

B.2 Experiments and Probabilities

An experiment is a process for which the outcome is not known with certainty. The *sample space* of an experiment is the collection of all possible outcomes of that experiment. A particular outcome is called a *sample point*.

Certain sets of sample points or collection of outcomes in a sample space are called *events*. An event occurs if the outcome of an experiment is one of the sample points in the set that defines the event.

B.2.1 Set Theory

The study of probability depends on the theory of sets. A set is a group or collection of distinct elements. A set is denoted by a capital letter and the collection is usually written enclosed within braces. For example, the set S is defined as $\{a,b,c,d,e\}$. A member of the set is an element that belongs to the set. If an element x is a member of set S, it is denoted as: $x \in S$. If element y is not a member of set S, it is denoted as $y \notin S$.

Some of the common set operations are described next.

- An empty set is denoted as $\emptyset$ and is also a valid set. This set contains no elements and is known as the *null* set.
- The union of two sets A and B is denoted as $A \cup B$ and is a set with all the elements contained in either of the two sets A and B.
- The intersection of two sets A and B is denoted as $A \cap B$ and is another set with only the elements contained in both sets.
- The subset S of a set A is denoted as $S \subset A$ and is a set with the elements that are also contained in a set A. Set S contains some or all the elements in A.
- The universe is denoted as Ω and is a set that contains all possible elements.
- The complement of a set A is denoted as $A \cap B = \emptyset$ and is another set with all the elements that are not contained in set A.
- Two sets A and B are mutually exclusive if they contain no common elements. The intersection of A and B is the null set, $\emptyset$. This is denoted as $A \cap B = \emptyset$.

B.2.2 Probabilities

The probability of an event is defined as the relative likelihood that it will occur when the experiment is performed. By default, probabilities take values between 0 and 1.

The relative frequency of an outcome is represented by the probability measure. It is defined by a function P that assigns a real number to an event. The probability of event A is denoted $P(A)$. Let Ω denote the entire sample space. The following are the most common properties of probabilities:

1. For every event A, $0 \leq P(A) \leq 1$
2. $P(\Omega) = 1$
3. If A and B are mutually exclusive events, then

$$P(A \cup B) = P(A) + P(B)$$

4. The conditional probability of event B given that event A has occurred, denoted by $P(B|A)$, is defined by

$$P(B|A) = P(A \cap B)/P(A)$$

5. Two events A and B are independent if their occurrence are unrelated and the relation is defined as
$$P(B|A) = P(B)$$

or
$$P(A|B) = P(A)$$

If events A and B are independent then

$$P(A \cap B) = P(A) \times P(B)$$

In studying the behavior of systems, simulation models are used to represent the behavior of systems over multiple experiments. Each experiment defines several possible outcomes. Therefore, the relative frequency of an outcome is what is important in probability theory. This is the number of occurrences of a particular outcome in a large number of repetitions of the experiment. An event is a set of outcomes.

B.3 Random Variables

A random variable is a function that assigns a real number to each sample point or outcome in the sample space. This function assigns a real number to an event.

The probability that a random variable X does not exceed a real value x, is defined as a function $F(x) = P(X \leq x)$. The function $F(x)$ is known as the *cumulative distribution function* (CDF) of the random variable X. The function $F(x)$ has the following properties:

- $F(-\infty) = 0$
- $F(\infty) = 1$
- If $x \leq y$ then $F(x) \leq F(y)$.

A random variable is *discrete* if it can take at most a countable number of values, $x_1, x_2, \ldots$. The cumulative distribution function of this random variable only changes value at certain points $x_1, x_2, \ldots$ and remains constant between these points. The function $F(X)$ has values $p_1, p_2, \ldots$ at these points, and $p_1 + p_2 + \ldots = 1$.

A random variable is *continuous* if it can take on an infinite number of different values, which are all nonnegative real numbers. The cumulative distribution function of a continuous random variable is continuous everywhere.

The *probability density function*, $f(x)$, for the continuous random variable X, is defined as the derivative of the cumulative distribution function, $F'(x)$. It follows that $F(x)$ can also be derived from the integral of $f(x)$. Then the probability that the random variable X has a value in the interval (a, b) is calculated by:

$$P(a < X < b) = F(b) - F(a) = \int_a^b f(x).$$

The cumulative distribution functions are normally useful for calculating probabilities, and probability density functions are normally useful for generating random numbers in a simulation model.

B.4 Other Properties of Random Variables

The *expected value*, also known as the *mean*, of a random variable is the weighted sum of all its values. The weight of a value is the probability of that value of the random variable.

If the random variable X is discrete, and has values $x_1, x_2, \ldots$ with probabilities $p_1, p_2, \ldots$ the expected value of X is defined as:

$$E[X] = \sum_{i=1}^{\infty} p_i x_i.$$

If the random variable X is continuous, the expected value of X is defined by the integral:

$$E[X] = \int_{0}^{\infty} x f(x) dx.$$

The *variance* of the random variable X is defined as:

$$\mathrm{Var}[X] = E[(X - E[X])^2] = E[X^2] - (E[X])^2.$$

The variance of the random variable X is a measure of the spread of X around its mean. The standard deviation of X is defined as the square root of its variance, and is denoted by σ.

The *covariance* of two random variables X and Y that are not uncorrelated, is defined by:

$$\mathrm{Cov}[X, Y] = E[XY] - E[X]E[Y].$$

If random variables X and Y are uncorrelated, then their covariance is zero.

B.5 Stochastic Processes

For the models of systems studied in this book, the long-term behavior of the systems is the main focus. Therefore, it is very important to observe how a system behaves over some period, instead of any particular observation at some instant. To study the long-term behavior of a system, a series of independent repetitions of an experiment is carried out, of many different aspects (random variables) of the system. Each repetition generates an event corresponding to a random variable defined for the experiment.

A stochastic process[1] is a series of repetitions of an experiment over time. These repetitions result in a sequence of events observed through time. More formally, a stochastic process is a set of random variables as functions of time. Note that some

---

[1] The term *process* used here has a statistical meaning.

random variables are continuous-time, that is, defined for any value of time (for $t \geq 0$); other random variables are discrete-time, defined only at specific instants.

B.6 Random Numbers in Simulation Models

The simulation models studied in this book are the models for the simulation of stochastic processes. For these models, it is necessary to generate the values for the various random variables that represent the different *events*. To accomplish this, almost all the programs for the simulation models include calls to routines that generate random numbers based on appropriate distributions.

The basic generation of random (or more precisely, pseudo-random) numbers is carried out from a uniform distribution. The generation of pseudo-random numbers with the other distributions uses transformation methods starting with the uniform distribution as a base. The run-time simulation package in OOSimL provides not only routines for the generation of pseudo-random numbers with a uniform distribution, but also routines for the most common probability distributions. Each time a routine that generates pseudo-random numbers is called, it generates a number. A sequence of these numbers will be generated by successive calls to the appropriate routine that generates pseudo-random numbers.

The main characteristic of a pseudo-random stream of numbers is that the stream or sequence of numbers will be the same each time the program, which calls the routine to generate these numbers, is executed. When there is need to generate a different sequence of such numbers, the value of the seed has to be changed. But when there is need to reproduce the same sequence of numbers, a seed is usually set to an odd value.

Appendix C
Bibliography

1. Almeida, V.A.F., D.A. Menasce, and D.W. Dowdy. *Capacity Planning and Performance Modeling: from Mainframes to Client-server Systems*, 1994. Englewood Cliffs: Prentice-Hall.
2. Ash, Carol. *The Probability Tutoring Book*, Piscataway, NJ: IEEE Press, 1993.
3. Banks, J. J., S. Carson, and B. Nelson *Discrete-Event System Simulation*. Second ed. Englewood Cliffs, NJ: Prentice-Hall, 1996.
4. Booch, Grady. *Object-Oriented Analysis and Design*, 2nd ed. Reading, MA: Addison-Wesley, 1994.
5. Budd, Timothy. *Understanding Object-Oriented Programming With Java*. Updated Edition. Reading: Addison Wesley Longman, 2000.
6. Dale, Nell, Daniel T. Joyce, and Chip Weems. *Object-Oriented Data Structures Using Java*. Sudbury, MA: Jones and Bartlett Pub., 2006.
7. Davis, Alan M. *Software Requirements Analysis and Specification*. Englewood Cliffs, NJ: Prentice-Hall, 1990.
8. Deitel, H. M. and P. J. Deitel. *Java: How To Program*. Third ed. Upper Saddle River: Prentice Hall, 1999.
9. Douglas, Bruce, P. *Real-Time UML Second Edition Developing Efficient Objects For Embedded Systems*. Reading: Addison Wesley Longman, 2000.
10. Fishwick, Paul A. *Simulation Model Design and Execution Building Digital Worlds*. Englewood Cliffs, NJ: Prentice-Hall, 1995.
11. Fowler, Martin. *UML Distilled Third Edition: A brief Guide to the Standard Object Modeling Language*. Boston: Addison-Wesley Pearson Education, 2004.
12. Garrido, J. M. *Object-Oriented Discrete-Event Simulation with Java*. New York: Kluwer Academic/Plenum Pub., 2001.
13. Garrido, J. M. *Practical Process Simulation Using Object-Oriented Techniques and C++*. Boston: Artech House, 1999.
14. Goodman, Roe, *Introduction to Stochastic Models*, Reading, MA: Addison-Wesley, 1988.
15. Harrel, Charles, Biman K. Ghosh, and Royce Bowden. *Simulation Using ProModel*. New York: McGraw-Hill Higher Ed., 2000.

16. Harrington, Brian E. and Paul A. Fishwick. "A portable Process-Oriented Compiler for Event Driven Simulation," *Simulation*, Vol. 60, No. 6, June 1993, pp 393-409.

17. Hortstmann, Cay S. and Gary Cornell. *Core Java 1.2 Volume 1 — Fundamentals*. Upper Saddle River: Sun Microsystems Press, Prentice Hall, 1999.

18. Hortstmann, Cay S. and Gary Cornell. *Core Java 1.2 Volume 2 — Advanced Features*. Upper Saddle River: Sun Microsystems Press, Prentice Hall, 1999.

19. Hyde, Paul. *Java Thread Programming*. Indianapolis: Sams Publishing, 1999.

20. Jain, Raj. *The Art of Computer Systems Performance Analysis*. New York: John Wiley, 1991.

21. Jia, Xiaoping. *Object-Oriented Software Development Using Java. Principles, Patterns, and Frameworks*. Reading: Addison Wesley Longman, 2000.

22. Kafura, Dennis. *Object-Oriented Software Design & Construction with Java*. Upper Saddle River: Prentice Hall, 2000.

23. Kelton, W.D., R. P. Sadoswki, and D.T. Sturrock. *Simulation with Arena*. Fourth Ed. New York: McGraw-Hill, 2007.

24. Khoshafian, Setrag. *Object Orientation*. 2nd ed. New York: John Wiley & Sons, 1995.

25. Kleijnen, Jack P. C. *Simulation: A Statistical Perspective*. New York: Wiley, 1992.

26. Law, Averill M., and W. David Kelton. *Simulation Modeling and Analysis*. Third Ed. New York: McGraw-Hill Higher Education, 2000.

27. Martin, James, and James J. Odell. *Object-Oriented Methods: A Foundation, UML Edition*. 2nd ed. Englewood Cliffs, NJ: Prentice-Hall, 1998.

28. Medhi, J. *Stochastic Processes*. 2nd ed. New York: John Wiley, 1994.

29. Meyer, Bertran. *Object-Oriented Software Construction*. Hemel Hempstead, Herts: Prentice-Hall International (UK) Ltd., 1988.

30. Mitrani, I. *Simulation Techniques for Discrete Event Systems*. Cambridge: Cambridge University Press, 1982 (Reprinted 1986).

31. Molloy, M.K. *Fundamentals of Performance Modeling*. 1st ed. 1989. New York: MacMillan.

32. Nelson, Barry L. *Stochastic Modeling, Analysis and Simulation*. New York: McGraw-Hill, 1995.

33. Norton, Scott J. and Dipasquale, Mark D. *The Multithreaded Programming Guide: Threadtime*. Upper Saddle River: Prentice Hall PTR, 1997.

34. Pedgen, C. D., R. E. Shannon, and R. P. Sadowski. *Introduction to Simulation Using SIMAN*. Second Ed. New York: McGraw-Hill, 1995.

35. Pohl, Ira and Charlie McDowell *Java by Dissection: The Essentials of java programming*. Reading: Addison Wesley Longman, 2000.

36. Piroumian, Vartan. *Java GUI Development*. Indianapolis: Sams Publishing, 1999.

37. Rumbaugh, J., M. Blaha, W. Premerlani, F. Eddy, and W. Lorensen. *Object-Oriented Modeling and Design*. Englewood Cliffs, NJ: Prentice-Hall, 1991.

38. Savitch, Walter. *Java: An Introduction To Computer Science & Programming*. Upper Saddle River: Prentice Hall, 1999.

39. Schwetman, Herb. "Using CSIM to Model Complex Systems." *Proceedings of the 1988 Winter Simulation Conference*. San Diego, CA, December 1988, pp. 246-253.
40. Selic B., G. Gullekson and P. T. Ward. *Real-Time Object-Oriented Modeling*. New York: John Wiley, 1994.
41. Tanner, Mike. *Practical Queuing Analysis*. New York: McGraw-Hill, 1995.
42. Yourdon, Edward. *Object-Oriented Systems Design: An Integrated Approach*. Englewood Cliffs, NJ: Yourdon Press Prentice-Hall, 1994.

Index